Satirical Tibet

Studies on Ethnic Groups in China

Stevan Harrell / *Editor*

Satirical Tibet

The Politics of Humor in Contemporary Amdo

Timothy Thurston

University of Washington Press
Seattle

Satirical Tibet was made possible in part by a grant from the Association for Asian Studies First Book Subvention Program.

This work was also supported by a UKRI Future Leaders Fellowship (grant number MR/V026348/1). The open access edition was supported by funding from UKRI and the University of Leeds.

Copyright © 2025 by the University of Washington Press

Design by Mindy Basinger Hill

Composed in 10.75/15pt Adobe Text Regular

The digital edition of this book may be downloaded and shared under a Creative Commons Attribution Non-Commercial No Derivatives 4.0 international license (CC-BY-NC-ND 4.0). For information about this license, see https://creativecommons.org/licenses/by-nc-nd/4.0. This license applies only to content created by the author, not to separately copyrighted material. To use this book, or parts of this book, in any way not covered by the license, please contact the University of Washington Press.

UNIVERSITY OF WASHINGTON PRESS / *uwapress.uw.edu*

LIBRARY OF CONGRESS CATALOGING-IN-PUBLICATION DATA

Names: Thurston, Timothy, author.
Title: Satirical Tibet : the politics of humor in contemporary Amdo / Timothy Thurston.
Description: Seattle : University of Washington Press, 2024. | Series: Studies on ethnic groups in China | Includes bibliographical references and index.
Identifiers: LCCN 2024033913 (print) | LCCN 2024033914 (ebook) | ISBN 9780295753102 (hardcover) | ISBN 9780295753119 (paperback) | ISBN 9780295753126 (ebook)
Subjects: LCSH: Amdo (Tibetan people)—Ethnic identity. | Tibetan wit and humor—Political aspects. | Tibetan wit and humor—Social aspects. | Satire, Tibetan. | Popular culture—China—Amdo Xian. | Amdo Xian (China)—Social life and customs.
Classification: LCC DS731.A53 T48 2024 (print) | LCC DS731.A53 (ebook) | DDC 305.895/41—dc23/eng/20241101
LC record available at https://lccn.loc.gov/2024033913
LC ebook record available at https://lccn.loc.gov/2024033914

∞ This paper meets the requirements of ANSI/NISO Z39.48-1992 (Permanence of Paper).

To all who have,
    at any time,
been a part of my village . . .

But especially
        Tsomo and
        Yangsi

Contents

Foreword by Stevan Harrell *ix*

A Note on Language, Methodology, and Ethics *xiii*

Acknowledgments *xix*

Introduction: Doing *Zurza* *1*

1. *Dokwa*: "Eating the Sides" in Oral and Literary Traditions *18*

2. *Khashag*: Language, Print, and Ethnic Pride in the 1980s *43*

3. *Khashag* on Air: Solving Social Ills by Radio in the 1990s *67*

4. *Garchung*: Televised Sketches and a Cultural Turn in the 2000s *98*

5. *Zheematam*: Tibetan Hip-Hop in the Digital World *119*

Conclusion: The Irrepressible Trickster *144*

Glossary *153*

Notes *161*

References *169*

Index *201*

Foreword
Stevan Harrell

We usually think of Tibetans in the People's Republic of China as an oppressed people. This is not wrong. Their religious activities and institutions are carefully monitored and severely circumscribed; their ability to use their own language in education and government is progressively constrained; they are denigrated as "backward" and in need of help from the Han-dominated regime; and their almost universally revered leader, His Holiness the fourteenth Dalai Lama, is excluded from his homeland and denigrated as a traitor to China and a dangerous "separatist." For some people, this oppression sometimes becomes unbearable, and their most extreme reactions include self-immolation in protest.

Because Tibetans are an oppressed people, we can easily assume that there is little joy or laughter in their lives, and that we should approach their predicament with uniform solemnity. This is wrong. Tibetans deal with the tragedy of Communist oppression as they have dealt with the vicissitudes of life on Earth for centuries—not only with "quiet desperation" or extreme religious devotion but also with uproarious comedy and biting satire. That satire, *zurza* in the Amdo dialect, is the topic of Timothy Thurston's *Satirical Tibet*, based on his decade-plus of observing, listening to, recording, questioning, and even performing Tibetan comedy and satire.

To illustrate the continued salience of humor and satire in the cultural life of Amdo (northeastern Tibet, now mostly in Qinghai Province), Thurston leads us through a historical progression of satirical genres. He shows us first how zurza was present in traditional Tibetan folklore, and then presents detailed analyses of the specific forms that satirical performance has taken from the 1980s to the present. Focusing on extended passages from specific works, laid out in parallel columns of Tibetan text and his own English translation, Thurston demonstrates how the form and content of satire has changed as the medium has changed.

The first post–Cultural Revolution format for zurza was scripted, staged performances of *khashag* "crosstalk" dialogues (which Thurston helpfully compares to Abbott and Costello). These made fun of the politics of language and ethnicity in the emerging post-Mao order, as when an ethnic Tibetan Communist Party secretary will speak only broken Chinese to incomprehending Tibetan herders but insists on speaking Tibetan with his Han superiors, demonstrating his importance by employing an interpreter.

Khashag continued its popularity in the 1990s as audiocassettes and recorders became widespread, and the focus turned to the social ills of Amdo society as it began to experience modern economic change. Satirists directed their mockery at official malfeasance and corruption, village and clan feuds exacerbated by new opportunities for economic gain, the uncertain prestige of real lamas and their impersonators, and continued discrimination against girls in education.

In the early 2000s, as televisions and VCRs became widespread, the medium for satire changed to video discs, requiring much more preparation and better acting, since audiences would see as well as hear the performers, whose acts were now known as *garchung*. These concerned the increasingly precarious state of Tibetan culture, with many barbs directed at both Chinese and foreigners who began to view Tibet as a source of religious and ecological inspiration, often aided by Tibetans eager to benefit from their national and cosmopolitan connections.

Finally, after protests and repression across the whole Tibetan Plateau in the run-up to the 2008 Beijing Olympics, hip-hop came belatedly to Amdo. But Thurston points out that performances during this phase were not as funny as their predecessors, as Tibetan cultural activists found their creativity increasingly circumscribed not just by repression of outright dissent but also by the very waves of digitalization that made their performances possible. To this day, many of them plaintively and mordantly, sometimes desperately, call for the preservation of Tibetan culture, even if they have to concentrate on such relatively neutral topics as language and secular folklore, and cannot mention more contentious aspects of religion, let alone Tibetan nationalism.

As Thurston makes clear, zurza has continued, sometimes more and sometimes less humorously, to be a channel for social critique and on occasion for understandable social resentment. But hilarious as it sometimes is, zurza always has a serious purpose. We see no examples as nonsensical as "Who's on First?" or Gracie's Allen's malapropisms. Absurdity abounds, but frivolity is absent. Every dialogue, skit, and rap is about a social problem of some sort. In contemporary Amdo, comedy and laughter exist not so much in spite of repressive politics but because of it. Where direct critiques might be dangerous, the indirection embodied in zurza takes advantage of its own ambiguity (and of course of its frequent hilariousness) to serve a serious purpose of saying what needs to be said but cannot be said in plain words. While zurza brings levity into the lives of the audience and gives direction to the creative impulses of the writers and performers, that is an extra benefit, a psychological uplift in dark times and an indicator of the strength of character of people who are, as we know, living under an oppressive regime. The important thing is to be able to criticize.

As Thurston also recognizes, not all overseas audiences will appreciate the ways in which creative comedians and writers deal with oppression through satire. Some will see the situation in Tibet as so dire as not to admit anything humorous. But people living there have little choice. And Tim Thurston shows us this through his meticulous scholarship and infectious sympathy for those of whom he writes. We are proud to present *Satirical Tibet* as the twenty-sixth volume of Studies on Ethnic Groups in China.

A Note on Language, Methodology, and Ethics

The chapters of this book open us onto a complex Tibetan world featuring multiple ethnic groups, languages, dialects, and registers. In order to convey concepts, performances, and people "on their own terms," I have favored many Chinese and Tibetan terms over imperfect English equivalents. In some instances, I have provided English translations followed by Tibetan and/or Chinese originals in parentheses. Some terms, like the names of administrative units (counties, prefectures, provinces, etc.) have both Chinese and Tibetan equivalents; others are specifically Tibetan. Some of the Tibetan terms are common across dialects and have accepted written forms; others are specific to the Amdo dialect and have no commonly accepted written form. This complicated situation means that I have spent far too much time considering how best to portray these terms in a way that is accessible to readers but also does justice to the communities and the individuals. There are no easy answers, and surely someone will be disappointed. If someone *is* to be disappointed, though, I would rather it be the readers than the people who kindly shared with me their time, food, tea, liquor, experiences, knowledge, and dreams. These speakers deserve to be read and heard in their words, their language, and their culture.

Chinese terms are relatively straightforward; they are also in the minority. I use the pinyin romanization system for all such terms and mark these terms with "Ch." For example, when describing the 1950s ethnic identification projects, I write: "ethnic identification" (Ch. *minzu shibie*). Where Tibetan terms are involved, however, this commitment to the words of my interlocutors presents at least two immediate difficulties. First, there is no commonly accepted system for rendering Amdo Tibetan speech with the Latin alphabet. The most common romanization systems render Tibetan based on either normative pronunciations of the Lhasa dialect or the Tibetan writing system. Neither of these really makes sense. A book about Amdo—a region of northeastern Tibet now split between modern-day Qinghai, Sichuan, and Gansu, possessing a range of dialects largely unintelligible to Tibetans from other regions—can hardly employ a romanization based on the Lhasa dialect, like the Tibetan and Himalayan Library's Online Tibetan Phonetics Converter. The Extended Wylie Transliteration System (see Anton-Luca 2006), while dialect neutral, portrays words and concepts as they are written in Tibetan. This would solve the problem of dialect but yields unwieldy consonant clusters that some English-speaking readers may find off-putting.

If neither of these, then what? The best solution I have found is to render Tibetan names and terms in the body of the text in something resembling the Amdo Tibetan pronunciation based on how I, as an American from Ohio, hear them. Because the comedians, rappers, and tradition bearers with whom I spoke are primarily from pastoral communities, I especially privilege pronunciations from their subdialects. In cases where I am trying to make a specific linguistic point, I have also included Tibetan script in parentheses immediately following the romanized term. For longer quotations of Tibetan texts, I have placed English translations and Tibetan script together. After all, any book about modern Tibetan cultural production and language's important role in this can hardly proceed by erasing Tibetan language.

I have made two major exceptions to this practice. For proper nouns sufficiently well known to my expected English-speaking audience to have other popularly accepted romanizations, I have used the more common ones, even where they differ from the Amdo Tibetan pronunciation. For example, I have written the name of the Central Tibetan region "Ü-Tsang" instead of the Wylie *Dbus* (or *dBus*) *gtsang* or the Amdo pronunciation of Wetsang. Additionally, if a living person has expressed a particular preference for how to write their name in English, I have followed that. Comedian-poet-actor-director Shidé Nyima, for example, uses this spelling when writing his name with the Latin alphabet, though I might render it differently if trying to faithfully replicate some Amdo dialects. Failing specific requests, I have rendered names phonetically as I heard them. The Tibetan script for personal names and specific terms can be found in the glossary.

Rendering Tibetan script throughout the text should not be off-putting. For a book about Tibet, it is little different than including Greek script in a text about Greece, except that a Western reader's eyes are less accustomed to it. The same applies to Chinese characters. Meanwhile, in a moment in which we seek to recognize and be transparent about the construction of knowledge, there is a strong decolonizing argument that my interlocutors be heard as well as possible and on their own terms. This will help to ensure that speakers' words can be examined and that my own interventions and decisions are more available to readers.

Having made this decision, my second immediate difficulty is that, despite a few attempts at writing in Tibetan "vernacular" (some of which are mentioned in this book), there remain few commonly accepted ways of *writing* colloquial Tibetan. The conventions in this book follow those I have seen employed in textbooks, scripts, and vernacular literature. Where Tibetan performances quoted derive from poetry, comic scripts, and other written documents, I have replicated the spelling in the originals. For transcriptions of oral performances for which I have no scripts, the Tibetan provided represents my best efforts to render specific features of the Amdo dialect's grammar, often in collaboration with Tibetans from the region. A nonexhaustive list of some conventions would include verb aspect markers like *ki/gi* (ཀྱི or གི) for the present tense, *tha* (ཐལ) for completed actions, and *ni re* (ནི་རེད) for the simple past aspect. The following phrase from "Gesar's Horse Herder" (the performance discussed in chapter 4) illustrates this approach:

In my opinion there's a lot that you don't know.

ངས་བསྔས་ན་ཁྱོས་ཤེས་གི་མེད་ནོ་མང་གི

This one sentence illustrates many of the concerns and interventions unique to the Amdo dialect. Here, the syllable *no* (ནོ) is used as a nominalizer (Dpal ldan bkra shis 2016, 540) to construct the relative clause "what I'm talking about." The syllable ཁྱོས། is the second-person pronoun (locally pronounced *cho*) with the agentive particle affixed, rendering the new pronunciation *chee*, creating the subject of the verb "to know." The final two syllables of the phrase, *mang gi* (མང་གི), join a single syllable adjective *mang* 'many' with *gi*, which in Dpal ldan bkra shis's (2016, 48) terminology is the "reportive mood," used by a speaker to report what the speaker thinks to be the case. Most of these features are specific to the Amdo dialect. At the same time, the verb "to speak" has a commonly accepted spelling, and I preserve this even though it differs from the pronunciation.

Toponyms and names for administrative units and government media companies present further problems. With both Tibetan and Chinese names, I have chosen to use Tibetan pronunciations for cities, towns, counties, and prefectures, Chinese pinyin in parentheses at the first usage, and characters in the glossary.

Due to the very real potential for political fallout associated with any study of China's ethnic minority populations, I have done my utmost to protect the identities of my consultants. Most interviews were conducted in Tibetan, and only rarely in English or Chinese at the interviewee's preference. If done in English or Chinese, I have marked the quotes as such at the end of the quotation. Under the terms of IRB protocol 2012B0466, and due to the potentially sensitive nature of the project, I transcribed all interviews myself, without the aid of a research assistant. All interviews were conducted in spaces chosen by the interviewee, often teahouses or cafés. As such, there were certain segments of conversations that were difficult to understand. These indistinct portions are marked with question marks. Any mistakes in the transcription and translation are entirely my own.

It should also be noted that, due to the scope of this thesis and the regional nature of its analysis, I have sometimes generalized based on the informed opinions of my interlocutors. I am fully aware of the dangers of overgeneralization, but, over the course of countless conversations throughout the region, I have come to believe that the views contained in their responses are representative of those held by many (especially lay) Tibetans in Amdo.

The selection of interlocutors was limited to my own networks and my own ability to meet people. They are overwhelmingly male, first-generation-urban Tibetans who, when asked about their home areas, are more likely to say the name of a county in the Tibetan countryside than the provincial capital of Ziling, in which most of the interviewees live. I also conducted interviews with people from a variety of areas in the countryside.

Most of my interviewees are bilingual in Amdo Tibetan and some form of Chinese; some are trilingual. Their opinions, and my subsequent deductions, certainly do not reflect the experience or opinions of every person on the plateau. To wit, there is a small—but growing—population of one-and-a-half- and second-generation urbanites who are unable or unwilling to speak Tibetan, and not as concerned with the issues being articulated here. I conducted no formal interviews with such people, as they admitted no interest in these performances, due to their inability to understand both the language and the content.

Acknowledgments

Some people are master storytellers. They have command over a full complement of culturally defined tools to weave masterful narratives. They manipulate speech, silence, pacing, volume, and myriad other vocal qualities to keep an audience's rapt attention, while the words themselves join to form meaningful tales that may comment on important situations. I, sadly, am not one of these people. My interest in humor and satire stems in no small part from the fact that I have never been that funny or a good storyteller. If brevity is the soul of wit, then my family and I are notably unwitty: we never fail to use twenty words where five will do. (For proof, see that last sentence.) The *bon mot* and other forms of banter, meanwhile, are almost entirely absent from my verbal arsenal. I was so bad at telling jokes in high school that my friends at one point considered delegating one member of the group to listen to the joke once *before* allowing me to tell the joke to the group, so as to make sure I would relate it properly. Even now, the only humor I can reliably muster is self-deprecating. This is all to say that if I have succeeded in portraying the traditions and performances examined in this book as humorous, it is probably in spite of my own capacities and because of those who have helped me along the way: audience members, performers, friends, reviewers anonymous and otherwise. Any remaining errors and infelicities are entirely my own.

Additionally, as a folklorist both by training and by habit, I take great interest in what people say, and how they say it. This book's examination of satire across traditional forms, post-Mao Tibetan comedy, and emerging forms like hip-hop, developed naturally from these two broader interests in humor and verbal art. I use methodologies of participant observation, ethnographic interviewing, and textual criticism to diachronically analyze Tibetan comedic performance at various moments in the post-Mao reform era and tie them back into larger cultural trends. In the end, I recorded over one hundred hours of interviews, attended the tapings of four shows in which comedies were featured, collected a corpus of over ninety comedic scripts and recordings, and had countless unrecorded conversations with Tibetans from all walks of life and on a variety of topics, some of which led back to satire, comedy, hip-hop, and oral tradition. I learned some basic comedic arts from comedian-poet-actor-director Shidé Nyima, and performed with him for the 2015 New Year's variety show on Qinghai Tibetan television. Through this performance, I became the fifth "student" in his artistic lineage. I am still only beginning to understand what this entails.

But these statistics fail to describe the debts accrued and friendships forged in Western China. Indeed, one does not complete over four nearly uninterrupted years of fieldwork, ten years of graduate school, or really any significant social endeavor without doing so. This book is no different, and the assistance of dozens of friends, colleagues, mentors, teachers, institutions, and funding bodies has been crucial. There is insufficient space to thank all those who have helped with their time, thoughts, advice, and fellowship. Moreover, out of concern for the privacy of my consultants, I cannot credit them fully here. If you graciously agreed to share with me your invaluable thoughts, opinions, and knowledge, I am eternally grateful, and the first thanks goes to all of you.

Beyond consultants from the "field," I am incredibly thankful to Professor Mark A. Bender, who has, at varying points served as adviser, teacher, mentor, friend, gentle nudge in the ribs, and swift kick in the (insert synonym for donkey here). His careful reads of early drafts were essential to the dissertation on which this book is based. I also owe immense gratitude to other members on the committee: Professor Kirk Denton, who gave consistently excellent advice and meticulous edits both before and throughout the writing of the dissertation; Professor Dorothy Noyes, whose long conversations, frequent emails, and comments on a number of drafts were essential to my understanding of the social life of genre from a theoretical perspective, as well as the discussion of enregisterment and language in society; and Eric Mortensen, for his constant encouragement, invaluable expertise, and careful reading of my dissertation.

Beyond my official advisers and committee, I have benefitted deeply from the friends and informal mentors who have shaped me and my research. I am thankful to Levi Gibbs, Ben Gatling, and Mario De Grandis for lending their expertise to this project through time-consuming reads and insightful comments. I am also grateful to the many friends and acquaintances, both local and foreign, with whom I have had numerous informal conversations about Tibetan culture, Tibetological approaches to culture, life in Tibetan areas, comedy, and theory. These include (in no particular order) Tshe dbang rdo rje, 'Phags pa don grub, Snying bo rgyal, Tsering Samdrup, Nyi ma rgyal mtshan, Dkon mchog dge legs, Skal bzang tshe brtan, Shidé Nyima, Sman bla skyabs, 'Jams dbyangs blo gros, Sog phrug shes rab, Detsaje, Sde btsan, Chos dpal, Rig grol, Grogs po, 'Jam dbyangs blo gros, Mona Schrempf, Charlene Makley, Isabelle Henrion-Dourcy, Françoise Robin, Janet Upton, Christie Kilby, Dawn Collins, Andrew Grant, Keith Dede, John Huntington, and Ariana Maki, to name but a few.

I would also like to thank my formal and informal language teachers, whose instruction made possible everything that followed: Klu 'bum thar (formerly of Qinghai Nationalities University); Shes rab lha mo (of Qinghai Nationalities University); Nyi ma rgyal mtshan, who has been the best friend, teacher, and debate partner I have found; Tsering Samdrup; Tshe dbang rdo rje; and O rgyan tshe ring. I am further indebted to Shidé Nyima and his lineage of students. He has been teacher, mentor, and friend, while his students all have helped me better to understand some of the linguistic and artistic nuances of modern Tibetan culture. Amalia Rubin kindly read through an entire draft of an earlier iteration of the manuscript and gave useful suggestions on English translations. Tsering Samdrup kindly checked the Tibetan script and corresponding English translations.

I also thank colleagues and friends at the Smithsonian Institution's Center for Folklife and Cultural Heritage, where I spent part of my time as a postdoctoral research fellow and preparing this manuscript, and colleagues at the University of Leeds, where the manuscript was completed. I am especially incredibly grateful for the support and comments of, and conversations with, Michael Mason, Robert Leopold, Amalia Cordova, Mary S. Linn, Suonan Wangjia, Frances Weightman, Sarah Dodd, David Pattinson, Przemyslaw Nornicki, Amalia Rubin, Thea Pitman, and others.

Portions of this book, meanwhile, have been presented as papers at annual meetings of the Association of Asian Studies, American Folklore Society, and American Anthropological Association, and at the International Association of Tibetan Studies meeting in 2015, as well as at invited talks at Columbia University, Cambridge University, and King's College London. Comments and questions from those audiences have helped to develop this book into its present form. Series editor Stevan Harrell, University of Washington Press editors Caitlin Tyler-Richards and Lorri Hagman, copy editor Richard Isaac, and two peer reviewers meanwhile have played crucial roles in helping to shape the monograph.

Next, I must acknowledge with gratitude the financial support provided by the Institute of International Education's Fulbright grant (during which I initially learned about the performances discussed in the dissertation), as well as FLAS and Fulbright-Hays DDRA grants from the US Department of Education. For their extensive logistical support, I thank Joanna Kukielka-Blaser from The Ohio State University's Office of International Affairs, and various staff members at Qinghai Nationalities University for hosting me. I am grateful for a UKRI Future Leaders Fellowship (and COVID-enforced absence from China) gave me the time and headspace to re-write the monograph.

Lastly, I thank my families for their constant support throughout my graduate training and academic career. My parents have given me the support and freedom to continue studying something that is, quite frankly, a little unusual. I thank my brother, David, whose own (sometimes) uncompromising pursuit of his passion is a constant source of inspiration. As for my family in China, I am eternally grateful to Tsedar and A ma Tsering Yangstso, who took me in and have always treated me as their son. They may not have fully understood *why* I was doing what I was doing, nor why it took so long, but they were always welcoming and supportive. I thank Yangsi Yumtso Thurston for providing a source of joy, diversion, motivation, and wonder throughout this long process. But the last and most important thanks goes to my wife and best friend, Tashi Tsomo Thurston, without whose support, sacrifice, and encouragement this book would have been impossible.

Satirical Tibet

Introduction
Doing *Zurza*

There's no way to talk without joking.
There's no way to eat without making offerings.

གཏམ་ཀུ་རེ་མེད་ན་བཤད་སྟོལ་མེད།
ཟས་མཆོད་ཁ་མེད་ན་ཟ་སྟོལ་མེད།

Tibetan proverb

In the winter of 2010, a friend invited me to celebrate Losar, the Tibetan New Year, with his family in the grasslands of Tsongon (the Tibetan name for the province known as Qinghai in Chinese). I jumped at the opportunity for a true homestay there, and about a month before the festival was set to begin, I found myself sitting alongside my friend on a bus, winding westward and upward out of Ziling, the capital city. As we rode through the lower-altitude farming area of Trika County, I marveled at the sharp contrast between the barren red cliffs overlooking the murky Yellow River and the verdant grasslands, snow-covered mountains, and pure rivers that the name "Tibet" conjured in my mind's eye. From there we headed to the windswept town of Gomang in Mangra County, and then another thirty-minute drive in a private car on a bumpy dirt road took us southwest of town to my friend's home. The wintry grassland was a dull brown and adjacent to a gradually encroaching desert. This was not the picturesque Tibet memorialized in coffee-table books and postcards.

Over the next few weeks, my perceptions of the region's culture underwent a rapid transformation. I had come to the Tibetan Plateau to research the role of traditional tales about the well-known trickster, Uncle Tonpa (ཨ་ཁུ་སྟོན་པ།), in contemporary China's ethnic minority mediascape. I had even rationalized my trip by telling myself that I would probably spend evenings listening to elders telling stories around a warm stove or hearing songs being sung on the grassland—what I naively considered "real" folklore. I was hoping to document this, especially the trickster tales I was researching (the more ribald the better), to compare them with the sanitized versions in children's books, cartoons, and the work of an award-winning but controversial author. I thought that this might be the ideal opportunity to record some trickster tales in context. To my dismay, however, the telling of these and other folktales was far less common than the many printed collections had led me to believe.

Indeed, despite having read many accounts of evening storytelling, nocturnal visits to paramours in nearby villages, love-song soirees, and communal gatherings (all important parts of lived experience in the recent past), by the time I arrived in my friend's village in the winter of 2010, such practices were largely absent from the everyday experience of pastoralists. While material traditions and foodways persisted, many oral traditions seemed limited to particular contexts, especially "time out of time" (Falassi 1987) festival events and weddings. Instead, average evenings were spent around a softly flickering television. For weeks, after the sun had set and the family's livestock had been penned and fed, my hosts would gather around to watch the news and other programming on the Tibetan-language television station and, very occasionally, Chinese-language programming.

One night, instead of watching the regular Tibetan offerings, my hosts played a video compact disc (VCD) of sketch comedies. These portrayed contemporary Tibetan experience in ways simultaneously realistic and exaggerated, all featuring performances by a single comedian. It was like watching a "best of" compilation of *Saturday Night Live*. One particularly memorable sketch opens with a man, his back facing the audience, leaning against a structure that says *po* (men) on the door. Next, a woman walks on stage shouting at the man:

Aro! *Aro*! Did you hear me? This isn't the grassland! Ignoring the toilet to relieve yourself!

ཨ་རོགས། ཨ་རོགས། ཨེ་གོ་ཐལ། སྐྱོད་ཁང་ཆེབ་ནས་བཞག་བཏང་དེ་ཆེབ་བ་བཏང་དེ་རྩྭ་ཐང་ མ་རེད་མོ།

The characters are a study in contrast. The scene is some anonymous town. The audience recognizes that the woman wearing *jyala* (modern clothing, literally "Han clothing") must work as an attendant collecting money at the public toilet, while the man wearing a traditional robe must be a herder in town on some business. In saying that this is not the grassland, she is creating a moral geography in which one can urinate wherever one pleases on the grassland but not in the civilized city. The man, showing himself to be the argumentative type, replies,

Oh, I didn't know. With you just saying "*aro*," how can one know who you're talking to? My name isn't "*aro*," aro?

ཨོ་མ་ཤེས། རང་ང་ཨ་རོགས་ཟེར་ནས་ཨག་བཏབ་བཏང་ན་ངས་སུར་བཤད་གོ་གི་ཟེར་རེ། ངའི་ མིང་ང་ཨ་རོགས་མི་ཟེར། ཨ་རོགས།

The audience laughs, and the man turns to go into the toilet but is stopped again, this time because he has not read the sign saying it costs ¥2 to use the public restroom (as was common in many urban areas at the time). The man is miffed. For the remainder of the sketch, the two square off, the woman insisting that the man pay the amount required, and the man resisting hilariously. The herder takes the attendant to task both culturally and linguistically. To the audience's evident enjoyment—the video cuts to the audience at key moments, providing cues about how funny and clever particular turns of phrase are to other Tibetans—the man haggles over the correct terminology for the fee being assessed:

MAN: Nowadays one even has to pay a toilet tax!
WOMAN: It's not a tax
M: Right. It's not a tax. It's a rate.

4 INTRODUCTION

w: It's not a rate either
m: Then it *is* a tax.
w (annoyed): Call it a tax or call it a fee, you have to pay the price. It's two *mao*. That's it.
m: Price! So nicely said! A price means giving something and then getting something back. So if it's a price, then you still have to give me something.

འབྲོག་པ། དེང་སང་དུ་ཅིག་བཏང་ན་ར་ཁྲལ་འཛལ་དགོས་ནི་ཨེ་རེད།
བུད་མེད། ཁྲལ་མ་རེད།
འབྲོག་པ། བདེན་གི་ཁྲལ་མ་རེད། སྒླ་རེད་མོ།
བུད་མེད། སྒླ་ར་མ་རེད།
འབྲོག་པ། དེ་ན་ཡང་ཁྲལ་རེད་མོ།
བུད་མེད། ཨ་ཡ། ད་ཁྲལ་ཟེར་ན་ཆོག་གི་སྒླ་ཟེར་ན་ཆོག་གི་ རིན་སྟེར་དགོས་ནི་རེད། ཁོ་དོ་རེད། དེ་རེད།
འབྲོག་པ། རིན། ཡག་པ་ཡག་པ་ཞིག་བཤད་ལེ། རིན་ཟེར་ནོ་འདི་ཕར་ར་ཕྱིན་ན་ཕྱིར་ར་སྟེར་རྒྱུ་ཟིག་རེད་ཟེར་ན་མིན་ནས། རིན་གཟིག་ཡིན་ན་ད་རུང་ངར་ཅིག་སྟེར་དགོས་གི།

The herder concludes that if he has to pay to relieve himself, he'll just go behind the building.

Then there's a ¥10 fine!

ཆད་པ་བཅད་ན་བཅུ་ཐམ་པ་རེད།

The fines escalate if he ignores the attendant, and the herder begins to feel that it is all simply too ridiculous to be believed. At one point, things get so heated that the attendant locks the door.

The man, meanwhile, tries to bring the conversation back onto a cultural footing he understands: he talks about being a chieftain's son, about having urinated in some of Tibet's most illustrious locations, and that having to pay to carry out this most basic human act feels ridiculous. In the end, however, after several other twists and turns, the man leaves, having failed to use the toilet. As he goes, the attendant sends an ominous warning:

Say, uncle, and go and tell the others: "If you don't get used to paying the price, in the future you might not be able to pee freely on the grassland."

ཨ་རོགས་ཨ་ཁུ་བཟེ་ཡ། སོང་ད་ཀྱད་པོ་ཚོ་ཧོད་ལ། རིན་སྟེར་རྒྱུར་ལོབ་གི་མ་བཞག་དུས། གཞུག་ནས་རྩྭ་ཐང་ནས་ར་རང་ང་རང་ང་བཏང་ན་མི་ཆོག་ན་ཐང་བཟེ་གོ

The sketch ends with the herder saying that such a custom will never spread on the grasslands and trudges off.

Moments later, the next comedy begins. This time, it portrays two salesmen trying to bilk a hard-of-hearing pastoralist and his friend into selling his traditional robes to be repurposed as modern leather goods, only to find that they are not such easy marks as the salesmen imagined. Even though my hosts were already familiar with this performance and the other sketches on the VCD, evening activity came to a near standstill while the comedies played. Adults and children alike laughed freely at misunderstandings between characters, particularly well-worded comebacks, puns, and artfully crafted parallelisms. Looking away from the screen briefly, they smiled and repeated favorite lines to each other appreciatively.

In noticeable contrast to the conversations that frequently drowned out everyday television watching, these comedies brought ambient conversation to a halt. More than mere entertainment, it was also immediately clear to me that these comedies were conveying important messages about contemporary Tibetan life and shaping attitudes about language, culture, urbanization, and more. In the first sketch described above, the behavior of both characters is placed on display for audiences, who laugh not only at the pastoralist's inability to navigate the urban environment but also at the bathroom attendant's unstinting adherence to seemingly arbitrary rules. More ominously, they hear foreboding comments about the increasing privatization of space on the grassland. The performances may not be "real" or "true" stories, but they were "realistic," and many Tibetans would know well—perhaps viscerally—the feelings and situations portrayed on stage and on screen. In short, these sketches appeared to be the new stories Tibetans were telling about their contemporary selves. I was hooked and determined to better understand what and how these comedies "mean" to performers and audiences alike.

Between 2011 and 2015, I collected over one hundred recordings and scripts of comedy performances and attended live performances whenever I had the opportunity. I met many of the most prominent comedians and chatted with dozens of self-described fans. From both my own reading of the performances and the testimonies of Tibetan interlocutors, I learned that these comedies engage in a wide-ranging social critique about issues facing Tibetan society. I also noticed that both comedians and their fans consistently stated that "good" comedic performances *zurza ye* (ཟུར་ཟ་བྱེད།), that is, they "do *zurza*." When pressed about the term, my interlocutors often translated into Chinese as *fengci* or—less frequently—into English with "satire" or "sarcasm" (see, for example, Goldstein 2001), but these translations failed to account for the nuance with which people used the term. During follow-up field trips in 2016 and 2017, I also heard Tibetans use *zurza* in relation to obscure oral traditions, socially critical works of modern Tibetan literature, and the latest in Tibetan hip-hop. To hear the comedians and rappers tell it, zurza is part of what makes their work in new genres and emerging media uniquely Tibetan. This book presents the first study of this underappreciated expressive concept and its importance to post-Mao Tibetan cultural production.

•

Zurza and the laughter that frequently accompanies it are hardly the first things most people think about when they hear the words *China* and *Tibet* in the same sentence. And why should they be? Many in the Euro-American "West" may hear the word *Tibet* and think of a traditionally Buddhist society, perhaps oppressed by a colonizing Chinese Communist Party. The same people may think of recent news reporting about Tibetans self-immolating, and Tibet's Nobel Prize–winning exiled religious leader. For many who have grown up in China, meanwhile, images may range from a feudal society liberated by and incorporated into the People's Republic in the 1950s, to news spots showing Tibetans dancing happily in displays of gratitude to the Communist Party for the "gift" of modernity (Yeh 2013b), to a pristine environment for young Han to conquer as they escape from China's heavily polluted coastal metropolises. These descriptions, all carrying elements of truth, select some of the most contrasting images possible to make a rhetorical point. But the discourses of modernity and progress, and of traumatic experience and dramatic resistance, all emphasize grand narratives that leave little room for zurza.[1]

Set against the background of these ongoing and well-publicized cultural and political tensions, a book about a topic as seemingly trivial as zurza and humor can come across as being in poor taste. And yet, laughter has served as the soundtrack to almost every one of my experiences of Tibet. This also manifests in everyday life. During dinners among friends, the seemingly endless toasting with liquor—almost always three cups at a time—often lowered inhibitions to the point at which teasing and reminiscing might devolve into uncontrolled hilarity. At traditional weddings, women from the host village may use humor and wit to demand some sort of payment or gift from the visiting representatives of the person marrying into the village (usually the maternal uncles of the bride). In the valley of Rebgong, interludes in the annual harvest festival featuring inebriated villagers—sometimes cross-dressing or wearing monks' robes—may make fun of the behavior of certain members of the community, to the applause and laughter of all in attendance. Tibetan communities possess a diverse vocabulary for humorous activity that mirrors the diversity of ways that laughter appears in everyday life, including *kure* (joking), *labjyagpa* (boasting), *tséwa* (play), and *zurza*. This humor frequently accomplished important social work: to entertain, mask existential pain, serve hegemonic forces, speak the otherwise unspeakable, provide a "steam-valve" for social discontent, and/or to project and reflect worldviews (Rea and Volland 2008, x).

Among these arts of Tibetan humor, zurza, in particular, has emerged as an important principle guiding contemporary Tibetan cultural production in the modern era. Zurza—literally "eating sides"—refers to the arts of Tibetan satire and sarcasm. *The New Dagyig Dictionary* defines it in the following terms: "the name for words that criticize or expose the truth about another's actions through relying on meanings other than what is actually said with examples or exaggeration" (Dag yig 'di'i rtsom sgrig tshan chung 1979, 693). *The Great Tibetan-Chinese Dictionary* further defines the term as "to abuse with indirect language or to speak something meaningful" (Zhang 1985, 2467).

These two definitions emphasize two major characteristics: first, the practice of critique, and second, the use of indirection and inversion. When used in a sentence, *zurza* takes the verb *ye* (to do, བྱེད།), which is classified in Tibetan grammar as a *ta dadpa* verb—what we might imperfectly translate into English as a transitive or agentive verb. The subject of these sentences is marked with an ergative marker, which emphasizes the agency of the satirist. In short, a speaker or author "does zurza" to a target when critiquing their appearance, attitudes, or behavior with indirection and inversion.

Primarily associated with the literary register of Tibetan, many illiterate or less educated Tibetans in Amdo may not immediately recognize the term. Nevertheless, they would be familiar with the activity, as many oral traditions use zurza to poke fun at the behavior and appearance of others through indirection and inversion. In this way, zurza operates more like a master trope, similar to African American "signifying" (Gates 1983; Abrahams 1962), and the people who "do zurza" act—as do comedians and satirists around the globe—as vernacular ethnographers (Brodie 2014) and "*ipso facto* moralists" (Levin 1987, 197). When famed trickster Uncle Tonpa tricks a landlord or merchant, or makes a king bark like a dog, he "does zurza." When the seventeenth-century lama Shar Kalden Jyamtso (1607–1677) composed songs poking fun at the behavior of monks, he was also "doing zurza." And when a contemporary comedian mocks people whose behavior seems out of touch in the contemporary moment, they too do zurza.

In the post-Mao period, zurza became a topic of explicit concern for a new generation of intellectuals and cultural producers, who use it as an expressive resource to simultaneously access state-run media and advocate for Tibetan causes. Working across media, genre, and moments, they weigh in on and shape popular attitudes toward the issues Tibetan communities face at various moments. Cultural producers, however, must get things exactly right as they create works that entertain and instruct Tibetan audiences on the one hand and meet government expectations for content on the other. Failure to do so can land a performer in jail, as happened with the famed comedian Menla Jyab (Donyol Dondrup and Makley 2018, 6).

That humorists living in authoritarian contexts potentially face reprisal for their jokes is not new (Oring 2004), but when they get the balance right, they can create memorable and meaningful texts that have potential to influence society. Seen from this perspective, zurza provides the tools for ensuring Tibetan presence contemporary media. This book explores the changing uses and meanings of zurza across different media and various moments of the post-Mao era. In doing so, it becomes possible to recognize how "cultural producers" (Abu-Lughod 1999, 113–14) from the ethnolinguistic region Tibetans call "Amdo" have used the concept to create work that is both entertaining and meaningful, reshaping Tibetan society in the process.

•

Amdo is a geographical, linguistic, and cultural identity for Tibetans living in northeastern areas of the Tibetan Plateau, across parts of what are now Sichuan, Gansu, and Qinghai. Amdowas (people from Amdo) speak a variety of subdialects of Amhkel, or the Amdo dialect. The subdialects spoken in Amdo are nontonal and compensate for this with complex initial and final consonant clusters (Makley et al. 1999), leading some to postulate that Amdo's spoken languages are more conservative or archaic than the Lhasa and Kham dialects. Estimates for the number of Amdo dialect speakers range from roughly one million (Huber 2002, xvi n5) to 1.8 million (Reynolds 2012, 19; see also Wang 2012).

Tibetans in Amdo further differentiate between *ronghkel* (farming dialects) and *ndroghkel* (nomad dialects), which constitute emically distinct sociolects (Reynolds 2012, 5). Linguists in China further recognize phonological and lexical differences between northern and southern versions of each, creating a four-part, etic distinction between northern and southern versions of farming dialects, and northern and southern versions of nomad dialects. Though the regional sociolects within Amdo are, to a large extent, mutually intelligible, each has its own expressive practices, as well as pronunciations that can confuse people from other parts of Amdo.

Along with the Eastern Tibetan region of Kham and the Central Tibetan region of Ü-Tsang, Amdo is one of the *chol kha sum*, the three regions traditionally recognized as being part of the Tibetan cultural world (Yang 2016). These are defined as follows:

> It is known that when dividing the three regions, [the land] from Ngari and Gung thang to Soglakyawo is Ü-Tsang, the land of religion. And from there to the bend in the Yellow River is Dohtod [Kham], the land of men, and from there to China's white stupa is Dohmad [Amdo] the land of horses. (Brag dgon pa dkon mchog bstan pa rab rgyas 1987)

This quote from the nineteenth-century *The Political and Religious History of Amdo* continues to influence Tibetan self-definitions and experiences to this day. It defines the regions according to altitude, with the highest in western and Central Tibet. Next come the higher-altitude valleys of Kham (Dohtod, literally "upper valleys"), then Amdo (Dohmad, literally "lower valleys") as the lowest and easternmost of the three. Each region is then associated with a characteristic. Central Tibet, home to Lhasa and many of the most significant monasteries, is the land of religion. Renowned for its pugnacious inhabitants, Kham earns recognition as the land of people. Amdo is the land of horses, a nod to the region's lush grasslands.

By the time I arrived in Amdo to begin my research, however, conditions on the Tibetan Plateau had changed, and some people had reworked the original chol kha sum formulation in recognition of this. One parody that I heard popularly during my fieldwork went as follows:

> Ü-Tsang is the land of politics
> Dohtod [Kham] is the land of wealth
> Dohmad [Amdo] is the land of scholars

དབུས་གཙང་སྒྲིག་གི་ཆོལ་ཁ།
མདོ་སྟོད་ནོར་གྱི་ཆོལ་ཁ།
མདོ་སྨད་ཤེས་རིག་གི་ཆོལ་ཁ།

In reformulating the chol kha sum definition, we simultaneously recognize the incredible staying power of these emic definitions, and the changing ways in which each region is viewed in relation to the current socioeconomic climate. Ü-Tsang, home to the historic capital of Lhasa, is the most politically sensitive; Kham is a land of economic development; and Amdo is a hub of contemporary Tibetan intellectual activity.

In the process of modernizing a traditional wedding speech," meanwhile, a Tibetan comedian parodied the original idea, describing various inhabited areas:

> In Lhasa, there are many pilgrimage sites,
> In Ngawa, there are many merchants,
> In Ziling, there are many scholars,
> And in Tibet in general, it should be said that there are many monks (Sman bla skyabs 1996f)

ལྷ་ས་ན་མཇལ་ས་མང་ནི་རེད་གི།
རྔ་བ་ན་ཚོང་པ་མང་ནི་རེད་གི།
ཟི་ལིང་ན་མཁས་པ་མང་ནི་རེད་གི།
སྤྱིར་བོད་ཡུལ་ན་གྲྭ་བ་མང་ནི་རེད་གི་རེད་ཟུས།

In mentioning Ziling, one of the major urban centers in Amdo, and long a place where Tibetan cultural producers from the region gathered and worked, this version of the three-provinces model speaks to an emerging realization of the intellectual ferment and scholarly activity developing in Amdo. In the recorded comedy performance, the statement elicits laughter from the studio audience of Ziling-based Tibetans, many of whom would themselves be intellectuals. They simultaneously recognize the intertextual relationship with the original chol kha sum idea and appreciate that it has been reworked into an image that they understand.

Further complicating this already complex description is the fact that Amdo, which was never a concrete political entity (Huber 2002, xiii), now exists across multiple administrative boundaries, including parts of China's present-day Qinghai, Gansu, and Sichuan. Local provincial and prefectural administrations interpret policy directives differently, and implementation may also vary by county or even township. Nevertheless, Amdo remains a salient regional and linguistic identity for many Tibetans in the region.

In the 1950s, the new government of the People's Republic of China further complicated regional identities when it undertook an ambitious nationwide "ethnic identification" (Ch. *minzu shibie*) project that sought to scientifically identify the ethnic composition of the people living in China (Mullaney 2010; Ramsey 1992) on the basis of four criteria: shared language, locality, economy, and psychological makeup (Gladney 2004, 151; Harrell 2001, 39–42). The project whittled an initial number of over four hundred applications (Davis 2005, 17; Litzinger 2000, 7) to the more manageable official recognition of fifty-five minority groups and one majority (Han) group who are all considered part of one Chinese nation-race, the *Zhonghua minzu* (Leibold 2007; Mullaney 2004).[2] On the basis of this work, the Chinese government officially recognized Tibetans, regardless of where they are from, with the umbrella term *Zangzu*, translated into Tibetan as *Bod* (བོད་།) and pronounced in Amdo as *wod* or *wol*. This official recognition appears on national identification cards, and various prefectures and counties are classified as "Tibetan autonomous," with guarantees of Tibetan representation in local government.

From some perspectives, this might seem natural. Tibetan oral tradition includes formulae like *gonak wol* (black-headed Tibetans, མགོ་ ནག་བོད་།) and *dongmar wol* (red-faced Tibetans, གདོང་དམར་བོད་།), by which Tibetans referred to themselves. Religious writing often began with a Sanskrit phrase followed by a translation into *wolhkel* (the Tibetan language, བོད་སྐད།). Seen from another perspective, however, the state's use of the term *Bod*—which also referred more specifically to Tibetans from the central regions, including Lhasa and Zhigatse—gave new political status to a reified and translocal identity (Makley 2007; see also Tuttle 2010) that arguably did not exist in this fashion before. These historical and contemporary complications make Amdo a difficult and awkward scale for contemporary academic study.

With its lower altitude and location at the peripheries of both Tibetan and Han cultural spaces, the region plays an important role as an interethnic "contact zone" (Sulek and Ptackova 2017, 11) about the size of modern-day France, which is also inhabited by a number of ethnic groups, including the Hui (China's largest Muslim ethnic group),[3] the Tu (also known by a number of autonyms, including Monguor, Mangghuer, Monghuor, and Mongghul),[4] Salars,[5] Kazakhs, Mongolians,[6] and China's majority ethnic group, the Han (Zenz 2014, 36–42; Roche 2011, 8). Historically, for example, Tuttle recognizes that Amdo Tibetans, as well as Mongolian and Monguor practitioners of Tibetan Buddhism in the Amdo region, acted as brokers in the development of the modern Chinese state, not least by serving as important mediators between Tibetan communities and the Chinese state (Tuttle 2005). The Amdo dialect of Tibetan, meanwhile, has traditionally been the "model language" of what is often called the Amdo *sprachbund* (Sandman and Simon 2016; Dwyer 2013; Janhunen 2004, 2005), which includes the languages spoken by the various groups living in the region. This continued into the 1950s, when the People's Liberation Army formally—and sometimes violently (Li 2016; Weiner 2020)—incorporated Tibetan communities in Amdo within the nascent People's Republic of China.

Under the auspices of the United Work Front, the Chinese Communist Party initially promoted a gradual implementation of socialist collectivization, and area religious and secular elites were recruited into local government leadership (Weiner 2012). Then, in 1958, disaster struck. A failed uprising saw the party scrap the gradual policies of the United Work Front and implement full collectivization in line with the rest of the nation. In the aftermath, the Tibetan religious and secular elite fled to India and established a government in exile, and many monasteries were forced to close their doors. In Qinghai, for example, which had once boasted a robust 722 monasteries and nearly sixty thousand monks and reincarnate lamas prior to 1958, only 11 monasteries remained open after this date; the number rose to 137 in 1962 after the Northwest Nationalities Work Conference (Pu 1990, 3–4). Statistics from neighboring Gansu tell a similar story: the 369 pre-1958 monasteries were reduced to only 8 after that date; again, the number rose to 107 in 1962 (Pu 1990 503–4). Similar stories apply to other Tibetan regions as well. Combined with Mao's ill-fated "Great Leap Forward" and a widespread famine, Tibetans in Amdo today still speak of 1958 as having brought such sweeping and traumatic changes for communities across Tibet that it remains the year that they recognize as a "change in worlds" (Hayes 2014): the year the "old world" ended and the "new world" began.

Between 1966 and 1976, the entirety of the People's Republic of China was gripped by the Cultural Revolution, and Tibetans in Amdo were no exception. This "ten years of turmoil," during which "the four olds" (old customs, old culture, old habits, and old ideas) were targeted for destruction, lingers in the region's cultural memory. The post-1958 closure of monasteries that had been so important to community life only intensified as village temples were demolished, monastery buildings repurposed (Makley 2007, 113–14), and religious writings destroyed (Willock 2011, 8). Pu Wencheng (1990) meanwhile notes that Qinghai and Gansu both closed all but one monastery, leaving open just Kumbum and Labrang Monasteries, respectively. In addition to targeting religion, Goodman (2004a, 388) points out that education was only to be conducted in Putonghua standard Chinese (Mandarin) rather than a bilingual education system that also taught Chinese.

Despite this commonly accepted narrative that cultural work and education came to a total standstill throughout the Maoist period, some did continue, and this is particularly true in Amdo, where a few dedicated teachers worked to, in the words of one former student, "save Tibetan" (Pema Bhum 2006, 2017).[7] In many pastoral communities, schools met in tents rather than in fixed buildings, and the conditions were basic at best, but the work of education continued. One notable cultural producer, who would have been ten years old before the end of the Cultural Revolution, described his early education as follows:

> After I was a little older than ten, after that I went to elementary school. Uh, at first, there wasn't exactly a clear school in our village. They pitched a tent, a cloth tent, and I went to that [tent] school.

Then, for one or two years, I went to the elementary school in the township, which is called the *xiang*. Then I went to the county middle school. Then I attended Tsolho Nationalities Normal School. And then at seventeen, I directly received a job, and came to Ziling and have been working at this post here since. (personal communication, March 11, 2013).

This type of anecdotal evidence appears time and again across Amdo. Under these difficult circumstances, Tibetan-language instruction often persisted due to the support of a single charismatic teacher, maybe a former monk. Those fortunate enough to attend these primary schools during the Cultural Revolution were well positioned to enter prefectural teacher training schools—like the famous Tsolho Nationalities Normal School mentioned above—and newly reopened universities when policies loosened again, beginning, for Tibetan regions, in the post-Mao period.

The above overview brings the narrative generally into the post-Mao moment, in which this book picks up the narrative: the period of Reform and Opening Up beginning in the 1980s. Against a background of intensifying social, economic, and cultural changes as the PRC shifted from a socialist to a market economy, Tibetans have been encouraged to resume Tibetan-language cultural production, including music (Morcom 2008; Adams 1996; Yangdon Dhondup 2008a), literature (Hartley 1999, 2003, 2007; Hartley and Schiaffini-Vedani 2008; Lama Jabb 2014; Yangdon Dhondup 2000, 2008b; Robin 2007, 2008), and art (Harris 1999), as well as the comedic and musical expressive forms detailed in this book. More recently, this has also spurred the development of a new film industry (Berry 2016; Frangville 2016; Lo 2016; Yau 2016; Grewal 2016).

The fortuitous confluence of educational opportunity, cultural policy, and the unprecedentedly bare cultural field in the wake of the Maoist period empowered a young generation of intellectuals to emerge as leaders of contemporary Tibetan experimentation with language, philosophy, and genre (Hartley and Schiaffini-Vedani 2008). Looking to both Tibetan traditions and more modern forms of cultural production, these intellectuals have played an immense role in shaping popular attitudes about the Tibetan present and expectations for a Tibetan future. Being seen and heard in media spaces, however, has often required working from within state-controlled institutions, including mass media. This book tells the story of how zurza provides cultural producers with a traditional resource to tell new Tibetan stories in post-Mao Amdo.

Amdo is a dynamic and diverse region undergoing rapid change, but studies have all too often examined contemporary Amdo Tibetan communities and their cultural practices synchronically and through festival moments. This approach produces "freeze frames" (Makley 2013b, 190) that obscure much of the region's dynamism and diversity. Similarly, the chapters of this book show that zurza is too fluid a concept for such an approach. A diachronic one as flexible as zurza itself is necessary to understand it and the various ways cultural producers have deployed it. This book follows zurza—formulated differently at different moments and in different media—and its development in a generally chronological order, from oral traditions linked to stage performances in the early post-Mao period, and then into twenty-first-century televised sketch comedies and online hip-hop. At each moment, the ability to use zurza allowed access to state-controlled media and performance spaces, making it a valuable expressive resource for Tibetan cultural resilience at a moment when many producers felt the culture to be under threat.

•

Sitting in a gleaming white Honda with a portly comedian and two of his trainees on the way to a performance, I was admiring the northern Sichuan countryside when the comedian Jamyang Lodree twisted back from his shotgun seat (one of his students was driving) and said, "If you want to be an artist, you have to be a bad person." Something in his voice told me that he considered this an important idea. He used the word *jyutselpa*, which refers not just to painters or sculptors but to culture brokers who may engage in a variety of forms of production, including writing, acting, and singing. People like him. The word *ngen pa*, which I translate as "bad person," was tinged with moral judgment.

Over the next few days, I watched as he seemed to put his words into embodied action. Over this time, he ate dinner with a local paramour (and tried to introduce me to her sister), consumed impossible amounts of liquor with a lama while the cleric's Han devotees served them both, and got into arguments on the popular social media platform WeChat.

I should also note that he is a former monk who left religious life and became an emcee, singer, and comedian. His early exposure to both monastic life and the oral and material ways of pastoral life underpin his reputation as a master wordsmith and a veritable repository of Tibetan folk knowledge. His breadth of experience also makes him a keen observer of Tibetan life in a rapidly changing world.

These culminated in his performance at the event we attended, in which he and his students performed a sketch hilariously targeting gambling (primarily), through a portrayal of a man losing progressively larger amounts of money at cards while seeking to influence his fortune with ever-more vigorous prayers between hands.

Jamyang Lodree passed away suddenly in 2019, and with him went a vast repository of folk knowledge. I have since come to understand this statement about being a bad person as saying that a contemporary Tibetan "artist" must be a trickster, living betwixt and between, and eschewing the accepted definitions of a good life. Taking on the role of modern society's trickster, the artist gains the experiences, critical eye, and expressive skill to create meaningful and entertaining stories. The foundation for all of this is the zurza as used in oral tradition. To begin the examination of zurza in post-Mao Amdo, then, requires first looking to still-present traditions of satirical humor in Tibet.

1
Dokwa
"Eating the Sides" in Oral and Literary Traditions

Two men meet while digging caterpillar fungus (also known as *Ophiocordyceps sinensis*, the Tibetan *yartsa gunbu*, or the Chinese *dongchong xiacao*), the medicinal herb that has grown so valuable in Tibetan communities in the twenty-first century that its harvest has become a key part of the local economy. Families from the areas where the fungus grows best may earn enough to live the rest of the year without working. Others keep their families afloat with proceeds from their harvest (Winkler 2013, 390). Tibetans now refer to the act of harvesting the medicine simply as "digging the bug" with no other modifiers necessary.[1]

Like the first day of deer hunting season in my native Ohio, schools close during the caterpillar fungus digging season, because many students simply will not attend, as their labor is needed elsewhere. For about a month in the late spring, entire families move to the highest altitudes of the Tibetan Plateau to dig for their fortunes in the form of this prized medicine. In doing so, they earn the disposable income that will be required to sustain them until the following spring.

The two men who meet on this day are a study in opposites. Drijya Yangkho, a bearded man, wears a traditional robe that has seen better days. Clean-shaven Ruyong Riglo sports the sort of modern style apparel that Tibetans in Amdo call "Chinese clothing." The former owns the land and now earns money by allowing prospectors to harvest its caterpillar fungus. The latter, who bears all the hallmarks of living in the town, has come to dig fungus to sustain his family during the coming year. The history of the two is evident even from their names: Drijya, means "one hundred female yaks" and suggests that Yangkho's family owns (or owned) a moderate-size herd, and is thus prosperous in traditional terms. Ruyong, by contrast, may refer to a family that has joined the community recently, perhaps due to conflicts in their original one.[2] Those who know the pair will also recall that there has previously been animosity between them dating back to the Cultural Revolution, when the once-wealthy Drijya Yangkho and his family were stripped of their property due to their class status, while the formerly penniless Ruyong Riglo was elevated.

Though they have each have their business to do, none of this should stop the two longtime rivals-turned-friends from having some fun while sitting on the grassland together. First, they reminisce about the old days, when they used to come to the grassland and play tug of war. They give it a go for old time's sake. Then, as they rest, Drijya Yangkho starts to compose a short poem on the spot to poke fun at Ruyong Riglo:

The one who goes crazy while talking about wealth,
The one who would jump [off a cliff] when he sees a [yartsa] bug,
The one acts as if released from being tied up.
The one who doesn't go unless it's to crawl [in search of yartsa],
From the figurative speech, I couldn't realize who it was.
When I meditated on it, [I realized] it was Ruyong Riglo.

རྒྱུ་ཞིག་བཤད་དུས་སྨྱོས་འཛིག་ནོ།།
འབུ་ཞིག་རིག་དུས་མཆོངས་འཛིག་ནོ།།
བཏགས་ནས་བཞག་སྟེ་ཁྲོ་འདུག་བོ།།
གོག་ནས་མིན་ནས་མི་འགྲོ་ནོ།།
ཚགས་བཞག་ནས་ཅེ་ཡིན་མ་ཤེས་ཐལ།།
མཉམ་བཞག་དུས་རུ་ཡོང་རིག་ལོ་རེད།།

The extemporaneously composed verse pokes fun at the man opposite him for his materialism, characterizing it as a mania. In doing so, the speaker is "doing zurza," sarcastically pointing out the flaws of another in a humorous and meaningful way.

Following this, the pair decide to engage in a friendly competition of poetry and trade several such poems back and forth. In one response, the digger, Ruyong Riglo, invokes the pastoralist's family name ("one hundred female yaks") to critique the latter's indolence—a common critique of Tibetans in China (Yeh 2013b, 163–89):

Ah, dear Drijya Yangkho,
whose hundred *dri* aren't on the mountain.
Hey, where have you put them?
When others don't buy the bugs
You'll certainly go hungry.

ཨ་འབྲི་བརྒྱ་གཡང་ཁོ་ལོ་ལོ།
འབྲི་བརྒྱ་བོ་རི་ན་མེད་ནོ།།
ཨ་དུ་བོ་གང་ལ་ཞོགས་ཐལ།།
འབུ་ཆ་བོ་ནོ་ནི་མེད་དུས།།
ཁྱོད་ཆ་བོ་ལྟོགས་རྒྱུ་ལོས་ཡིན།།

Later, Ruyong Riglo picks up the same thread and also alludes to government subsidies that makes the pastoralist's comfortable life possible, saying:

Don't tell about how there is fungus
in the uninhabited grassland.
If those above [meaning the government] knew that there
 is wealth here,
Would they still give you what they have given?

སྦྱི་ཅང་མེད་རྒྱུ་སའི་ནང་ན།།
འབུ་ཡོད་ནོ་ཅང་ལ་མ་བཤད།།
རྒྱ་ཡོད་ནོ་གོང་ལ་གསལ་དུས།།
ཁྱིའ་གནང་ནོ་རང་དགར་ཆེ་སྟེར།།

The pair continue back and forth for several minutes in this vein, sometimes pausing between poetic performances to discuss the last poem, their history, or modern life. Each laughs at the other's poems, apparently appreciative of the art, and neither takes offense at the gentle teasing.

Zooming out, we see that the old acquaintances are not on the grassland at all. In fact, they are on a stage in a television studio, and this is a staged performance, scripted by the comedian Menla Jyab in 2011. In this sketch, Menla Jyab and his partner Namlha Bum reprise two favorite roles from performances past. The live studio audience and the viewers watching the prerecorded sketch at home both know the characters' backgrounds and are intimately familiar with the sort of exchange and context before them. They laugh and applaud as the two stars use poetry to banter back and forth.

On stage, the performers call their poems *dokwa*, though in other parts of Amdo, Tibetans call them by the related names *daksa*, *dakree*, and *dokra*. This rare form of extemporaneously composed, sarcastic verse pits folk poets against each other, mercilessly making fun of each other's appearance and behavior. In writing, intellectuals may render the term as *btags pa* (བཏགས་པ།). *Btags*, the verb also used for naming an individual, suggests that name-calling, or poetically naming someone as the possessor of certain traits, is an important part of the genre.

Amdo boasts an incredible array of oral and festival traditions. Just focusing on the oral ones, Tibetans in Amdo are known to perform a variety of secular and religious verbal arts, including but not limited to *tamhwé* (proverbs),[3] *tamshel* (speeches),[4] *khel* (riddles),[5] *laye* (love songs),[6] and *lushag* (antiphonal song duels). These sit alongside a much broader array of oral and festival practices from across the Tibetan cultural world. Euro-American scholarship on these is only piecemeal at best, with much recent research centering on a few locations most easily accessed (Henrion-Dourcy 2017b, 9–10).

Among these, dokwa are an obscure and little-studied genre of Tibetan oral tradition. The only English-language description I have yet found defines the poems as follows:

verbal sparring matches characteristic of nomad herdsmen. These are intensely amusing encounters where the participants trade highly potent verses in order to belittle each other. These stinging caricatures are unforgiving and make frequent reference to the other's physical traits. (Anton-Luca 2002, 183)

And yet, despite its relative absence from the Tibetological literature, the poems combine several values that Tibetans seemed to admire in speech: a quick wit and turn of phrase, the ability to put ideas into verse, and using both in the service of humorous critique. As such, dokwa and other sarcastic and satirical forms of traditional expression serve as an entry point to the Tibetan concept of zurza in traditional contexts as a way of making both person-specific and more general societal critiques. Note that although the examples here stem primarily from my fieldwork in the twenty-first century, the focus on a range of traditional oral and literary practices is intended to underscore the historical importance of zurza, which continues to shapes the attitudes and practices of modern Tibetan cultural producers in the present.

•

Amdo Tibetans are not the only folk artists to compose humorous oral poems. In Lhasa, Tibetans traditionally sang humorous "street songs" written by performers (Goldstein 1982), and Tibetans around the plateau sing lushag (see Anton-Luca 2002). In exile, performers of Ache Lhamo opera may parody and satirize others in performance (Calkowski 1991, 653; Henrion-Dourcy 2017a). Elsewhere in the People's Republic of China, the Nuosu branch of the Yi in Sichuan perform poetic *kenre*, used to "both welcome and cajole guests" (Bender 2019, xvi; see also Bamo Qubumo 2001, 2008), while the Dai in Yunnan also use verbal dueling in courtship rituals (Davis 1999). In another part of the world, Basque *bertsolari*s create their own poetic dueling performances (see, for example, Barandiaran 2009; Egaña 2007; White 2003; and Pagliai 2009), while verbal dueling is also part of "the dozens" in African American and white American (Bronner 1978) communities, and in Tuscan *contrasto* (Pagliai

2009). Not all traditions rely on spontaneous duels, though. For example, the *haló* of the Anlo-Ewe people in Ghana may be carefully prepared ahead of time (Avorgbedor 1994, 92–93; 1999; 2001). These traditions may be spoken, sung, or performed with musical accompaniment. There may also be rules regarding the gender and age of performers in verbal exchanges. Each, however, comes with genre- and culture-specific rules for performance and interpretation.

Recited as if extemporaneous—though in actuality part of a scripted performance—the sarcastic poems from the sketch about digging caterpillar fungus are only imitations of true dokwa poems. To really understand the genre- and culture-specific "keys" (Bauman 1977) of dokwa performance, original texts would almost undoubtedly be better. They were not easy to find. In the farming area of Rebgong, I spoke to people who had heard of the extemporaneously composed satirical poems but was told that nobody actually performed them there. Not anymore. They suggested that I seek out performers in the nomadic areas. The accepted logic in Amdo is that pastoral communities have long been famed for their command of oral traditions, and this ideology persists into the present. So I went to Malho Mongolian Autonomous County, colloquially known simply as Sokdzong (meaning "Mongolian County"). There I was again told that people *used* to perform these traditions but now did so only rarely. Instead, they suggested I go to Golok. Even further from the urban center of Ziling, Golok remained a repository of oral tradition in the Amdo Tibetan imaginary.

The road from Ziling to Golok is better than it used to be. What was once a tortuous bus ride taking at least twelve hours on narrow roads twisting up one side of mountains and back down another is now an eight-hour jaunt along smoothly paved roads. The capstone to this engineering feat is a ten-kilometer tunnel through Laji Shan (which Tibetans call Goméla)—part of a mountain range, running roughly from the northwest to the southeast, that many of the roads to southern and western Qinghai must cross—that cuts under what was once the most dangerous and time-consuming part of the journey. In addition to considerably shortening the drive time, the tunnel also shaped how Tibetan travelers experienced the landscape. Those who get carsick still retch as the bus navigates bends in the road, but they no longer throw windhorses—*lungta*, small, colorful pieces of paper with scriptures printed on them—at the highest point of the mountain pass. Buses still stop for meals at roadside noodle houses, but they no longer need to make an overnight trip. All things considered, I think most travelers willingly accept the tradeoff.

My last such trip was in 2017, when a friend introduced me to a local government official who had agreed to introduce me to some people with knowledge of dokwa, which locals call *dokra*. The next day, after a two-hour drive to a town even farther out in the country, I found myself sitting in the living room of the lavishly decorated but little-used apartment that the official kept in his local county seat. There was nothing to suggest that we were in an area of the Tibetan Plateau that had, until recently, been relatively underdeveloped. Outside, a bright sun bathed the town and the surrounding mountains in golden light, but inside the curtains were drawn. We could have been anywhere.

I spoke with the middle-aged official who had agreed help me on my way, as well as another man who worked for the local government in dispute mediation, a role that required knowledge of both national law and local proverb lore. We discussed verbal art in Golok Prefecture and the mediator's work in a role that spans tradition and modernity. The mediator's experiences were interesting, but I was not in Golok to talk about proverbs or the law. Instead, I had been introduced to this man because people said he could tell me about dokwa. After a fair amount of discussion, he gave a classic disclaimer that he was unable to perform them himself, but that he knew of some, and then he began to tell a rather scatological story:

> Once, this thing happened in my place. My father's name was called Adri Topa [to the cadre], you know that. When you ask what there was, an old woman with watery eyes, and a blue face, she was coming near a family in our place [in our community] called the Zhumar family. When she came to the edge of the that family['s land] . . . she found a red padmaraga stone,[7] so one from our place spoke a dokwa like this:

You have sent a green round [woman] over here.
You have found a red round thing,
Turning and tossing it a bit.
What is it, white-watery woman?
What kind of shit is it, shitty-blind woman?

He said like this. Then what the woman replied was this (Adri Topa was a person who knew a thing or two about *gzi* and agates):

A green and round woman came over,
Found a red and round thing,
Tossed and turned it, and
Showed it to Adri Topa.
[He] said it was worth hundreds of horses and mules.
If you add your black tent over your head,
As a bonus, it would make a difference.

She said like that. So, for example, those two going back and forth, is called a dokra.

ཆག་འཛོག་ཁ་ཐུས་ད་སྔུན་ཆད་ཅིག་ག་དེད་དོ་ས་ཆ་དེ་མོ་ཅིག་ཡོད་ནི་རེད། དའི་པ་ཀུན་གི་སྡིང་ལ་ཨ་དྲིས་སྟོད་པ་ཟེར་ནི་རེད།...དེ་ཐུས་ཤེས་ནི་རེད། ཆེ་ཅིག་ཡོད་ནི་རེད་ཟེར་དུས་ཨ་ཡེས་སྙིག་རྒྱ་ཡོད་འདུག་ནི་...དོ་སྟོན་པོ་ཅན་ཅིག་དེ་མོ་ཅིག་བརྒྱགས་ཡོད་ནི་...དེད་དོ་གི་བཞུར་མར་ཆོང་བཞེ་ཅིག་ཡོད་ནི་རེར་...དེ་ཆོང་གི་མཐའན་ཀ་ནས་ཡོད་གོ་དུས་གི་ནས་ད་དེ་མོ་གི་པད་མར་ཀ་ཅན་པོ་དོ་མོ་དམར་དྲིས་ཅིག་ལོན་རེད། དི་གི་དེད་དོ་གི་གཅིག་གིས་འདོགས་ར་ཅན་པོ་ཆེ་བཞེ་ནི་རེད་ཟེར་དུས་ན།

ཁྱོད་སྨན་ལྗང་རིལ་རིལ་ཅིག་བཀྱངས་ཡོང་ཐལ།
ཐུས་དམར་རིལ་རིལ་ཅིག་ལོན་ཡོང་ཐལ།
ཡར་རིལ་མར་རིལ་ཆ་ཅིག་ཡས།
དེ་ཆེ་ཞིག་རེད་གོ་རྒྱ་དཀར་མ།
སྒྲུག་རེ་རེད་གོ་སྒྲུག་ཞར་མ་...དེ་མོ་བཞེ་ནི་རེད།

དེ་ཨ་ཡེས་དེས་ཧུར་ར་ཆེ་བཞེ་བཞེ་བཞེ་དུས།

དེད་དེ་ཨ་དྲིས་སྟོད་པ་ཅན་པོ་དེ་ཅིག་གཉེ་དང་མཆོང་སླ་ཤེས་ནི་ཅིག་ཡིན་ནི་རེད།

སྣན་ལྕང་རིལ་རིལ་ཞིག་བརྒྱངས་ཡོང་ཐལ།
དམར་རིལ་རིལ་ཞིག་ལོན་ཡོང་ཐལ།
ཡར་རིལ་མར་རིལ་ཚ་ཅིག་ཡས།
མོས་ཨ་ཉིས་སྟོད་པ་སྟོན་ན་ད།
རྟ་རྡེལ་བརྒྱ་རེ་གནས་གི་བཟེ།
ཁྱིའི་མགོ་མགོ་སླུ་ད་ད།
ཁན་ཞིག་བཞག་ན་ཁ་ཁ་རེད།

དེ་མོ་བཟེ་ནི་རེད་...ད་དཔེར་ན་དེ་གཉིས་ཏུར་ཆུར་ར་བབ་ནོ་...འདོགས་ར་ཚན་པོ་དེ་ཇེར་གོ་ནི་རེད་...

The poems themselves do not seem particularly funny in translation. The first makes a slur against the woman's appearance, and the response wittily and poetically answers the first to brag—in verse form, no less—that she has just obtained something of great value. Nevertheless this narrative about the initial dokwa and the woman's level-headed response—versions of which were shared as exemplary of the genre by speakers from multiple areas of Golok—provides valuable perspectives on the genre. Dokwa, referring to both the initial poem and the response, may denote any extemporaneously composed, spoken, and critical poems. Second, the poems themselves were composed of groups of lines that usually ranged from six to eight syllables each, a meter that is common in folksong traditions (Sujata 2005; Ramble 1995; Sangs rgyas bkra shis, Qi, and Stuart 2015) and secular oratory (Thurston 2012, 2019). The syllables are grouped into phrases and formulae of two or three as, for example, the three-syllable phrases "you have sent" (བརྒྱངས་ཡོང་ཐལ།, *jyang yong ta*), and "you have found" (ལོན་ཡོང་ཐལ།, *lon yong ta*) above, in which the first syllable is the main verb, the second indicates movement with the verb "to come," and the third is a perfective marker. The initial poem uses parallel lines and may repeat syllables either within the same line or across lines. The first poem in the above exchange, for example, repeats *ril ril zig* (རིལ་རིལ་ཞིག, translated above as "something round") in each of the first two lines and ends each with *yong ta*. The third line continues to repeat the syllable *ril*, but this time in the phrase *yar ril mar ril* (ཡར་

རིལ་མར་རིལ།, translated as "turning and tossing"). These forms of wordplay sound pleasing and can be used to make the same Tibetan syllables humorously take on a range of meanings.

While dokwa do not always require a response, the most noteworthy exchanges all seem to feature a retort, and the example from this is no different. The response need not be metrically identical to the initial dokwa but should play off of and invert some of its grammar and language. The second poem in the narrative above, for example, repeats the first three lines verbatim, essentially accepting its premise, but then uses the remaining lines to invert the critique. The intertextual link to, and inversion of, the first poem helps to underscore the second speaker's impressive command of verbal art and generates some of the humor in the performance through its wordplay.

A final point about the poetics of dokwa is that unlike Tibetan folk singing and oratory traditions, which deploy a variety of formulae to satisfy the metrical requirements of traditional verse, these dokwa do not. Instead, the performances are so specific to the moment of their creation that they maintain the verse but often dispense with the register of oral tradition. For example, the speakers rarely compare their targets to animals or to deities, nor do they use traditional formulae about the earth, sky, or mountains common in wedding speeches and praises of place. The vertical, tripartite division of upper, middle, and lower prevalent in vernacular representations of territory (Ramble 1995, 87) is also absent. Instead, the speakers use a lower register, a more colloquial idiom full of repetition and inversion, to make their case as cleverly and succinctly as possible. Additionally, unlike folk singing traditions, which are also metrically limited by the songs themselves, dokwa poets can switch between seven-, eight-, and nine-syllable lines within the same poem as fits their needs.

Notice, also, that rather than simply retelling the poems, speakers who told me about exemplary dokwa performances of the past embedded the poems in narrative. At first, I thought that the narratives were added for my benefit. After all, good storytellers around the world are known to take the audience into account during the emergent storytelling performance. But then I found a published collection of these poems that did the same thing, and these were almost certainly aimed at Tibetan audiences. Whereas collections of love songs or song-dueling regularly only include pages upon pages of lyrics with no further information, this collection also uses narratives to contextualize the poems, as with the following example, which is illustrative:

YOU WON'T GET FAR

One day, a young man who particularly enjoyed banter was riding a blue-black horse and holding a riding crop. As he was bringing the horse to a walk as he went around a camp, the horse's hoof gave way at a family's cattle pen, and he tumbled to the ground. A witty nomad woman spoke this dokwa:

> Hey uncle!
> [Your] black horse was galloping, and
> When it arrived in the black-earth enclosure,
> The black horse did a full prostration.
> And though your crop sounds on its rump,
> You won't go very far!

When she said this, that young man looked closely at the woman and saw that she didn't have a sash around her waist but had tied a rope. Knowing that it was a poor family, he immediately spoke this dokwa back:

> Hey sister!
> Tying a black string as a waist sash,
> Doing a dokwa of someone you've just encountered.
> When you have enough to eat and drink,
> No one will be able to subdue you.

When he said this, the girl was left speechless.

ཐག་རིང་ལ་བློན་ས་མེད་ཀི

ཉིན་ཞིག་གསར་བུ་ཁྱད་ཆོས་རྒྱག་རྒྱུར་དགའ་བ་ཞིག་གིས་རྟ་སྦོ་ནག་ཅིག་ཞོན་ནས་རྟ་ལྕག་ཅིག་
ཐོགས་ཏེ། རྟ་གོམ་པ་ཁྱེར་ནས་དུ་འདབས་ཞིག་བརྒྱུད་ནས་འགྲོ་དུས། བྱིས་ཆུང་ཞིག་གི་ཕྱགས་
སླས་ནས་རྟ་ལྕག་རིབ་བྱུང་ནས་ས་ལ་འགྱེལ་བ་ན། འབྲོག་མོ་ཁ་བདེ་ཞིག་གིས་འདི་ལྟར་བཏགས་
པ་བྱས།

ཨ་རོགས་ཨ་ཁུ།
རྟ་གྲོ་ནག་ལ་གོམ་པ་འགྲོ་གི།
ས་སླས་ནག་གི་ནང་ལ་ཕྱིན་དུས།།
རྟ་གྲོ་ནག་གིས་བརྒྱངས་ཕྱག་འཚལ་གི།
ཁྱིའི་སྔག་རིང་ལ་གཞུག་རྒྱུ་བྱགས་སུང་།།
ཁྱོད་ཐག་རིང་ས་བློན་ས་མེད་ཀི།

ཞེས་བཏད་པ་ན། གསར་བུ་དེས་བུ་དེར་ཞིག་ལྟ་ཞིག་བྱས་པ་ན། སྐུ་རགས་མེད་པར་བྱུ་གུ་ཞིག་
བཅིངས་ཡོད་པ་མཐོང་ནས། རྒྱ་ནོར་གྱིས་དབུལ་བའི་བྱིས་ཆུང་ཞིག་ཡིན་པ་ཤེས་ནས། དེ་ལ་ཐག་
ཕྱིར་འདི་ལྟར་བཏགས་པ་བྱས།

ཨ་རོགས་ཨ་ཅེ།
ཐིག་ནག་གིས་སྐུ་རགས་བཅིངས་ནས།།
ཐུག་ཐུག་པོར་བཏགས་པ་བྱེད་ཀི།
ཆ་འབྱུང་གི་མགོ་རྟ་འཛོམས་དུས།།
མགོ་ཅིག་གིས་ནོན་ས་མེད་ཀི།

ཞེས་བཏད་པ་ན་བུ་མོ་དེར་ཁ་གགས་རྒྱུ་མེད་པར་གྱུར།

(Lha sde nyi ma tshe ring 2013, 16–17)

In this second example, the woman teases the man whose horse has fallen, saying that his horse has prostrated itself. The second half of the poem, meanwhile, notes that no amount of whipping the horse will make a difference, suggesting a rebuke of the man's response to his animal's misfortune. In the response, meanwhile, the man points out the girl's poverty—indexed by her clothing—and suggests that an adequate amount of food and drink might help her wits. People in glass houses, he would seem to say, should not throw stones.

The humor and appreciation, however, derives only partly from the content of the poems. The poetry itself and the quick wits to create it are also part of the appeal. The two dokwa in "You Won't Get Far" maintain many of the characteristics as the one before it, including parallelism, repetition, and intertextual reference from the first poem to the second. The first poem also evidences a head rhyme popular in Tibetan oral traditions, with the first three syllables of each line paralleling one of the lines adjacent to it. For example, the first and third lines begin with *shta gyo nag* (རྟ་རྒྱོ་ནག་, black-haired horse), where *shta* means "horse" and *gyo* is the writer's approximation of the Amdo pronunciation of the word for horse hair. The second line begins with *sa lhee nag* (ས་སླས་ནག་, black-earth enclosure). The three syllable phrases rhyme *shta* (horse) and *sa* (earth), and end with the color *nag* (black). The parallelism, head rhyme, and repetition further mark the performance as poetic.

In performance, speakers distinguished the poetry from the narrative in several ways: poetic lines were more measured and spoken at an even cadence, and the speaker's voice started each line a little higher before gradually lowering his intonation toward the end. This cadence is almost identical to the vocal features used in the "caterpillar fungus" sketch and imitates how these dokwa would have been performed in the moment. In a written publication, they are introduced with a brief statement saying that the speaker "did a dokwa," and then the lines are indented and marked (as with other poetry) with two vertical lines at the end of each. These create aural and visual distinctions between prose and poetry in line with the conventions of their respective media.

But beyond their incorporation of formal features of oral poetry, the narratives in which the dokwa are embedded also encode important information for understanding the genre, not least through pointing directly to questions of immediacy, wit, and (in some written narratives) zurza. First, notice that in both the written "You Won't Get Far" and the orally performed "Adri Topa," the narratives are extremely brief. Because the characters were less important than their words, they only provide enough information—about appearance, actions, etc.—to ensure that the poetic humor makes sense to audiences who were not physically present at the original. In doing so, they focus all attention on the poems, and include no extraneous information beyond what is needed for the audience to make sense of the poems. "You Won't Get Far," for example, tells audiences that the young man likes banter, and explains the circumstances surrounding his horse's tumble, which provided the fodder for the first poem. The girl, meanwhile, is described primarily based on her appearance, and particularly the rope she used to tie her robe, on which the second poem hinges. After the poem or poems are retold, speakers provide very little extra information to conclude the narrative beyond a brief statement about how those present reacted to the poem.

Some information, however, is not directly relevant to understanding the poem, and these evaluative words also provide valuable information about some of the other skills deemed necessary for a successful dokwa performance. For example, in "You Won't Get Far," the woman who spoke the first poem is described as being a "a witty nomad woman." Wit or eloquence, translated from the Tibetan *khabde* (ཁ་བདེ།, literally "good mouth"), is not limited to dokwa but can refer to wittiness or competence in a variety of poetic speech genres.

Tibetans find khabde to be such a valuable quality that it is even enshrined in a Tibetan proverb, which states:

The eloquent are leaders, and
the handy are servants.

ཁ་བདེ་པོ་མི་ཡི་དཔོན་པོ་དང་།།
ལག་བདེ་པོ་མི་ཡི་གཡོག་པོ་ཡིན།།

The proverbial wisdom quickly breaks down in real life. Few of those identified as eloquent in the dokwa narratives above have any real social power within their communities, except that the quick-witted speaker temporarily gains the upper hand in their encounters. While it rarely provides any material benefits, however, recognition as being khabde does provide some degree of social status. In the narratives, a character is often described explicitly as being khabde, but even when they are not, audiences recognize that the characters in these narratives are to be favorably evaluated for their wit.

Immediacy is often important as well. The young man who ultimately wins the encounter, for example, leaves the "witty nomad woman" speechless with his "immediate" response. Both terms appear time and again in the written edition. The oral narratives, meanwhile, may not emphasize these factors in the same way, but consultants also emphasized the same qualities in conversations as well. Not all dokwa require such an immediate response, though. Many narratives tell of a single poem to which no reply is given. Less commonly, a consultant told me that a response may come only hours or even days later. Nevertheless, the best dokwa, the most exemplary performances (and therefore memorable, durable, and repeatable), include quick responses that further cement a person's reputation as being khabde.

But, as one consultant emphasized, "doing dokwa has verse and meaning. You might speak very articulately, but if it doesn't have meaning, it's not good, right? First, it must have meaning, and second, the poems have to be related" (personal communication, April 28, 2016). The poetics of dokwa are, then, fairly straightforward. Meaning, meanwhile, comes from the poem's humorous and indirect critique of another's appearance or behavior.

Indirection refers to "the capacity for presenting, mentioning, or alluding to matters in a roundabout way: either by touching on them obliquely, metaphorically, and unspecifically; by implication, allusion, or analogy; or by the formalization or ritualization of discourse. Indirect discourse is subtle, suggestive, or circuitous, rather than bold and direct" (Young 1978, 51) In "You Won't Get Far," instead of directly saying the woman is poor, the second speaker's response hinges upon the mutual recognition that the rope the woman uses to tie her robe is a sign of her poverty. In "Adri Topa," the woman responds with humor to an attack on her physical appearance and indicates her recognition that her fortunes might have just changed. In other performances, a woman turns a hunter's own boasts against him when he returns home wounded and empty-handed. In the dokwa from the 2011 sketch about caterpillar fungus, the poems focus on the behaviors and attitudes of diggers and of the people who let others dig on their land without ever directly saying that the practice is good or bad. Indirect, sarcastic critique of another is at the center of these performances.

As the dokwa poems demonstrate, poets may rely on a number of speech functions, including punning, parody, synecdoche, metonymy, repetition, and inversion, as well as Tibetan tropes like *khamtshar* (witticisms) and *labjyagpa* (boasting) in order to make a critical point, and the term may appear in collocation with other expressive practices like "bad-mouthing" and "disparaging." Such insults and critiques often, though not always, form an important part of verbal dueling traditions around the globe. Like Basque *bertso*s, for example, Tibetan dokwa might be considered improvisation within "a pre-established framework of entertainment wherein their relationship with themselves and their surroundings can be resolved dialectically" (Egaña 2007, 117). Unlike the more formulaic *bertso*s, however, or even Tibetan lushag traditions, these performances emerge from the conditions of everyday life, and their insults are highly specific to the performance context. Instead, zurza is perhaps best seen as a Tibetan practice similar to the African American art of "signifying."

Writing on the African American verbal dueling practice known as "the dozens," Abrahams (1962, 212) argued that it uses signifying as "a technique of indirect argument or persuasion." Notice the parallels between Tibetan dictionary definitions of zurza and Abrahams's discussion of signifying. Through this indirection, signifying "destabilizes the stable relationship between signifier and signified. Signifiers are interrupted, deferred, or relocated." (Venturino 2008, 278). Zurza, too, makes traditional Tibetan poetic practice "meaningful" by destabilizing this relationship. For example, in "You Won't Get Far," the rope that the nomad woman ties around her waist to secure her robe ceases to be a useful tool in everyday pastoral life, and instead becomes a marker of poverty and shame.

Abrahams's focus on indirection, however, refers only to a single and limited version of signifying (Gates 1983). Signifying also is a tool of parody and intertextual revision of key tropes in African American literature, a "master trope" for African American expressive art. Zurza, too, features in other forms of traditional Tibetan expression, including *nahtam*, the word Tibetans in Amdo use for folktales. Literally meaning "old speech," nahtam provide one entertaining source for the transmission of fundamental ideas about human and more-than-human relations in the

Tibetan physical and cosmological world, about compassion within the Buddhist framework, about appropriate and inappropriate behavior, and more. Through the feats and exploits of heroic kings, famous Buddhist teachers, beloved buffoons (like Arik Lenpa), and tricksters like Uncle Tonpa, these tales provide traditional "equipment for living" (Burke 1973) in the Tibetan world.

Around the world, traditional tales about tricksters and fools—like the Native American Coyote (see, for example, Toelken and Wasson 1999; Tedlock [1978] 1999; and Ballinger 2006), the Tibetan Uncle Tonpa (Dkon mchog dge legs, Dpal ldan bkra shis, and Stuart 1999; Rwa se dkon mchog rgya mtsho 1996; Rinjing Dorje 1997; Sichuan Sheng Minjian Wenyi Yanjiu Hui 1980; Aris 1987), and the Uyghur trickster Afanti (Yu 1991)—appear to upend social order. These same upheavals often define and reinforce the boundaries of acceptable normal human behavior. At the same time, their life on the "tolerated margin of mess" makes them broker characters, who carry with them possibilities for change (Babcock-Abrahams 1975, 183–86). Stories about tricksters and buffoons frequently accomplish this through doing zurza.

Uncle Tonpa—Tibet's most renowned trickster (Dkon mchog dge legs, Dpal ldan bkra shis, and Stuart 1999)—is a man of uncommon wit. He steals from the wealthy (Tshe dbang rdo rje et al. n.d., 43), makes fools of lamas, slaughters animals whose lives have been compassionately spared (Sichuan Sheng Minjian Wenyi Yanjiu Hui 1980, 26–28), and makes kings bark like dogs (Benson n.d., 26). In his more bawdy exploits, he sleeps with nuns and with royalty (Rinjing Dorje 1997). To the average Tibetan, these behaviors are incongruous. No king would bark like a dog. It would be undignified and inappropriate to the office! No merchant would give up his belongings without a reasonable hope of return (and profit)! *Tsétar*—the compassionate Buddhist act of freeing a life so that a particular animal will never be slaughtered (Tan 2016)—would normally preclude all Tibetans from daring to slaughter an animal, even to feed others.

Uncle Tonpa is frequently believed to have been either a single historical figure from Central Tibet (Rwa se dkon mchog rgya mtsho 1996) or an amalgamation of the adventures of many quick-witted Tibetans from the region (Löhrer 2012–13). Whatever the trickster's true origins, his stories are now known across the Tibetan Plateau, including Amdo (Dkon mchog dge legs, Dpal ldan bkra shis, and Stuart 1999, 6), as with, for example, this story excerpted from a textbook for Tibetan students of English:

> Uncle Tonpa's neighbor planted a juniper tree near Uncle Tonpa's window. As time passed, the tree grew bigger and bigger, while Uncle Tonpa's home became darker and darker.
>
> Uncle Tonpa decided that he must do something, broke a branch off the tree, and then went to his neighbor's home. When the neighbor saw Uncle Tonpa holding the branch, he asked, "Where are you going with that juniper branch?"
>
> Uncle Tonpa replied, "A trader is coming to town today. He is buying juniper branches. I am going to sell it to him. One branch is worth ¥100."
>
> The neighbor said, "I have a tall juniper tree with many branches. I'll sell it to him and earn a lot of money."
>
> Uncle Tonpa said, "True. You probably will get a lot of money. But you'd better hurry, because won't be in town long."
>
> His neighbor quickly cut down the tree, cut off all the branches, tied them together in bundles, loaded the bundles on a horse, and led it to town. But when he got there, he couldn't find any trader willing to give him a large amount of money for his juniper branches. Finally, he exchanged all the branches for a donkey.
>
> When he got back, he went to Uncle Tonpa's home and angrily said, "You tricked me! There was no juniper dealer in town!"
>
> Uncle Tonpa said, "I didn't trick you. I told you he wouldn't be in town for long."
>
> Afterward, sunshine bathed Uncle Tonpa's home.

ཨ་ཁུ་སྟོན་པའི་ཁྱིམ་མཚེས་ཀྱིས་ཨ་ཁུ་སྟོན་པའི་སྐྱེའུ་ཁུང་གི་ཉེ་ས་ནས་ཤུག་སྡོང་ཞིག་བཙུགས། དུས་ཀྱི་འགྲོས་དང་བསྟུན་ནས་སྡོང་པོ་རྗེ་ཆེ་ནས་རྗེ་ཆེར་སོང་བས་ཨ་ཁུ་སྟོན་པའི་ཁང་པའང་སྨུག་རྗེ་ནག་ནས་རྗེ་ནག་ཏུ་སོང་།

ཨ་ཁུ་སྟོན་པས་ཁོས་བྱེད་ཐབས་ཤིག་འཐེན་དགོས་པ་བརྒྱ་གིས་བཅད་ཅིང་སྡོང་པོའི་ཡལ་ག

ཞིག་བཅགས་ནས་ཁོའི་ཁྱིམ་མཚེས་ཚང་དུ་སོང་། ཁྱིམ་མཚེས་ཀྱིས་ཨ་ཁུ་སྟོན་པའི་ལག་ལ་ཡལ་
ག་ཞིག་བཟུང་ཡོད་པ་མཐོང་ནས་ཁྱེད་ཀྱིས་ཡལ་ག་དེ་བཟུང་ནས་གང་ལ་འགྲོ་ཞེས་དྲིས།
   ཨ་ཁུ་སྟོན་པས་ཚོང་བ་ཞིག་དེ་རིང་གྲོང་བརྡལ་དུ་ཡོང་ཡོད། ཁོས་ཤུག་སྡོང་གི་ཡལ་ག་ཏོ་
བཞིན་ཡོད། ངས་ཡལ་ག་ཁྱེར་འཆོང་རྒྱས་བྱེད་བཞིན་ཡོད། ཡལ་ག་གཅིག་ལ་སྒོར་མོ་བརྒྱ་སྦྱེར་
ཞེས་ལན་བཏབ།
   ཁྱིམ་མཚེས་ཀྱིས་ང་ལ་ཡལ་ག་མང་པོ་ཡོད་པའི་ཤུག་སྡོང་མཐོན་པོ་ཞིག་ཡོད། ངས་སྡོང་པོ་
ཁོར་བཅོངས་ནས་སྡོང་མོ་མང་པོ་རིག་རྒྱུ་ཨིན་ཞེས་ལབ།
   ཨ་ཁུ་སྟོན་པས་བདེན་པ་རེད། ཁྱེད་ཀྱིས་ཁྲིགས་ཁྲིགས་མེད་ན་སྡོང་མོ་མང་པོ་རིག་ཐུབ།
དེན་ཀྱང་ཁོ་གྲོང་བཟས་ནས་ཡུན་རིང་པོར་མི་འདུག་པས་རབ་ཡིན་ན་ཁྱེད་ཀྱིས་མགྱོགས་པོ་བྱེད་
དགོས་ཞེས་ལབ།
   ཁོའི་ཁྱིམ་མཚེས་ཀྱིས་མགྱོགས་པོར་སྡོང་པོ་བཅད་ཅིང་ཡལ་ག་ཚང་མ་གཞགས་ནས་དོས་
པོར་བསྒྲིལ། དོས་པོ་ཚང་མ་ཁལ་བཀལ་ནས་སྡོང་བདལ་ལ་སོང་། དེན་ཀྱང་ཁོ་སྡོང་བདལ་ལ་
ཕྱིན་པ་ན་ཁོའི་ཤུག་སྡོང་གི་ཡལ་ག་ལ་སྒོར་མོ་མང་པོ་སྤྱེད་འདོད་པའི་ཚོང་བ་གཅིག་ཀྱང་མ་རྙེད།
མཐར་མར་ཁོས་ཡལ་ག་ཚང་མ་སོད་དུ་ཞིག་བཞེས།
   ཁོ་ཕྱིར་ལ་ཐོན་པ་ན་འཆིག་པ་ཟ་བཞིན་དུ་ཨ་ཁུ་སྟོན་པའི་ཁྱིམ་དུ་སོང་ནས་ཁྱེད་ཀྱིས་ང་ལ་
མགོ་སྐོར་བཏང་སོང་། གྲོང་བདལ་ན་ཤུག་སྡོང་གི་ཉོ་མཁན་མེད་ཅེས་བཤད།
   ཨ་ཁུ་སྟོན་པས་ངས་ཁྱེད་ལ་མགོ་སྐོར་མ་བཏང་། ངས་ཁྱེད་ལ་ཁོ་གྲོང་བདལ་ནས་ཡུན་རིང་པོ་
མི་འདུག་ཅེས་ལབ་སྟེ་ཞེས་ལས་བཏབས།
   ཟེར་སོར། ཨ་ཁུ་སྟོན་པའི་གནད་བར་ནི་འདི་རྟག (Tshe dbang bsod nams 2006, 64–65)⁸

Tibetans find favorite exploits like this one to be hilarious, but the enduring feature is their ability to use humor to instruct—to do zurza. In this case, Uncle Tonpa uses the neighbor's avarice and credulity against him, thereby instructing Tibetans. I have found versions of this story reworked as cartoons and in children's books. These stories remain essential equipment for living in Tibetan society.

Importantly, the critique in these stories is often far more indirect than in dokwa. Like the unidentified neighbor, the kings and nobles targeted are not historically identifiable individuals but generic character types who draw attention to and motivate Uncle Tonpa's tricks. The neighbor conned into cutting down his own juniper tree could be your own neighbor who builds a new addition to his or her home that blocks the sunlight from reaching your kitchen. The king who is made to bark like a dog could be any king. Uncle Tonpa's religious victims are similarly never named but are intended to represent generic monks and lamas. Instead, the witty trickster's actions parody normative social relations through "ludic inversion" (Bauman 2004, 2) of the established order. In doing so, the stories create critiques in which the powerful people receive the comeuppance their inappropriate behaviors deserve, and provide instruction for audiences about appropriate behaviors. The generic satirical critique seen in Uncle Tonpa's narratives points to a second—and no less important—form of zurza, which makes a broader and more generic social critique.

Not limited to the oral tradition, Tibetan poets and authors like the renowned early-twentieth-century polymath Gendun Chopel also traditionally used zurza in satirical poems to criticize the behavior of others, including powerful monks. One example is his "Katsom to Labrang" (Labrang la kurwee katsom). Using a traditional form of poetry called *katsom*, in which each line begins with the next letter of the Tibetan alphabet in order, the iconoclastic intellectual and author sarcastically targets the monastic community in Labrang Monastery, where he had studied until being expelled in 1926. Toward the end of the poem, for example, he writes:

> Rather than expelling to distant mountain passes, valleys,
>   and town
> One who takes pride in studying the textbooks of Rwa and Bse,
> Would it not be better to expel to another place
> Those who take pride in selling meat, beer, and smoke?
>   (Lopez 2006, 9–10)

ར་བསྲུས་བསེ་བསྲུས་ཤེས་པའི་ང་རྒྱལ་ཅན༎
ལ་ལུང་ཡུལ་གྲུ་གཞན་ལ་སྐྱོད་པ་ལས༎
ཤ་ཆང་དུད་ཆོས་བྱེད་པའི་ང་རྒྱལ་ཅན༎
ས་ཆ་གཞན་དུ་བསྐྱད་ན་ཅིས་མ་ལེགས༎ (Dge 'dun chos 'phel [1926] 2017)

Labrang Monastery is one of the key monastic institutions in Amdo and follows the Gelukpa sect of Tibetan Buddhism, which has historically discouraged monks from engaging in income-generating activities. Gendun Chopel compares how he was expelled despite his own pursuit of more praiseworthy activities, while monks who misbehave remain.

The sale of meat—which begins with the sinful act of slaughtering a sentient being—and beer would be particularly egregious examples of unbecoming behavior.

Notice that Gendun Chopel's critique operates differently from the dokwa described above. While dokwa performances target specific individuals, the satiric poem targets a community. The satire, meanwhile, focuses less on individual appearances, and instead on actions perceived to be unbecoming of the religious: the mercantilist practices of the "impure" monks from their community at Labrang, and the blind eye that the monastery's leaders seem to direct toward them. If even the monks of this prestigious institution engage in such acts, readers are left to conclude, along with the author, that these activities will "destroy the religious teachings," an accusation made several times throughout the poem. Seventeenth-century Amdo Tibetan Buddhist adept Shar Kalden Jyamtso wrote many songs and poems in which he criticized the behavior of other monks (Sujata 2005, 11) and satirized the wealthy but impious Mongol communities living in Amdo (Sujata 2005, 5). Again, these often critiqued generalized behaviors rather than the appearance or attitudes of specific individuals.

Combined with verbal dueling discussed earlier, Uncle Tonpa's exploits, Kalden Jyamtso's songs of spiritual realization and Gendun Chopel's poems reveal zurza as an important expressive practice for Tibetans in Amdo to create "meaningful" and humorous critiques of others across genre and media. These examples provide a valuable sense of zurza's flexibility and its links to critique. This included both bitingly sarcastic and person-specific jokes, and more generalized satire targeting behaviors of a broader community or subset of a community. However, with the establishment of the People's Republic of China, and its incorporation of Tibetan land and communities within its borders, Tibetan traditions and those who practiced them came into sustained contact with political structures, ideologies, and Han cultural practices that authorized new forms of artistic expression.[9]

Recall from the introduction that Chinese and Tibetan societies were in no way isolated from each other prior to the establishment of the People's Republic (and especially not in the cultural borderlands of Amdo).

The Qing dynasty (1644–1912) stationed "Ambans" and a garrison in Lhasa to represent the Manchu emperor's government. For centuries, the Amdo region was dotted with local rulers, many of whom held power at least partly thanks to recognition by "China-based imperial states" like the Yuan, Ming, and Qing dynasties (Weiner 2020, 27). Tibetan religious leaders, both in Amdo and in Lhasa, had long maintained contacts with Chinese patrons—including emperors—and viewed China as a Buddhist country (Tuttle 2005, 2). But when the People's Liberation Army entered Amdo and other Tibetan regions in the 1950s, the Chinese Communist Party began exerting direct control over them to an unprecedented degree, extending into all areas of Tibetan life, including pastoral practice, education, religion, and expression.

In the early years of the People's Republic of China, as leaders sought ways to promote its Marxist-inspired ideology to Tibetan communities, leaders turned to satire as one potential avenue of expression. In this case, the notion of acceptable satire came filtered through the tentatively sanctioned Chinese concept of *fengci*, itself a relative neologism used to translate Western words for "satire" (Tian 2014, 3). Mao Zedong in particular embraced fengci-as-satire in his famous wartime "Talks at the Yan'an Forum on Literature and the Arts," saying:

> Should we abolish satire (*fengci*). No. Satire is always necessary.[10] But there are several kinds of satire: There are the ones dealing with enemies, dealing with allies, and dealing with one's own team, and the attitudes of each is different. We should not, in general, oppose satire, but we must abolish the satire's indiscriminate use.

In explicitly embracing certain satirical expression, these talks, which shaped much of Mao-era cultural policy, created a space for humorous and artistic expression within the closely monitored Mao-era cultural sphere. This contact with Chinese concepts of satire became so important that many Tibetans and dictionaries now translate *zurza* into Chinese simply as *fengci*.

Seizing on this support for satirical cultural production, scholars and collectors of Tibetan culture promoted traditional tales that seemed to satirically target traditional society. The stories of Uncle Tonpa, for example, found advocates who saw them as signs of a nascent class consciousness already existing in Tibetan society. As the introduction to one volume of collected Uncle Tonpa narratives points out, the stories of the trickster's more Robin Hood–like exploits could

> express the irresolvable contradiction between the rulers and the ruled, the serfs and the lords; reflect the suffering Tibetan people's desire to break their fetters, to liberate themselves, and the unstoppable desire for a better life. The loves and hates of their class are completely clear. (Sichuan Sheng Minjian Wenyi Yanjiu Hui 1980, 3; translation by author)

First published in the immediate aftermath of the Maoist period, during which almost all minority oral traditions were denigrated as "old culture," this introduction conflates the zurza of Uncle Tonpa narratives with Chinese fengci, suggesting how government support elevated some traditions associated with zurza, while making more personal forms of it even more dangerous.

The emphasis on satire's appropriate use, aimed at the correct targets, has been an important feature of officially sanctioned cultural production in China for decades. In Tibetan communities, though, where policies essentially layered fengci atop the preexisting concept of zurza, official attempts to cultivate particular forms of satire essentially flattened zurza through deemphasizing personal critique and traditional practices of "signifying" to fit the political expectations of fengci, which targets the enemies of a modern society. At the same time, fengci did not displace Tibetan notions of zurza. Instead, official government support created new opportunities for authors, comedians, and other eloquent young cultural producers to access state-sponsored media channels to use in novel ways. In this way, zurza became a source of Tibetan persistence and presence on media and in everyday life. Even in the most difficult moments of the Maoist and post-Mao reform eras—periods when the Tibetan language and portrayals of Tibetan traditions in media faced tight restrictions—zurza served as one valuable tool for authors, folktale collectors, and others to be seen and heard.

These oral and written traditions demonstrate that rhetorical and discursive practices that Tibetans associate with zurza are traditionally—meaning historically—a natural part of how those in Amdo understand and inhabit their complex social worlds. Though the examples are decidedly contemporary, they are meant to reference traditional practices dating back to "the old society" before the establishment of the People's Republic. As with the historical dokwa retold to me as narratives, after the performance, audiences still memorize these poems and repeat them to each other when out on the grasslands or just chatting with friends. They may use them just for general levity, or they might invoke the poems to critique the behaviors and attitudes of their peers.

The continued existence of these forms, alongside the Chinese government's support for satire, helps to make zurza a potent expressive resource that carries with it the potential for both person-specific and more general behavior-oriented critiques. The poems in the performance described at the beginning of this chapter are illustrative of this. For example, the first poem directly critiques the person of Ruyong Riglo (by name, no less) for his obsession with making money.

> The one who goes crazy while talking about wealth,
> The one who would jump [off a cliff] when he sees a [yartsa] bug,
> The one acts as if released from being tied up.
> The one who doesn't go unless it's to crawl [in search of yartsa]
> From the figurative speech, I couldn't realize who it was.
> When I meditated on it, [I realized] it was Ruyong Riglo.

རྒྱུ་ཞིག་བཤད་དུས་སྨྱོས་འཛིག་ནི།།
འབུ་ཞིག་རིག་དུས་སྐྱབས་འཛིག་ནི།།
བཏགས་ནས་བཤག་སྟེ་ཁོར་འདུག་ནི།།
གོག་ནས་མིན་ནས་མི་འགྲོ་ནི།།
ཚགས་བཤག་ནས་ཅི་ཡིན་མ་ཤེས་ཐལ།།
མཉམ་བཤག་དུས་རུ་ཡོང་རིག་ལོ་རེད།།

Placed on stage, however, and satirizing the behavior of a fictional character, the personal critique also makes a broader one about changing Tibetan attitudes in the twenty-first century.

Nevertheless, dokwa and many other oral traditions do face strong headwinds. Again, the old frenemies Ruyong Riglo and Drijya Yangkho provide some clues about this as they wrap up their verbal duel and move on to other topics. At the end of their duel, the pastoralist Yangkho reaches a point at which he runs out of steam and lamely says:

Look! Today it doesn't come like that into my mouth.

ལྟོས་དང་། དེ་རིང་ཁ་ནང་ལ་དེ་མོ་ཞིག་མ་ཡོང་ཐལ།

In response, the caterpillar fungus digger casually throws out an opinion:

These days, as we live and live, our mouths and tongues
     become inept.

དེང་སང་བསྡད་ཀྱིན་བསྡད་ཀྱིན་དེད་ཚོའི་ཁ་ལྕེ་སྨུག་གོད་གི

The conversation eventually heads off in other directions, but the idea that Tibetans have, in recent years, become inarticulate or verbally incompetent (in the sense of being less able to fluently perform traditional genres) contrasts starkly with the notion of khabde, discussed above, as a key element of Tibetan verbal art. As people's livelihoods change, and as younger generations increasingly spend time away from their home communities to attend schools, traditional ideas of eloquence are likely changing. Scripted eloquence seems to largely replace impromptu performance, and the understandings and expectations surrounding zurza change. Chapter 2 begins the discussion with the emergence of satirical comedic dialogues in the 1980s, when zurza becomes a crucial tool for comedians and authors to envision new, Tibetan forms of modernity in the post-Mao period.

2

Khashag
Language, Print, and Ethnic Pride in the 1980s

Two speakers, identified in the script only as Ka and Kha (the first two consonants in the Tibetan syllabary), greet each other:

KA: Ya, *aro*! What's rattling around in your thoughts these days? There's nothing wrong with your health, is there?

KHA: There's nothing wrong with my health, but my mind really isn't able to settle itself.

KA: It's said that

> Clothes with patterns are worth looking at, and
> words with roots are worth listening to.

And don't I know it? Your words might be worth listening to.

KHA: That's for sure. Haven't you it heard the saying

> Butter is at the heart of a tub of yogurt, and
> meaning is at the heart of one hundred spoken words?

You've got good eyes. With my mouth open, you can see into my chest.

KA: It's really difficult to see your chest. Haven't you heard it said that

> Livestock's *khya khya* [colors] is on the outside, and a person's *khya khya* is on the inside.
>
> I'm not a person with great perception, and I don't know whether birds in the sky are male or female, but I do know about moods of the black-headed people [Tibetans].
>
> KHA: Yes, That's really good. So, you should know what's rattling around inside my thoughts.
>
> KA: By the three jewels! When you have something to think about you, it should be these crooked letters. (Don grub rgyal [1980] 1997, 43)[1]

ཀ༎ ཨ་རོ། ཉེ་མ་འདི་ཚོ་ཁྱེད་འདང་རྒྱུག་ཟིག་གི་ནང་ང་སྣང་རེ་བསྟོད་ཡོད་ནོ་ཚེ་ཡིན། ལུས་འབྱུང་གཞན་གནོད་མི་བདེ་རྒྱུ་མེད་ལ།

ཁ༎ ལུས་འབྱུང་གཞན་ད་མི་བདེ་རྒྱུ་མེད་ཀྱི་ར། སེམས་བསམ་པ་གནོད་ཆ་བདེ་ལ་འབབ་མི་ཐུབ་ཀྱི།

ཀ༎ གོས་རེ་མོ་ཆན་ན་ལྷ་རྒྱུ་ཡོད་དུ། ཆིག་རྒྱ་བ་ཆན་ན་ཉན་རྒྱུ་ཡོད་ཟེར་ནི་རེད། ངས་མ་ཤེས་ནི་མེན་ན། ཁྱིའི་ཆིག་དེ་ར་ཉན་རྒྱུ་ཡོད་ན་ཐང་གི

ཁ༎ དེ་ལོས་ཡིན། ནོ་བཀུ་དགོག་གི་སྙིང་པོ་མར་དུ། ཆིག་བཀུ་བཤད་ཀྱི་སྙིང་པོ་དོན་ཡིན་ཟེར་ནོ་ཁྱིས་མ་གོ་ན། ཁྱེད་གནོ་སྒྱུ་རེག་ཡག་ཟིག་རེད། ངས་ཁ་གདངས་རུང་གི་ཡིག་པ་རེག་གི་བསྟོད་ཡོད་ག

ཀ༎ ཁྱིའི་ཡིག་པ་རེག་རྒྱུ་གནོ་རོ་མ་དགའ་མོ་རེད། ཟེག་གི་ཁྱུ་ཁྱུ་ཡི་ར་ཁྲུ་གི་ཁྱུ་ཁྱུ་ནང་ཟེར་ནོ་མ་གོ་ནས། ང་ཁྱུ་རེག་ཡག་ཟིག་ཚོ་ཨིན་ར། ནམ་མཁའི་བྱ་གི་ཕོ་མོ་མི་ཤེས་རུང་། མགོ་ནག་ཁྱི་གི་རྣམ་འགྱུར་ཤེས་ནི་ཟིག་ཡིན།

ཁ༎ ཡ་དེ་ཡིན་ན་དེ་མ་ཏུ་གི་ཨོ་ན། ཁྱིས་ང་འདང་རྒྱུག་གི་ནང་ང་སྣང་རེ་བསྟོད་ཡོད་ནོ་གི་རྒྱུ་མཚན་ར་ཤེས་རྒྱུ་རེད་ལ།

ཀ༎ དེ་ད་མི་ཤེས་ན་དཀོན་མཆོག་གསུམ། ཁྱེད་འདང་རྒྱུག་རྒྱུ་ཟིག་ཡོད་དུ། ཡིག་འབྲུག་དེ་ཚོ་ཡིན་རྒྱུ་རེད།

Crooked letters, he says. With this, the true focus of the dialogue takes center stage. The second speaker (the one identified as Kha) immediately responds with his dislike of the term "crooked letters," and clarifies the meaning of the term for any audience members who may not understand, saying:

I completely disagree with calling the writing of Tibet, the land of snows, "crooked letters." (Don grub rgyal [1980] 1997, 44)

བོད་གངས་ཅན་གྱི་ཡི་གེ་འ་ཡིག་འཁྱོག་དེ་ཚོ་བརྗོད་ཟེར་ན། ང་འཐད་དུང་རྒྱུ་སྙུ་ཚམ་ཞིག་ར་མེད་ཀྱི

Now the performers change to a discussion of politics and language. Though the first performer insists that he is not devaluing the Tibetan language, he believes that there is abundant evidence that Tibetan is somewhat obsolete in New China. In fact, the local party secretary, Secretary Wangchen, whose name literally means "very powerful," speaks exclusively in Chinese to his fellow Tibetans in the countryside, thus requiring someone to translate for him.² The second speaker is understandably taken aback, saying,

What did you say? Secretary Wangchen doesn't know Tibetan? (Don grub rgyal [1980] 1997, 44)

ཁྱོས་ཅི་གཟེ། དབང་ཆེན་ཧྲུའུ་ཅི་གི་བོད་སྐད་མི་ཤེས་ནི་རེད།

The first speaker quickly reassures the second that Secretary Wangchen (as a Tibetan) certainly *does* know Tibetan, very well in fact:

KA: Where are there Tibetans who don't speak Tibetan? He speaks Tibetan better than I do!
KHA: If he knows Tibetan, then why do you have to translate?
KA: The reason cannot be expressed in one or two words, right? Don't tell anyone, but Secretary Wangchen is really interesting. When he's with Tibetans, he speaks nothing but Chinese. When he's in Chinese places, he speaks nothing but Tibetan.
KHA: What are you talking about?
KA: It's really hilarious if you think about it. Last year we went to the pastoral areas to do propaganda for the Party's economic policies...
KHA: That's good. If the pastoral and farming masses know the Party's policies, then all the agricultural and pastoral work will develop. Moreover, the lives of the pastoral and agricultural masses can get richer.

KA: That's right. Except the masses were unable to clearly understand the Party's policies.

KHA: Why not?

KA: The document was in Chinese, Party Secretary Wangchen proclaimed in Chinese, and there are very few among the masses who understand Chinese.

KHA: You couldn't interpret?

KA: Who would have a Tibetan interpret for a Tibetan? Also, I myself am not very capable, and afterward Secretary Wangchen would say, "This was an error and that was wrong."

KHA: Then there's nothing you can do. Well then, can't Secretary Wangchen speak in Tibetan?

KA: How could Party Secretary Wangchen speak Tibetan, you old fool?

KHA: Why's that?

KA: If he spoke Tibetan, then it would dull the shine of being a party secretary.

KHA: Stop being silly.

KA: I'm telling it like it is. If a Tibetan speaks Tibetan, then he can't signal that he is a party secretary.

KHA: I've never seen or heard anything like it. It's really difficult if you have a party secretary like that.

KA: Actually, Secretary Wangchen speaks broken Chinese. Unless you're accustomed to listening to it, it's very difficult [to understand]. (Don grub rgyal [1980] 1997, 44–46)

ཀ། བོད་ཀྱིས་བོད་སྐད་མི་ཤེས་ན་གང་ན་ཡོད་ཀྱི་བོད་སྐད་གཉོ་བཤད་ན་ང་བསླབས་ན་ར་དག་གི་ཡ།

ཁ། བོད་སྐད་ཤེས་ན་ཁྱོས་ལོ་རྩྭ་ཡིད་ལེ་ཆེ་གོ་ནས།

ཀ། དེའི་རྒྱུ་མཚན་གཙོ་ཆེག་གཅིག་གཉིས་གཉིག་གི་ནད་དཔོན་ནི་མ་རེད། ཨ་རོ། ཁྱོས་སྨྲ། གཞན་པ་གཉོ་མ་བཤད་དུ། དབང་ཆེན་ཧྲུའུ་ཅི་དྲོ་མ་སྐྱུ་ཡ་མཚར་ཅན་ཞེར་ནི་ཡིན་རྒྱུ་རེད། བོད་ཀྱི་ནང་ང་ཡོང་ན་རྒྱ་སྐད་མིན་འདའ་བཤད་ཀྱི་མ་རེད། རྒྱ་ཡི་གྱུན་བ་སོང་ན་བོད་སྐད་མི་འདའ་བཤད་ཀྱི་མ་རེད།

ཁ། ཁྱོས་ཆེ་གཏེ།

ཀ༏ འདད་བརྒྱབ་ན་ངོ་མ་དགོད་རྒྱ་ཡོད་ཀྱི་ན་ཞིད། གང་སྨྲེ་ཧྲུའུ་ར་རེད་ཆེ་གསུམ་པོ་ཏུ་ནང་གཉིག་ག་སོང་དེ། ཧང་གི་དཔལ་འབྱོར་སྲིད་ཧྲུས་ཐྲིལ་བསླགས་ལེ་ནས།

| ཁ། དེ་དུ་གི་མོ་རོང་འབྲོག་པ་མང་ཚོགས་ཀྱི་དུང་གི་སྙིད་དུས་ཤེས་ན་ད་ཞིང་ཕྱུགས་ལས་ཐམས་ཅད་གོང་འཕེལ་ལ་འགྲོ་རྒྱུ་རེད། དེས་མི་ཚང་རོང་འབྲོག་པ་མང་ཚོགས་ཀྱི་འཚོ་བ་ར་རྗེ་ཕྱུག་ག་འཕྲུབ་རྒྱུ་རེད།
| ག ཡིན་རྒྱུ་དེ་རེད། དེ་རེད་དུ་ར། མང་ཚོགས་གྱིས་དུང་གི་སྙིད་དུས་གསལ་པོ་ཤེས་མ་ཤེས་མ་ཐུབ་ཟེར་
| ཁ། ཅི་ཟེར་ག
| ག ཡིག་ཚ་རྒྱ་ཡིག་རེད། དབང་ཆེན་ཅུའུ་ཅི་གི་རྒྱ་སྐད་གྱི་བསྒྲགས་ནི་རེད། མང་ཚོགས་གྱི་ནང་ན་རྒྱ་སྐད་གོ་ནི་དོན་ད་ཐུང་གི
| ཁ ཁྱེས་ལོ་ཙཱ་ཡེ་ན་མི་ཚོགས་ནས།
| ག བོད་ཅིག་གི་བོད་ཟིག་ག་ལོ་འཛུགས་ནི་ཤུ་རེད། ང་རང་གི་ཡོན་ཚད་དབང་ནི་རེད། དུས་འདོད་དབང་ཆེན་ཅུའུ་ཅི་གི་འདི་འཕུགས་ཐལ་ར། གཞན་བོར་ཐལ་ཟེར་གྱི་བསྡད་ན་དགའ་མོ་རེད་ཨ་རོ།
| ཁ། དེ་ཡིན་ན་ཁྱོར་ཁག་མེད་གི་དོན་དབང་ཆེན་ཅུའུ་ཅི་ཁོ་གིས་བོད་སྐད་བཤད་ན་མི་ཆོག་གི་རེད།
| ག ཨེ་སྐྱིའུ་ཉན། དབང་ཆེན་ཅུའུ་ཅི་གིས་བོད་སྐད་བཤད་ཁ་ཉན་ནེ།
| ཁ། ཅི་ཟེར་ག
| ག བོད་སྐད་བཤད་ན་ཅུའུ་ཅི་གི་གཟི་བརྗིད་ཉམས་འགྲོ་གི་མོ།
| ཁ། ཕྱུག་གཉིས་མ་བཤད།
| ག དོམ་བཤད་ན་ཡ། བོད་ཟིག་གི་བོད་སྐད་བཤད་གོ་གི་རེད་ན། ཅུའུ་ཅི་ཡིན་ནོ་གི་རྟགས་རིག་མི་ཐུབ་གི
| ཁ། རིག་ད་ཇེ་སྐྱིད་ར། གོ་ར་མ་སྐྱིད་ནི་གཟིག་རེད། ཅུའུ་ཅི་དེ་མོ་གཟི་ཡོད་ན། དོམ་དགའ་རྒྱ་རེད།
| ག དང་མོ་བཤད་ན་དབང་ཆེན་ཅུའུ་ཅི་གི་རྒྱ་སྐད་བཤད་ན་ད་མ་ཅིག་རེད་ཡ། ཉན་ནས་ལོངས་བསྡད་ཡོད་ནི་ཟིག་མིན་ན། དོམ་གོ་དགའ་རྒྱ་རེད་གོ

So even if listeners *could* understand Chinese, they might not understand *the party secretary's* Chinese. To combat this, the secretary devises a workaround. After he finishes in his broken Chinese, he asks "Secretary Zhang," a Han subordinate of Secretary Wangchen's, to interpret in Tibetan. Although Secretary Zhang does speak some Tibetan, when called on to interpret, he simply says:

Well, I'm not very good at translation, and there were many mistakes! But you get the general idea! (Don grub rgyal [1980] 1997, 46)

ད་ང་ལོ་ཙཱ་ཨ་རྩ་མི་ཤེས། འཕུག་སོང་ནོ་མང་གི་ཡ། ད་དེ་ཁྱོད་ཚོ་ཤེས་གི་མོ།

Then, when speaking with Han officials on trips to Inner China, Party Secretary Wangchen only speaks Tibetan and requires the first speaker (and not Secretary Zhang) to interpret for him. This patently ridiculous linguistic situation (and not the Party's policies), it is implied, is one reason Tibetan regions lag behind the rest of the country in terms of economic development. Facing this, the first speaker concludes that learning Tibetan is useless in the present moment.

The second performer then takes it upon himself to disabuse the first of these errant notions about the utility of the Tibetan language in the dawning post-Mao period:

> KHA: You've got the wrong idea. These years, Lin Biao and the Gang of Four have caused many misfortunes and done damage, and in general, the country has gone horribly backward. Especially minority nationalities' education and culture were made to go backward. For Tibetan culture, before the greater five and lesser five cultures are famous,[3] but you certainly know that during the Gang of Four, people weren't even allowed to look at long books, let alone study culture.[4] And there's no need to say that it wasn't only Tibet at that time—the entire country was like that. But these days, for example, it's a good time: people are happy, the policies are good. What do you think? Is it like that?
>
> KA: That goes without saying.

ཁ། ཁྱོད་བསམ་བློ་དེ་ནོར་འཁྲུལ་རེད། ལོ་འདིའི་ཚོའི་རིང་ད། ལིན་པིའོ་ར་སྐྱི་བཞི་ཚོགས་ཁག་གིས་བར་ཆད་ར་གཏོར་བརྒྱག་ཡེ་ལས། སྤྱིར་ན་རྒྱལ་ཁབ་ཅུང་ད་མི་རིག་ནི་རིག་གི་ལོག་ཡོད་ཀྱི་སློས་སུ་གྲངས་ཆུང་མི་རིགས་ཀྱི་སློབ་གསོ་ར་རིག་གནས་ཀྱི་ལམ་དོན་འདི་ཅུང་ད་རིག་ནི་ཉིག་གི་བཟང་ཡོད་ཀྱི་བོད་ཀྱི་རིག་གནས་གཙོ་མཆོན་ན། སྔོན་ཆད་གཙོ་རིག་གནས་ཆེ་བ་ལྔ་ར་ཆུང་བ་ལྔ་བཞི་སྙད་གྲགས་ཆེ་ནི་རེད། རེད་ད་ར། སྐྱི་བཞི་ཚོགས་ཁག་གི་རིང་ད། རིག་གནས་སྦྱོང་རྒྱུ་ད་པར་ཞོག་དཔེ་ཆ་སྤྱ་རིང་ཞིག་རིག་མི་ཆོག་ཁོ་སྐྱི་ཉེས་ཟེར་རྒྱ་ཆེ་ཡོད། སྐབས་དེ་དུས་གཉོ་བོད་ཁེར་རྐྱང་ཞེར་རྒྱ་ཆེ་ཡོད། རྒྱལ་ཁབ་ཆེན་མ་དེ་རེད་ད་དེང་སང་གཉོ་མཆོན་ན་བསྐལ་བ་བཟང་གི་ལྗང་བ་སྐྱིད་ཀྱི་སྲིད་ཧྲུས་ཡག་གི་ཁྱོད་བཤད་ན་དེ་མོ་ཞིག་མི་རེད།

ག། དེ་ད་ཅི་བཤད་ཀྱི (Don grub rgyal [1980] 1997, 47–48)

Such is the accepted logic of the moment that the first speaker is forced to agree. Having gotten his interlocutor's approval for the first set of statements, the second speaker then notes that in this better era, Tibetan culture remains very great, and worthy of study. Again, the first agrees. Once he has done so, he is on the hook for the rest.

KHA: Okay, and moreover, we have everything, from Tibet's own religious and political histories, to biographies and hagiographies, to maxims and treatises. Studying these is virtuous. Who could say that they have no benefit? What do you think? Is it like that?
KA: It goes without saying, that's for certain.
KHA: Well, beyond these, Tibetan folklore like epic and myths, folktales and speeches, songs and love songs, dances and games, jokes and sarcastic arguments, geomancy, and even milking songs, wedding songs, threshing songs — there are eighteen types of songs, one melody has eighteen variations. Studying all these is virtuous. Who could say that they have no benefit? What do you think? Is it like that?
KA: It goes without saying, that's for certain. (Don grub rgyal [1980] 1997, 48–49)

| ཁ། ཡ། ད་དེའི་མི་ཆད་ཀྱི་བོད་རང་གི་ཆོས་འབྱུང་ལོ་རྒྱུས་གནའ་རབས། རྣམ་ཐར་རྟོགས་བརྗོད་གནའ་རབས། ལེགས་བཤད་བསྟན་བཅོས་གནའ་རབས། དེ་ཆང་མ་མ་འཛོམ་ནི་མེད་ཀྱི། འདི་ཐམས་ཅད་སྦྱངས་ན་ཡོན་ཏན་རེད་ཕན་པ་མེད་ཀྱི་ཟེར་ཆེ་ཐུབ། ཁྱོད་བསམས་ན་དེ་མོ་ཟིག་ཨེ་རེད།
ཀ། ཅི་བཤད་ཀྱི། དེ་ད་ལོས་ཡིན།
ཁ། ཨ་རོ། ད་རུང་དེས་གི་མི་ཆད་ཀྱི་བོད་དམངས་ཁྲོད་གནའ་བོ་མཆོན་ན། སྒྲུང་རིང་སྒྲུང་ཐུང་། གནའ་གཏམ་འབེལ་གཏམ། གླུ་ར་ལ་ཡེ། བྲོ་ར་རྩེད་མོ། གནའ་ར་ཕྲག་འབེབས་སོ་དཔྱད་རྒྱུ། དཔྱད་ཐབ་ན་འོ་མ་བཞོ་བའི་གླུ། ཕྱུར་མ་ཡུར་བའི་གླུ། གཤུལ་ག་གཅིག་པའི་གླུ། གླུ་མི་གཅིག་གླུ་གཉི་བཅུད་ཡོད་ཀྱི། གདངས་མི་གཅིག་འགྱུར་ཁུག་བཅོ་བརྒྱད་ཡོད་ཀྱི། འདི་ཐམས་ཅད་སྦྱོར་ར་ཡོན་ཏན་རེད། ཕན་པ་མེད་ཀྱི་ཟེར་ཆེ་ཐུབ། ཁྱོད་བསམས་ན་དེ་མོ་ཟིག་ཨེ་རེད།
ཀ། ཅི་བཤད་ཀྱི། དེ་ད་ལོས་ཡིན། |

Then, moving back up in scale, the second speaker points out that the Party wants the people to develop both scientifically and culturally, and then links the study of the Tibetan language to these modern goals:

What we Tibetans have is Tibetan, what we speak is Tibetan. If we don't know how to speak and write Tibetan, how can we study culture? How can we understand science? If we don't have the proper levels of science and culture, we won't be able to realize the Four Modernizations.

ཉུ་ཚོ་བོད་ལ་ཡོད་ན་བོད་ཡིག་རེད། བཤད་ན་བོད་སྐད་རེད། བོད་སྐད་ར་བོད་ཡིག་མ་ཤེས་ན་བོད་ཀྱི་རིག་གནས་ཅི་ཞིག་སྦྱང་རྒྱུ། རིག་གནས་ཀྱི་ཡོན་ཚད་མེད་ན་ཚན་རིག་ཅི་ཞིག་ཤེས་རྒྱུ། ཚན་རིག་ར་རིག་གནས་ཀྱི་རྒྱ་ཚད་མེད་ན་དེང་རབས་ཅན་བཞིའི་བསྒྱུར་ཕྱུག་རྒྱུ་མ་རེད་ལ།

With this, the speakers have returned to the subject of language. Having already agreed to the previous arguments, they must also agree to this new assertion that the Tibetan language is indeed useful, and the speaker identified as Ka begins his now-habitual refrain:

It goes without saying, that's definitely true.

ཅི་བཤད་ཀྱི་དེ་ད་ལོས་ཡིན།

Having said this in response to every previous assertion the first performer makes, the second realizes he has been trapped and forced to contradict himself, and admits the errors in his thinking. By linking the Tibetan language to then-leader Deng Xiaoping's signature policy slogan—the Four Modernizations—as well as the entirety of the Tibetan written tradition, the speakers see that writing system (and by extension the Tibetan language) *is* important and that studying Tibetan *does* have value even in the modern era.

The performance ends when the second performer suggests that the first should no longer translate for Party Secretary Wangchen. Though the first begins to agree almost out of habit, and perhaps really wishes to defy the leader's orders, he realizes that Secretary Wangchen is too powerful a figure to confront, and he cannot really refuse the official's summons or requests. In the end, both performers laugh together.

This is "Studying Tibetan," (Woyik hlobpa)[5] a script of a *khashag* (ཁ་བཤད), a "comic dialogue," similar to the routines from the iconic American comedic duo Abbott and Costello, typically featuring two to three speakers and performed on stage or broadcast on state media.⁶ The script was written by Dondrup Jya, the iconoclast poet and author (and Amdowa) frequently credited as one of the founders of "modern Tibetan literature." Sent to school at a young age, he later worked for Tibetan radio—one of the few spaces for approved public use of minority languages (Si and Li 2013)—reading and translating the news during much of the Cultural Revolution, and studied in Beijing, pursuing an MA there in 1978. In the early years of the post-Mao era, he became one of Tibet's first published authors.

Dondrup Jya's influence on modern Tibetan literary arts is difficult to overstate. As an expert in the Indic Ramayana and its influence on classical Tibetan poetics, he was keenly attuned to Tibetan oral and literary traditions. His education and upbringing, meanwhile, provided access to the resources and means of more modern literary production. The short story "The Tulku" (Htruku) depicting a thief and lecher who preys on a community's piety by pretending to be a *tulku* (reincarnate lama) now shines within the gradually developing canon of modern Tibetan literature, along with others of his works.⁷ Students recite his iconic, free-verse poem "The Waterfall of Youth" (Langtsee babchuh) at school events, and treat the song "Tsongonpo" (meaning "Koknor" or "Qinghai Lake") as a sort of unofficial anthem for Tibetan communities (Stirr 2008, 305). The controversial essay "The Narrow Footpath" (Hkang lam tramo) enraged more conservative Tibetans (Shakya 2008, 80) and inspired other authors through its experimentation with both form and content (Sangye Gyatso 2008, 264).⁸ "Studying Tibetan," by contrast, is a relatively obscure part of Dondrup Jya's prolific body of work.⁹ Written in 1980 and subsequently published in the journal *Folk Art*, this script is one of the earliest dialogues in my corpus, making it highly instructive for understanding both comedic dialogues in post-Mao Amdo, and some of the prevailing intellectual trends among Tibetophone intellectuals at that time.

・

Khashag, the term most frequently used for this form of comic dialogue in Amdo, derives its name from the words *kha* (ཁ, mouth) and *shag*

(འགས།), a term that the Rangjung Yeshe dictionary translates variously as "joke, jest," "to rally maliciously," "cause of contention," and "quarrel in general" (Kunsang 2003, 2713). The latter term can be traced at least to an ancient document of "maxims" (Stein 2010, 38), found in the caves at Dunhuang. This Dunhuang document attests to the historical presence of shag as a speech style, without necessarily creating a link between the form as practiced now and that recorded in the documents. By at least the twentieth century, the term *shag* was used to reference oral duels between two performers (or two groups of performers) and was commonly associated with "antiphonal singing" (*lushag*). The preceding *kha*, meanwhile, distinguishes it from, but also ensures a relationship with, antiphonal singing. In the narrowest sense, then, khashag are verbal contests or duels between a set of speakers.

The precise origin of khashag, in its present form as staged, scripted comic dialogues, is a matter of some debate among Tibetan intellectuals. The nature of the debate demonstrates the high stakes the Chinese Communist Party places on identifying "true" or "authentic" origins of cultural phenomena, and how the Party's own emphases create spaces for Tibetan intellectuals to complicate established narratives. To this end, Tibetan writing and interviews suggest two competing narratives about the origins of khashag. The most commonly accepted—the one that comedians tell about themselves—holds that khashag is a uniquely modern form of cultural production based on the Han *xiangsheng* (crosstalk) tradition in which "two performers . . . stand before an audience and tell jokes, recount humorous anecdotes, sing songs, do imitations, recite tongue-twisters, engage in contests of vocal pyrotechnics, verbal wit, and wordplay, and in general do their best to provoke laughter" (Moser 1990, 45–46).[10]

Shortly after the establishment of the People's Republic of China in 1949, Mao, who was himself reported to have been a fan of xiangsheng (Link 2010, 210), as well as famous author Lao She, saw the potential for these comic dialogues to spread the social and political ideologies of the Chinese Communist Party. They sent comedians to perform in the countryside, and to China's margins (Wang, Wang, and Teng 2011,

191). During this period, authors and performers began to write new performances featuring revolutionary content, although that content was carefully monitored so that it fulfilled the key political criterion of the moment: that all art serve the people.[11]

The alliance between professional satirists and state ideological interests finally came to a head in 1955 with "Buying Monkeys" (Ch. Mai hou'er), a crosstalk performance by He Chi and Ma Sanli, which indirectly satirized party members and officials who did not live according to the communist ideal. In showing "the vulnerabilities of the new society—on problems either that did not exist in the old society or that did exist but now seemed to grow worse" (Link 2010, 229), He Chi, a longtime party member, opened himself to significant criticism from authorities. Thus, in spite of the performance's popularity, He and Ma were both criticized and labeled "rightists" in the ensuing Anti-Rightist Campaign in 1957, thus sending a clear message to performers: while satire remained possible, the ideological work of art outweighed all other concerns (Kaikkonen 1990). As comedians went to the countryside, they also went to ethnic minority communities, creating performances in Mongolian, Tibetan, and other ethnic-minority languages (Link 2010, 214). One Tibetan comedian, for example, described the genre's history in the following terms:

> Well, for Amdo Tibetan comedies, originally, long, long ago, well, before me, in the 1960s, during that time, in Qinghai there was something called a theatre troupe. It was called a *hua ju tuan*, right? They translated Chinese khashag about the situation in Tibet into Tibetan, and then performed them. They did it like that. They also told folktales and the like on stage. In the past, folktales were told in the home, but now they performed them on stage. However, there were no real comedies in the strict sense of the term, except for translated ones—there were some translated ones. Later, at the beginning of the 1980s, there were ones like Rinchen Dorje, my personal teacher [who] also [worked] in the radio station. That one and the one called Phurwa. Before, they wrote one or two comedic

dialogues. They did it like that. And after that, I myself first wrote comedies, beginning in the 1980s. (personal communication, November 21, 2013)

The timeline presented here gives the suggestion of a state-imposed change in the contexts and practices of storytelling, moving first from the house to the stage (from intimate domains to public ones) and then from traditional narrative forms like folktale to emergent stage performances. In this way, it may be valuable to understand Amdo Tibetan khashag as a sort of successor genre to traditional storytelling. Such a genre, in this sense, not only follows and (to some degree) displaces its predecessor but also fills a similar cultural role. In this case, folktales have an important didactic function within Tibetan communities, and audiences similarly expect the comedic performance to both entertain and to instruct.[12]

Comedians from Central Tibet, not just Amdo, also accept the timeline presented above. Suoci, a prominent writer of Tibetan-language crosstalk dialogues in Lhasa, suggests a parallel historical progression for the first one in Lhasa, tracing that history back to the formation of propaganda troupes to pacify Tibet after the 1959 rebellion and a star performer with one of those troupes:

> The Eastern Lhasa Propaganda Team's primary performer and director [was] Lobzang Dorje—people all loved to call him King Zangmo, which is the name of a role in the Tibetan opera *Drowa zangmo*. He was a teacher: he studied at the Central Nationalities Institute and later also became a teacher there. Making use of the Tibetan language's rich layers of meaning and the performance principles of traditional Tibetan *shadgadpa* [comedy], he went on study and make use of the artistic characteristics of crosstalks from Inner China.[13] He began by translating the famous crosstalk performer Hou Baolin's[14] crosstalk, "Drunk," adding into this crosstalk a few phenomena found in contemporary Tibetan life. (Suoci 2004, 14–15, original translation in Thurston 2013)

Suoci also goes on to point out that original, Tibetan-authored, Tibetan-language crosstalks were not written in large volume until after the beginning of the period of Reform and Opening Up began in 1978.

Seeking earlier origins for khashag that might predate the arrival of Chinese propaganda teams, some Tibetan scholars proffer much earlier roots for the genre. One view, for example, looks for inspiration in Tibetan-language manuscripts found in the caves at Dunhuang that use the term *shag*. This, he believes, provides proof that "shag are not merely a form of play that has developed [recently] in Amdo but a part of cultural and political life in all of Tibet from ancient times" (Gdugs dkar tshe ring 2007, 319).

Other thinkers take this view a step further, attributing the first khashag to a little-known text in the collected works of the nineteenth-century religious leader Gungthang Tenpa Dronme, entitled "Gonpo Dorje's Tea Prayer" (Gonpo Dorje jamchol). This piece—written like a script, with Tibetan syllables *ka* and *kha* to designate the two speakers, and using Tibetan *phalké* (vernacular language) instead of the literary register—depicts the dialogue between a teacher and his pupil as they discuss how the latter makes a tea libation. Since the work is believed to have been written between 1800 and the cleric's passing in 1823, it is argued that Tibetan khashag (in form, if not in name) predated the existence of even Chinese xiangsheng, which the author dates as 1861 (Mog chung phur kho 2013).[15]

Regardless of which of these (if any) provides the "true" origins of khashag, this book tends to side with the comedians I interviewed, who believe that they are engaging in a form influenced by government's introduction of Han xiangsheng traditions. This is not least because their training and early performance stemmed from Chinese training and scripts. The official support that these new comedic forms received ensured that khashag were performed on stages, radio, and other contexts where they would be sure to have a sizable audience. Indeed, like xiangsheng in the People's Republic of China—which has migrated from streets to school auditoriums to radio, television, and the internet (Link 2010, 208)—many Tibetan comedies in Amdo have been performed primarily in government-sanctioned contexts. During the 1980s, this meant performing at schools and festivals, and on state-sanctioned radio broadcasts. Almost all performances required the government's blessing in advance, and there was little room for improvisation.

Tibetan comedians in Amdo (and beyond), however, believe that they are creating something uniquely Tibetan. For instance, Phuntsog Tashi, a comedian from Ü-Tsang, stresses that "the topics of the Tibetan comic dialogues [created by Tibetans] are different from those of the Chinese ones because [Tibetan people's] senses of humor are very different" (Phuntsog Tashi and Schiaffini 2006, 122). So how do Tibetan comedians in the post-Mao period make this transplanted art form into such a fully Tibetan phenomenon? Through zurza and *larjya* (ལ་རྒྱ།, pride), concepts that become increasingly important in the 1980s.

•

Although the political and economic disruption of the Cultural Revolution ended after Mao's death in 1976 and the nationwide economic and cultural reform period officially began in 1978, the reforms arrived in China's Tibetan areas somewhat later. Those monastic centers left standing at the end of the Cultural Revolution slowly began to reopen, with Labrang Monastery doing so in 1979 (Makley 2007, 76). A year later, Hu Yaobang, then general secretary of the Chinese Communist Party, gave a speech in Lhasa, encouraging Tibetans to exercise national autonomy, heralding a period of economic and cultural liberalism unprecedented before or since (Willock 2011, 28; Bauer 2005, 53; cf. Yao 1994). In the wake of this momentous speech, the number of open monasteries gradually increased, and monks renewed their vows—albeit under considerable scrutiny and with limitations placed on the number at a given monastery.[16] As lamas and other clerics reentered public life, they began to play an important role in establishing educational institutions and revitalizing monastic communities (Willock 2011). Communes officially began disbanding at around the same time, though Horlemann (2002, 252–53) notes that the process failed to reach remote pastoral areas of Golok Tibetan Autonomous Prefecture until 1984. The Tibet

Autonomous Region followed similar trends (Bauer 2005, 54; Goldstein and Beall 1989).

As more schools and universities reopened and began to operate at fuller capacity, those who were able to receive some education during the Cultural Revolution—and Amdo was the most progressive Tibetan region for this—found themselves ideally placed to take advantage of these emerging opportunities.[17] Among those being educated at this time, language and humanities majors dominated the course offerings at minority-serving institutions (Postiglione 1992, 27). Many Tibetan students, unsurprisingly, opted to study their own language and culture. But upon arrival at their universities, these students often found little pressure to prepare for lessons, because the education they had received at secondary institutions around Amdo gave them better command of the language (traditional grammars and the like) than their predominantly Han teachers (Wu Qi 2013, 196).

Without the pressing need to study, students read Chinese translations of Western literature and philosophy. Upon graduation, these young academics found relatively few business-related outlets in Western China's anemic economy (Wang 2013, 143), and many instead entered state-sponsored work units based around media, broadcasting, and translation. Meanwhile, the dearth of established cultural producers in Tibetan areas—Shakya (2008, 64) argues that there were no Tibetans writing in their own language by the 1980s—and the concerted effort to establish literary journals to nurture new Tibetan authors and readers created a space for young people to experiment with new expressive forms.

With access to education and to the means of disseminating ideas about culture through new media, these young scholars were poised to emerge as a new generation of Amdo Tibetan intellectuals, playing a "privileged role," in the words of Verdery (1991, 17), "in creating and disseminating ideologies that shape cultural values and influence identity formation." In the 1980s, at smoke- and drink-fueled gatherings, this new group tried to imagine a new *Tibetan* style of cultural production— broadly to include music, literature, comedy, and more—that would simultaneously meet Chinese state demands for new (and secular) cultural production, and Tibetan-audience expectations that this content be meaningful. The linguistic and cultural formations that survived the sometimes-violent contact with Mao-era policies evidenced both a radical rupture with the past and continuance of traditional forms and ideologies (Lama Jabb 2015). In larjya and zurza, aspiring Tibetan writers and intellectuals found discourses that could provide some inspiration for a modern, and uniquely Tibetan, cultural practice. It begins with larjya.

Larjya has alternatively been translated as "ethnic sentiment" (Yü 2006, 2013), "honor" and "allegiance" (Shakya 2008, 77), and "dignity" (Virtanen 2011, 84). When I first noticed the term sneaking into conversations, however, I was surprised by people's ambivalence toward larjya in the twenty-first century. One professor, for example, chatting in the comfort of his office, postulated that "speaking plainly, that thing called *larjya* is each person's own larjya. Uh, your own village, your own entire place, your own county, your own prefecture, your own land, your own country, these all have their own larjya. So, in Tibet, speaking plainly about Tibet is positive, but it is also very problematic" (personal communication, May 11, 2013).

Another consultant similarly distinguished between several types of larjya, saying, "Larjya has many divisions. Many: national pride, cultural pride, familial pride, school pride, personal pride. There are many kinds (personal communication, March 25, 2013). At each level of scale, larjya is, in the words of one recent college graduate, "about whether or not you benefit yourself or your group." Benefits to an individual, family, or community can be good for your own community but may come at the expense of others. For example, in one 1990s comedy performance, an elder justifies his village's continued fight with a nearby community by saying, "We mustn't lose our pride." These sorts of situations, then, suggest that larjya, at local levels of scale, has led to disharmony. Hence the ambivalence I heard from the interlocutors.

Moving up the scale, however, discourses of "national" or "ethnic" pride (*mirik gi larjya*) served as a prominent part of Tibetan intellectual conversations beginning in the 1980s (Shakya 2008, 77), especially among Amdo's emerging literary circle. In this moment of unprecedented—though still heavily restricted and monitored—cultural openness, Hortsang Jigmé remembers,

> [a]round that time, the phrase "national pride" ... began to appear with greater frequency in writings by young Tibetan intellectuals. When drinking or otherwise gathered together, certain young Tibetan writers, such as Döndrup Gyel [Dondrup Jya] would discuss "national pride" and related issues. (2008, 287)[18]

In many cases, this natively Tibetan discourse "paralleled state-sponsored discourse on modernization" (Shakya 2000, 36) and was therefore tolerated despite its simultaneous potential for mobilizing nationalist sentiment.

National pride continues to shape Tibetan intellectual conversations into the present, particularly around the questions of language, even—or perhaps especially—in the multiethnic city, where a localized version of standard Chinese is the primary language of everyday interaction, as I noticed one chilly windswept evening in 2012, when a group of Tibetan tour guides gathered to celebrate the end of the short but grueling tourist season in Qinghai. They met at a Tibetan restaurant located in one of Ziling's celebrated tourist streets to eat dinner, drink exuberantly, and share favorite stories about the tour guide life. The staff all wore Tibetan clothing, and the décor was in Tibetan style: customers sat on pine-wood benches topped with thin cushions and at on low tables intricately carved with Tibetan motifs; yak-hair slings for tossing rocks when herding and other Tibetan artifacts brought from the countryside hung on the walls. All these marked the restaurant as a distinctly Tibetan space in the predominantly Han city. Images of famous Tibetan customers—singers, comedians, and television presenters—adorned the restaurant's walls near the entrance, providing further testament to the establishment's popularity and authenticity. Many Tibetan-serving establishments in urban environments replicate this format, catering to a mix of Tibetans wanting a taste of home and tourists looking for an "authentic" experience.

As we were led into the private room reserved for our party, I noticed immediately posters with quotes from famous Tibetan intellectuals. One, attributed to the late Amdo cleric Jigme Rigpai Lodro, read:

> Because students these days from a young age learn only from textbooks that have been translated from Chinese, their compositions are influenced by translations; they never have the compositions written by our own Tibetan scholars, beautiful like the sound of buzzing bees' wings. So, we must not make the mistake of imitating—this is very important.

> དེང་སང་གི་སློབ་གྲྭ་བ་ལ་ཆུང་དུས་ནས་རྒྱ་ཡིག་ལས་བསྒྱུར་བའི་སློབ་དེབ་སྟེང་ནས་བསླབས་པ་དག་སྨྲག་ཡིན་པས། དེའི་ཆིག་སྦྱོར་ལ་སྒྱུར་ཚིག་གི་ཤན་ཡོད་སྲབས། བོད་རང་གི་མཁས་པས་བརྩམས་པའི་ཆིག་སྦྱོར་བུང་བའི་གཤོག་སྒྲ་ལྟ་བུའི་སྙན་ཆ་དེ་གཏན་ནས་མེད། དེའི་ཕྱིར་ཡང་མི་བྱེད་ས་དེ་འཁྱུག་མི་ཉན། འདི་ཧ་ཅང་གལ་ཆེན་གཅིག་རེད།

Another, from the tenth Panchen Lama, still much beloved in his home region of Amdo today, opined on the question of language:

> Tibetan is the language of our ethnic group. Because it is extremely useful, one must certainly study Tibetan.

> བོད་ཡིག་ནི་ང་ཚོའི་མི་རིགས་ཀྱི་སྐད་ཡིག་ལ་བརྒོལ་སློང་གི་རྒྱུ་མཚན་ཏུ་ཆེ་བས་དེས་པར་ཏུ་བོད་ཡིག་སློབ་དགོས།

A third poster featured a quote attributed to Dondrup Jya:

> Pride is our essence and patriotism our self-dignity. Our parents held their heads high and did not allow them to be trampled under the feet of others. If we can raise the shoulders of the Snowland's pride upon the heads of others, this is the self-dignity of our ethnic group, and our ancestors' pride.

> ལ་རྒྱ་ནི་རང་རེའི་བླ་སྲོག་ཡིན་པ་དང་། ད་རྒྱལ་ནི་རང་གི་གཟི་བརྗིད་རེད། ཕ་མས་སྒྱུད་པའི་མགོ་བོ་མཐོན་པོ་དེ། གཞན་གྱི་རྐང་འོག་ཏུ་མི་འཇོག་པ་དང་། ཁ་བ་ཅན་གྱི་ལ་རྒྱའི་དཔུང་བ་དེ། གཞན་གྱི་མགོ་ཐོག་ཏུ་བསྟུབས་ནུས་ན། རང་རིགས་ཀྱི་གཟི་བརྗིད་དང་། མེས་རྒྱལ་གྱི་ལ་རྒྱ་ཡང་རེད།

Our group ate and drank well into the night. The conversation and laughter reverberated around the small private room. All the while, these posters hung in the background, unacknowledged, literally surrounding our conversations and our meal. And yet, I found something strange in that combination of quotes juxtaposing the words of Dondrup Jya with those of religious clerics from the twentieth century: I was struck by the seeming incompatibility of these giants of the Tibetan intellectual world. On the wall of the private room, they sat silently and placidly, but I had trouble imagining they would be similarly restrained if they were physically present with us that evening. Nevertheless, the posters with their quotes blended to form a single (and predominantly male) logic of Tibetan culture that emphasized native language, education, and national-level pride.

Not limited to private rooms in restaurants, many of the same quotes also appear on the walls of Tibetan classrooms in urban universities and rural middle schools, where the next generations of Tibetans receive instruction. The posters seemed to literally frame our conversation on that night while reminding anyone interested about the foundational discourses of Tibetanness in the post-Mao era.

This sort of national-level pride is of particular importance for the production and reception of new Tibetan expressive arts. Audiences evaluate a work and its creator at least partly on the latter's perceived larjya and the degree to which it is included in the work. As one Ziling-based interlocutor suggested in an interview:

> I think, like, there's not like one single thing that's considered larjya, but there are many kinds of things. If you do it correctly, if you do it with your heart, . . . you're kind of making a kind of contribution to your ethnic group. Like, for instance, as a teacher, if you teach well, if you do all the jobs you need to do, you are making good things. As a singer, . . . if you sing good songs, or especially if you try to put some kind of . . . social things into your lyrics, it's also perfect. (personal communication, June 5, 2013, in English)

With "social things" meaning messages for the benefit of the Tibetan people (about ethnic unity, language, culture, etc.), ethnic pride is explicitly linked with socially conscious cultural production, in which the benefit that producers can bring to their nationality is demonstrated through the lyrics of their songs, the words of their characters, and the contents of their plots. Though not an essential element of Tibetan cultural production in the post-Mao period, this ethnic pride is reputational, earned over the course of a career, and plays an important role in the reception of a work. For example, *dunglen* music frequently expresses ideals of national pride (Lama Jabb 2011, 24), and the genre's most popular singers—including the late Dubhe—are often praised for their pride (Lama Jabb 2019, 12). The specific social issues targeted to demonstrate their pride, meanwhile, change at different moments of the post-Mao era in response to changes in Tibetan society. Zurza provided one way for aspiring Tibetan authors to demonstrate their pride and thread a very narrow and constantly moving needle between the government censors and audience expectations, through providing practices for articulating meaningful social critique in entertaining—and politically acceptable—fashion.

•

When meeting with Amdo's comedians, I had a choice: alcohol or tea. Alcohol deepened relationships, but tea often yielded the clearest information. Regardless of where we met—and it was almost always in a public place—the establishment often played loud music in the background. This made recording and transcribing a challenge. Nevertheless, I always felt it important to meet on the grounds they chose. Sitting in one such teahouse, with Maroon Five's "Moves like Jagger" blasting on the sound system, I asked one illustrious comedian to discuss the "artistic characteristics" of khashag comedic dialogues.

"If we speak about the main artistic characteristics of khashag," he began, "we can say that it really has to meet three primary conditions. One is verbal art."

"Mmm," I responded, nodding my head, keenly aware that Amdo Tibetan conversation expects frequent cues from listeners.

The comedian continued: "Verbal art, um, this is one. And what is the main part of verbal art . . . then, it is humorous art, making you laugh . . .

And then the condition that comes after humor is zurza [satire]. Zurza. It's called *fengci* [in Chinese], right?" After a brief exchange to make sure that I had understood the Chinese term, he continued: "So where does the humor come from? It comes from the zurza. So basically, there are these three major characteristics." He paused to take another sip of tea.

Rather than the imported formal features of the Han xiangsheng genre—like conversations between two or more speakers; self-referentiality (Moser 1990); long, rapidly delivered lists called "word fountains" (Tsau 1980), all of which also feature in popular khashag performances—this comedian's definition of khashag comedic dialogues focused on Tibetan expressive ideologies. The most important of these is zurza. The same comedian later drove this point home, when he said that comedies "all have a little criticism written in them. Moreover, they have a cultural foundation, and that cultural foundation is using zurza to solve problems."

"Studying Tibetan" includes all three components of the comedian's definition. "Verbal art," for example, features from the earliest lines of the performance. Dondrup Jya, who is famous for his skill with proverbs, opens the dialogue with traditional proverbs like "Clothes with patterns are worth looking at, and words with foundations are worth listening to." The author continues to use other forms of verbal artistry throughout, to win the audience's attention and appreciation. By referring to Tibetan writing as "crooked letters" and other forms of figurative language (talking about seeing into one's chest at the beginning), the performance again taps into popular discursive practices. The debate through which the language advocate convinces his opponent of the value of the Tibetan language (and specifically writing), meanwhile, uses a classic strategy of circuitous arguments to eventually turn an initial supposition on its head.

The author matches these more traditional forms of verbal art with novel interventions as well. The script is somewhat uniquely composed entirely in a form of colloquial Tibetan that approximates the author's native dialect rather than the more commonly used literary language.[19] Though Dondrup Jya's other writings occasionally use colloquial Tibetan for dialogue between characters, very rarely does he use it to this extent. This, in turn, provides interesting insights into the linguistic practices and limits on expression in the early 1980s. "Studying Tibetan," for example, frequently makes reference to the policy goals of its time, including Deng Xiaoping's signature policy, "the Four Modernizations" (Don grub rgyal [1980] 1997, 49)[20] and "Lin Biao and the Gang of Four" (47), who Communist Party history labels as the main antagonists of the Cultural Revolution. The speakers also refer to each other as *lomtun* (comrade), language that largely disappeared from common parlance during the 1980s, and, with the exceptions of meetings and government leaders, is rarely used unironically in daily communication (including even broadcast media). While audiences may find some humor in the language play, Dondrup Jya also created humor through the party secretary's bizarre language practices and the way it produces humorously incongruous circumstances that motivate the entire performance.

Finally, Amdo's comedians and audiences will not appreciate a script or performance that fails to sarcastically target some sort of problem facing their communities. Although the party secretary's behaviors create a secondary critique about the behavior of local cadres (but never about central policy), the primary target of Dondrup Jya's zurza—from the comedy's title down to almost every line of the conversation—centers on those who would devalue the Tibetan language in modern society. Language provides an easy target. Sharing a common tongue was one of the primary criteria used to identify ethnic groups under the auspices of the "ethnic identification" project in the 1950s. In the context of Amdo at the beginning of the 1980s, meanwhile, the Tibetan language may well have seemed to be in a state of crisis as Tibetans began to debate its place and that of the culture in a modernizing society.

At the dawn of the post-Mao period, the government had just begun to allow Tibetan-language education and cultural production, and literacy rates remained low but were increasing. But decades of state propaganda emphasizing the backwardness of Tibetan society, plus government-imposed limits on minority-language expression (especially during the recently ended Cultural Revolution), had left a deep impression. Many Tibetans—Zenz (2014, 27) calls them "pragmatists"—might be forgiven for hesitating to invest too much time and effort in the Tibetan language.

But this exact situation also made it a valuable site for articulation on ethnic pride in Amdo.

"Studying Tibetan" models a riposte to the pragmatist position through using traditional verbal arts, including *tamhwé* (proverbs),[21] figurative language about Tibetan "crooked letters," and indirect arguments to satirize pragmatists and send a clear message to any doubters: the Tibetan language remains worthy of study in the modern era. In doing so, Dondrup Jya shows that Tibetans *can* speak their native tongue in a modern society. In fact, by explicitly linking the language—and the entirety of the Tibetan culture—with modern development policy, he contends that it is *necessary* for the development of Tibetan society. In short, Dondrup Jya uses zurza to offer a distinctly Tibetan solution. This contrasts markedly with the broader world around Tibetans.

•

Starting in the first years of the post-Mao era, zurza, in conjunction with content focusing on problems of local concern (larjya), provided Tibetan comedians, authors, and other artists with valuable expressive resources for creating new, meaningful, and specifically Tibetan cultural production in the early years of the post-Mao period. In doing so, they effectively localized the Han Chinese performance style of xiangsheng, transforming it into a uniquely Tibetan phenomenon: khashag. Not limited to this obscure khashag script, Dondrup Jya's use of zurza and larjya extend across his literary corpus. His landmark short story "The Tulku," for example, portrays a lecherous charlatan who masquerades as a holy man to dupe devout Buddhists and take their wealth (and sometimes their virtue). In doing so, he "does zurza" on people whose abundance of religious (generally Buddhist) faith leads them to make poor decisions (more on this later). Not limited to Dondrup Jya's work, these same concepts also figure heavily in the work of Amdo's other poets, authors, and singers, among others. These trends continue to this day. By ensuring access to state media, without compromising the linguistic and conceptual Tibetanness of these works, zurza and larjya form the grounds of Tibetan cultural survival even in Western China's highly constrained public sphere in the 1980s.

Returning to "Studying Tibetan," the critique Dondrup Jya makes in this comic script points to a few significant trends in the uses and understandings of zurza in the post-Mao period. First, the script's is locally focused. "Studying Tibetan" never criticizes central government policy but instead focuses on issues specifically facing Tibetan communities. In fact, where "Studying Tibetan" does mention central policies—either in general or by name, as with the script's reference to "the Four Modernizations"—the reference is exclusively positive. While the censorial standards of the day almost certainly influenced this, Dondrup Jya also used this as an opportunity to focus attention on issues that he believed to be directly affecting Tibetan society, like language that become central to emerging discourses on ethnic pride more generally.

Additionally, "Studying Tibetan" focuses its critique on generalized behaviors and stereotyped characters. Unlike the verbal dueling traditions discussed earlier, which may use zurza to comment on the attributes and behaviors of an individual, much of the critique in contemporary Tibetan cultural production satirizes general behaviors. Instead of directly lampooning the actions of an identifiable cadre, "Studying Tibetan" targets stereotyped and fictional characters. Party Secretary Wangchen, for example, serves as a stereotype of powerful (Tibetan) officials. His actions (only described) and his words (never quoted directly) cause no end of difficulties for those around him. Audiences may find this humorous in its own right, but the party secretary's actions, and those of other stereotyped characters, help to focus the satirical critique on broader issues facing Tibetan society. In this case, Dondrup Jya focuses it on people who harbor negative attitudes toward the Tibetan language and its continued value for society.

The focus on language continues, but it forms only one part of a broader intellectual critique of the issues facing Tibetan society in the post-Mao period. In the 1990s, when, if anything, comedy grows more popular, a series of four performances about a comedian's trip to a nomadic settlement reveals much about the satirical agenda of post-Mao intellectuals at the time.

3

Khashag on Air
Solving Social Ills by Radio in the 1990s

Two men stand on a stage holding pieces of paper and speaking into a pair of microphones. They greet each other as friends, and one can imagine the two are catching up in one of Ziling's many teahouses or having a chance meeting on the street. The first, the renowned comedian Menla Jyab, begins telling Pakmo Drashe the story of his recent trip to a fictional community called "Careful Village":

> MJ: Hey! This year, I went to the so-called Careful Village to write a khashag called "Careful Village."
> PD: Oh?! What was this so-called "Careful Village" like?
> MJ: Ah, ah, ah . . . it was a village!
> PD: When you said, "Careful Village," I knew it must be a village. But judging by the village's name, I bet you have to be very careful when you go there, right?
> MJ: Ah no, no. It's okay to let your guard down when you go there, I tell you!
> PD: That's right! You wouldn't dare go to a place where you would have to go in fear.

སློན་བྱ། ཨ་རོག་ད་ལོ་ངས་སེམས་ཆུང་སྡེ་བ་ཟེར་ནས་ཁ་ཤགས་ཤིག་འབྲི་རྒྱུས་བཟེས་ཆེད་དུ་སེམས་ཆུང་སྡེ་བ་གཅིག་ཡོད་དོ།

ཕག་མོ། ཡ། སེམས་ཅན་ཐྱང་སྟེ་བ་བདག་གོ་ཆེ་མོ་ཟིག་རེད།
སྨན་བླ། ཨ་ཨ་ཨ། སྟེ་བ་ཟིག་རེད།
ཕག་མོ། སེམས་ཅན་ཐྱང་སྟེ་བ་ཟེར་གོ་དུས་སྟེ་བ་ཟིག་ད་ཡིན་རྒྱའོ་རེད་དུ། སྟེ་བ་དེའི་ཁྱིད་ད་བསླུས་ན་ཞེ་གི་སེམས་ཅན་ཐུས་འགྲོ་དགོ་ནི་མིན་ན།
སྨན་བླ། ཨ་ཆེ་ཡིན་ཆེ་ཡིན། བབ་གི་སེམས་ལྡོང་ཞེ་བུད་སོང་ཚོག་གི་ཨ་རོག
ཕག་མོ། ཨ་ཨ་ཨ། ཨོ་ལེ་མོ། སྨག་དགོས་ས་ཟིག་ག་ད་ཁྱིད་འགྲོ་རོགས་མི་ཆེད་མོ། (Sman bla skyabs 1996e)

This is the opening to "Careful Village's Grassland Dispute" (Semchung déwee sahtsod), the first of a series of four wildly popular comic dialogues written and performed between 1992 and 1996, and later sold on audiocassette as an album entitled *The Colorful Nomad Camp* (Rudé tramo) (Sman bla skyabs 1996e).[1] The series is entirely in Tibetan, with each performance lasting between eleven and eighteen minutes and examining a variety of emergent problems facing communities in contemporary Tibet.

Over the next several minutes, Menla Jyab goes on to describe how the community—despite being embroiled in a violent grassland dispute with a neighboring village—greeted him with white silk scarves (called *khatak*) and plenty of tea. This is the sort of welcome usually reserved for honored guests. The audience soon learns why he received such special treatment, when the village leader—voiced by Menla Jyab, punctuating each line with hearty laughter—says that Menla Jyab is a lama, and that he will not accept any of the comedian's protests to the contrary:

> MJ: [as the village leader] "You shouldn't keep it a secret that you are a lama. This matter concerns all sentient beings. Hehe!"
> P: [chuckling] And you still haven't escaped [from the village leader].
> MJ: [in a normal voice] I was so scared that my hair stood on end. "Dear Village Leader, you seem like an intelligent person, so how can you say this? Look at the hair on my head, the clothes on my body, and the stubble on my face. Where is there a *lama* like me?"
> P: What did he say then?
> MJ: Hehe! He had some things to say, *aro*! [as the village leader]

"I've seen faces on *tangka* paintings, Tri Ralpachen's[2] head was like that. People say I don't know anything, but I've been around the block a few times. All those who don't like Tibetan clothes and don't wear modern clothes wear clothes like this, and don't seem to shave. Stubble grows on your face even if you are a lama; nobody is planting it."

P: That's right. I think that's definitely true.

MJ: [as himself] So then I also sincerely explained, "If I were a lama, then my monastery would be a distillery, my monks' perfection of wisdom studies wouldn't have been perfected, and they would have attained perfection only in smoking cigarettes. If there is a lama like this, let alone in the next life, would the government even recognize him?"

P: That was direct! What did the village leader say?

MJ: [as the village leader] "Huh! I know, I know. Then swear that everyone in your work unit doesn't call you 'Alak,'" (in a normal voice) he said.

P: But that's just a name your coworkers came up with themselves, right?

MJ: [normal voice] Eh, I said that too, but there was no changing that old man's mind.

སྨན་བླ། བླ་མ་ཡིན་ནོ་ཅིག་གསང་མི་ཉན་གི་སེམས་ཅན་ཐམས་ཅད་གི་དོན་དག་ག དེ་དེ་དེ་དེ།

པགས་མོ། ཡང་མ་ཐར་ཐལ།

སྨན་བླ། ང་བཟེས་ནོ་སྐུག་གི་མགོ་གི་སྐྲ་ཚོ་ར་ཕྱོགས་སོང་ཟིག་ཨ་ཁུ་སྟེ་དཔོན་ལོ་ལོ་ཁྱི་སྲི་མཁས་པ་ཟིག་ག་མ་རིག་ག དེ་མོ་དེ་བཤད་ཉན་ཞེས། ཁྱིས་དའི་མགོ་གི་སྐྲ་ལོས་ར་ཡུས་གི་ལུ་ལོས་ར་དོ་གི་སྦྱིའི་ལ་སྟོས་ར། ང་འདི་འདུ་བླ་མ་ཟིག་ཡོད་ཉེས།

པགས་མོ། དེ་བཟེས་ན་ཚེ་ཟེར་གི།

སྨན་བླ། དེ་དེ། སྟེ་གི་དེ་ཚོང་གི་བཤད་རྒྱུ་ཡོད་ཀྱི་ཨ་རོགས། ངས་ཐང་ག་གི་དོ་ནས་རིག་སྟོང་ཉེས། ཁྲི་རལ་པ་ཅན་གི་མགོ་ར་དེ་ཟིག་རེད། མི་ཤེས་བཟེས་རུང་བསམ་ཤེས་རེད། བོད་ལུ་མི་དགའ་ནོ། རྒྱུ་ལུ་མི་གོན་ནོ་ཚང་མས་དེ་མོ་གོན་ཡོད་གི། ཁ་སྤུ་དོ་སྤུ་གཟོ་བཏབ་ཉེ་མ་རེད། སྐྱེས་རྒྱུའི་རེད། བླ་མ་ཡིན་རུང་ང་། ཟེ་ཡ།

པགས་མོ། དེ་བཟོ་རེད། ལོས་བདེན་འདོང་ག

སྨན་བླ། ད་དས་ར་སེམས་གཏིང་ནས་འགྲེལ་བཤད་ཟིག་བཀུལ་བ། ང་བླ་མ་ཟིག་ཡིན་དུས། དའི་

དགོན་པ་དེ་ཆང་བཅགས་ས་ཟིག་ཡིན། དབི་གྲུ་བ་ཚོ་ར་པར་ཕྱིན་སྡངས་དེ་ཕེ་རོལ་དུ་ཕྱིན་
སོང་ནི་ཨིན། ཐ་མག་འཐེན་ནས་མཐར་ཕྱིན་སོང་ནི་ཨིན། དེ་མོ་བླ་མ་ཟིག་ཡོད་དུས་དུ་ཕྱི་མ་
ས་དགོ་གོང་མ་ཚང་གིས་ར་ཁས་ལེན་ནིས།

པགས་མོ། དུང་མོར་བཟད་ཟིག་གོ་ཨ་ཁུ་སྦེ་དཔོན་གིས་ཅི་ཟེར་གི
སྨན་བླ། ཤུ་ཤེས་ནི་རེད། ཤེས་ནི་རེད། ཁྱེད་ཚོ་ལས་ཁངས་གི་ཆང་མས་ཁྱིའི་སྒྱིད་ང་ལ་ལགས་མི་
ཟེར་བཟེས་མཐན་ཟིག་སློལ་ཟེ་ཡ།

པགས་མོ། དེ་ལས་ཁངས་གིས་དེ་ཚེས་རང་ད་བཏགས་ནི་རེད་མོ།

སྨན་བླ། ཨེ། ངར་ར་དེ་བཟེས་ར་ཀུད་པོ་དེ་སྒྱུལ་རྒྱ་མེད་ཀི (Sman bla skyabs 1996e)

Traditionally, communities might turn to elders and religious leaders for help mediating language disputes, as they were the only figures with sufficient authority and social capital to help the parties resolve such conflicts (Pirie 2006, 77–78). Menla Jyab decides to use the village's misplaced faith to trick them into solving their problems. To begin, he asks them to describe the problem's origins, and eventually he finds his answer in the village's response to a new policy:

MJ: [as the village leader] "Do you know the [government policy of the] household responsibility system?"
P: You certainly do know it.
MJ: [in the voice of the village leader] "*Ole!* When the livestock were divided up [among individual households], and they had constructed fences in each place, and each family was allotted a mountain pass, they let their horses stray into our sheep."
P: So, give them back!
MJ: "Ah, how much can a few horses eat? But we can't lose our pride! If they don't pay a fee, we won't return their horses."
P: So, they pay it, and that's that!
MJ: "Ah, they didn't pay, so we weren't happy, and so now we are at odds."
P: Now things have gotten worse.
MJ: "From that day on, we grew accustomed to taking turns slaughtering any who came onto our lands."
P: [addressing the village leader] What did you say? You slaughtered those that entered your land?

MJ: "We slaughtered them! We slaughtered as many as we could catch. If we couldn't catch them, then they got away."
P: [directly to the village leader] Oh, so if one rode a great horse, one would escape?
MJ: "Ah? What did he say? Where can you find livestock that ride horses?"
P: Who's saying that? Do your livestock ride horses?
MJ: [interceding as himself] Eh, the village elder was talking about [slaughtering] livestock!
P: [addressing MJ again] Oh, I thought that he was talking about slaughtering people.
MJ: [under his breath] Wouldn't that be a hospital [that slaughters people]?

སྨན་བླ། འགན་གཅུང་ལེན་ཁྱིས་ཤེས་ཀ་བཞེས།
པག་མོ། དེ་ལ་ཞེས་ནི་རེད།
སྨན་བླ། ཨོ་ལེ། རྒྱ་ཆོག་སྤྲིང་ར་བགོས། ས་རེར་ར་རེར་འཐེན་ནས་ཁྲིམ་རེར་ལ་བྱིད་ནས་བཞག་ཡོད་དུས་ལ་ལོ་ཚོ་ལ་ད་ཚོའི་ནང་ད་ཡོང་གི་གཤུག་བཏང་ནི་རེད།
པག་མོ། དེ་ཕྱིར་ར་སྦྱོང་ལ་ཐོངས་མོ།
སྨན་བླ། ཨ། ལ་ལོ་འགའ་གི་ཆི་ཐ་རྒྱུ་ར། ད་ཆོའི་ལ་རྒྱུ་འཆོར་མི་ཉན་གི་བླ་བྲེག་མ་བྱིན་ན་ཕྱིར་ར་མི་སྟེར་བཞེས།
པག་མོ།། དེ་བྱིན་བཏང་ན་ཆོག་གི་མོ།
སྨན་བླ། ཨ། མ་བྱིན་ནི་རེད། མ་དགའ་ནི་རེད། ད་མ་འགྲིག་ནི་རེད།
པག་མོ། ད་དོན་དག་ཇེ་ཆེར་བྱུད་ཐལ།
སྨན་བླ། དེའི་ཉིན་དགར་ནས་བྱུད་ལེ་ད་སུ་སུམས་ས་ཐོག་ག་སོང་ན་བཞའ་རེས་བྱེད་རྒྱུ་བྲེག་ལོབས་ཐལ།
པག་མོ། ཆི་བཞེས། ས་ཐོག་ག་བྱུད་སོང་ན་བཞས་འཛོག་ནི་རེད།
སྨན་བླ། བཞའ་ནི་རེད། དུ་ཟེན་དུ་བཞའ་ནི་རེད། མ་ཟེན་ཧོར་འགྲོ་ནི་རེད།
པག་མོ། ཨོ། ད་རྟ་བཅའ་ལ་བྲེག་ག་ཞིག་ཡོད་དུས་ཧོར་རྒྱ་རེད།
སྨན་བླ། ཨ། འདིས་ཆི་ཟེར་བྲེག་རྟུ་ཞེན་བྲེག་གང་ན་ཡོད་ཉེས་ཆི་ཁོ།
པག་མོ། སུམས་དེ་ཟེར་ཁྱེད་ཀྱི་བྲེག་ད་རྟུ་ཞེན་ནི་ཡིན་རྒྱུའི་རེད།
སྨན་བླ། ཨོ། སྨི་གི་ཀུན་པོས་བྲེག་ཟེར་ག་ནི་རེད་ཡ།
པག་མོ། ཨོ་དེ་བཞེས་སྨི་བཞའ་ཞེས་ན་འདོད་ལ།
སྨན་བླ། སྨན་ཁང་ཡིན་ས་ཡོད་ཀི་ར། (Sman bla skyabs 1996e)

Then Menla Jyab assigns members of the village a specific "karmic enemy." Each villager is only allowed to fight this one enemy.

> MJ: "First, that one with the long braid, stand up. [hastily] Oh, not that one, not that one. A kid with braided hair should be catching baby birds. The one behind him . . . not you, not you, what lady doesn't have a braid? The braided one behind her. Not that old man." I said, "The one young guy behind him, the one who's praying . . ."
>
> P: Ah, ah, ah. There are rows and rows of people with braids!
>
> MJ: [as himself] "Ah, speak up! Which is better: to enjoy your own life, or to destroy your own people?"
>
> P: That's not like what a real thief would say. What did he [the man with the braided hair] say?
>
> MJ: [in a different man's voice] "By my father's flesh, how should I know? But it must be that:
>
> 'Living in shame for one's whole life
> is not equal to dying nobly for a single day.'"
>
> P: Oh, so he's that type of person who is willing to die.
>
> MJ: [as himself in his role as lama] "Ah, noble son, if I tell you to run [to the battle, you will run to] the paths of the dead. If I tell you to hit, [you will hit] your father's head." Your karmic enemy is one who is deaf in his left ear, and who has a scar on his upper lip, and you're not allowed to fight with anyone else."
>
> P: That's precise; there can be no mistaking that!

སྨན་བླ། ཐོག་མར་རལ་བ་ཅན་པོ་དེ་ཡར་ར་ལོངས། ཨོ་དེ་བཟེས་ནི་མིན། དེ་བཟེས་ནི་མིན། ཨ་ཞེ་ཡིས་རལ་བ་ཅན་གྱི་ལས་ཀ་བྱིའུ་ཕྲུག་འཛིན་རྒྱུའི་རེད། དེའི་གཤུག་གི་དེ། ཨ་རེད། མ་རེད། ཨ་ཡིས་རལ་བ་མེད་ནོ་སུ་རེད་དེའི་གཤུག་གི་རལ་བ་ཅན་པོ། རྒན་པོ་དེ་མ་རེད་བཟེས་ན་དེའི་གཤུག་གི་གཤར་དུ་དེ། གསོལ་བ་འདེབས་གི་ནོ་དེ།

ཕག་ཨོ། ཨ་ཨ་ཨ། ད་རལ་བ་ཅན་པོ་ར་རབས་དང་རིམ་པ་ཐིག་ཡོད་ག།

སྨན་བླ། ཨ་ཙོས་ནོད། མི་ཚེ་ལོངས་སྤྱོད་བྱས་ན་ད་ག མི་རིགས་ཆར་གཅོད་བྱས་ན་ད་ག
པག་མོ། དེ་བཟོ་རྒྱུན་མ་དོ་མ་ཟིག་གི་སྨད་ཆ་མི་རིག་གི། ཅི་ཟེར་གི
སྨན་བླ། ཨ་རྒྱའི་དུ་གཅིག་ཤེས་ན། ད་ཚེ་གང་གི་བླ་སྐྱལ་ཡིད་རོག་གོ བསླས་ན་ཉིན་གཅིག་གི་ བླ་བསང་བྱེད་དགོ་ནི་ལོས་ཡིན།
པག་མོ། ད་བླ་བསང་བྱས་ན་ར་ཡིན་ནོ་བྱས་བྱུད་འགྲོ་ནོའུ་གྱུབ་ག་དེ་རེད་མོ།
སྨན་བླ། ཨ། རིགས་ཀྱི་བུ། རྒྱགས་བཟེས་ན་གཤིན་རྗེ་འཕྱང་། རྒྱབས་བཟེས་ན་ཨ་བའི་མགོ་རེད། ནུ་གཡེན་པ་འེན་པ་ཡིན་ནོ། ཡ་ཁ་ན་སྐྱ་ཁ་ཅན་པོ་ཅན་པོ་ཁྱིའི་འདུལ་སྐྱལ་ཡིན། དེ་མིན་ནས་ཁྱི་ཟིག་ག་བཏུད་ན་ར་མི་ཚོག
པག་མོ། ཏགས་ཅན་ད་རེད། འཁྲུག་ནི་མ་རེད། (Sman bla skyabs 1996e)

After repeating this process several times with different villagers, the audience notices a pattern: Menla Jyab has cleverly assigned each villager a target to whom they are related. The villager in the passage is assigned his maternal uncle, a family member with great significance in a Tibetan's life. Another villager is asked to fight his brother-in-law. These villagers cannot be asked to fight their own relations! Menla Jyab effectively reminds the villagers of how closely they are related to the neighboring village and dampens their desire to continue the feud.

Next, Menla Jyab reports that he went to the other village and gave a teaching, saying:

> MJ: "*Om Swa Ra Swa Sti* the land dispute, *Om Swa Ra Swa Sti* will end your grandchildren! *Om Swa Ra Swa Sti* the land dispute, *Om Swa Ra Swa Sti* will end your grandchildren! *Om Swa Ra Swa Sti* the land dispute, *Om Swa Ra Swa Sti* will end your grandchildren!" I chanted for the entire morning. In the afternoon, they all said that except for the [words of] praise [the mantra] and the "will end," they didn't understand anything.
>
> P: They probably didn't!
>
> MJ: Then I interpreted it clearly for them. I said, "This is not a prophecy that existed before but one that has just emerged for this time. As for the meaning, it says, 'If you fight over land with Careful Village land, your village will be finished.'" And everyone was afraid.

སྨན་བླ། ཨོཾ་སུ་ར་སུ་སྟི་ས་ཙོནྡྲ་ཀྱིས། ཨོཾ་ཚོ་བོ་ཚོ་མོ་ཚར་རྒྱུ་རེད།
ཨོཾ་སུ་ར་སུ་སྟི་ས་ཙོནྡྲ་ཀྱིས། ཨོཾ་ཚོ་བོ་ཚོ་མོ་ཚར་རྒྱུ་རེད།
ཨོཾ་སུ་ར་སུ་སྟི་ས་ཙོནྡྲ་ཀྱིས། ཨོཾ་ཚོ་བོ་ཚོ་མོ་ཚར་རྒྱུ་རེད།
ཕུ་དོ་ཟེག་གི་རིང་ང་བཏོན་བཏང་ང་ར།
ཕྱི་དོ་ཚང་ཨམས་ཅིག་ཆེད། ཟེག་ཚར་རྒྱུ་རེད་བཟེས་ནོ་མིན་ནས་གཅིག་ག་ར་མ་གོ་ཐལ་ཟེར།
ཕག་མོ། གོ་ས་ཡོད་དཱ།
སྨན་བླ། དེ་ནས་ད་དས་འགྱེལ་བ་གསལ་བོ་ཟེག་བྱུས། འདི་སྟོན་ཆད་ཡོད་ཉིས་ཡུད་བསྟུན་ཟེག་
མིན། ད་ལྟ་བབས་ཉིས་ཡུད་བསྟུན་ཟེག་རེད། ནད་དོན་མི་གོན་སེམས་ཆུང་སྟེ་བར་ས་བཅུད་
ན་ཁྱོད་ཚོའི་སྟེ་བ་ཚར་རྒྱུ་རེད་བཟེས་ནོ་རེད་བཟེས་ར། ཚང་མ་སྨུག་ཐལ།
(Sman bla skyabs 1996e)

With the two villages now unwilling to prolong their dispute, Menla Jyab has only brokered a temporary truce. He provides an extra solution that he expects really will reshape the future of the two villages and bring a lasting peace: using the money that they had given to him as a lama, he asked them to build a school on the land that borders the two villages.

•

The remaining three performances of the "Careful Village" series see Menla Jyab reprise his role as the comedian-turned-lama in subsequent trips to the village. In the second, "Careful Village's Bride" (Semchung déwee nama), Menla Jyab returns from another trip to Careful Village depressed, because a young villager named Zalejya is determined to marry the wrong woman. Not just any woman—a foreign woman! The village is in uproar. They refuse to accept this unprecedented event until Menla Jyab helps them see that couples should be able to choose their partners. As his partner says:

> But Zalejya loves her, and that's all that matters. It's none of Careful Village's business.

ད་ཟ་ལེ་རྒྱལ་གྱིས་བློར་བབ་བཏང་ན་དེ་རེད་མོ། སེམས་ཆུང་སྟེ་བ་མ་བབས་ནི་ཟེག་རེད།
(Sman bla skyabs 1996c)

In the series' third installment, "Careful Village's Wedding" (Semchung déwee htunmo), Menla Jyab orates a heavily modified wedding speech that he says he had given on a previous trip to the village:

> MJ: [as the village leader] "Ah, ah, ah, ah, wise lama! That was perfect! Such a fun wedding speech. Such a dear wedding speech, by my son's flesh!"
>
> PD: Oh! Without speaking it, I can't decide whether or not it's a dear wedding speech. I just hope that it's in language.
>
> MJ: The village leader spoke the truth! The form of my wedding speech is fresh so as to be in tune with a new era, and its meaning is easy to understand as it's close to real life.

སྨན་བླ། ཨ་ཨ་ཨ་ཨ། བླ་མ་མཁྱེན། མཁྱེན་ཤག་ག མཁྱེན་བདང་ཅིག དེ་མོ་སྟོན་བཤད་བསོ་མོ།
དེ་མོ་སྟོན་བཤད་ཐག་སྟེ། བུ་ཡུའི་ཤ་གོ་ཟེར་ཡ།
ཕག་མོ། ཨོ།ཁྱིའི་སྟོན་བཤད་དེ་མ་བཤད་གོང་གཅིག་གི་སྟོན་བཤད་ཤག་ཞེ་བདག་གོ་ཐག་གི་མི་
ཆོད་གི་སྨད་ཆ་གཅིག་ཡིན་ཞེས་སྟོན་ལས།
སྨན་བླ། ཨ་ཁུ་སྨྱེ་དཔོན་གྱིས་བཤད་ནི་བདེན་ནི་རེད། ངའི་སྟོན་བཤད་རྣམ་པ་སོ་མ་ཡིན་ནས་
དུས་རབས་གསར་བ་མཐུན་ཉི་རེད། ནང་དོན་གོ་བ་བླངས་ན་དངོས་ཡོད་འཚོ་བ་ཉེ་ནི་རེད་ཡ།
(Sman bla skyabs 1996f)

Mobilizing the authority of traditional oratory, Menla Jyab's speech raises a host of social issues facing Tibetan communities, with references to satellites, the influx of fake and counterfeit goods, the negative affects of alcohol, and the bad behavior of students and monks, as in the following example:

> Ya, so if I speak of the things of the world that are few,
> there are few villages that don't have grassland disputes,
> there are few monasteries that maintain pure religious doctrine,
> there are few schools with a good system of education,
> there are few leaders who only do public affairs,
> there are few lamas without beautiful consorts,
> and it should be said that they say that there are few children
>   these days who speak Tibetan.

ཡ་ད་འཛིག་རྟེན་གྱི་ཤུང་བ་རྣམས་གསུམ་གཉོ་ཅིག་བཤད་ན།
རྒྱུས་ཆོད་སྒྲོང་མེད་ཉེས་སྟེ་བ་ཤུང་ཉེས་ཟེར་གྱི
ཆེས་ཁྲིམས་གཅོང་མ་ཚན་གྱི་དགོན་སྟེ་ཤུང་ཉེས་ཟེར་གྱི
རིག་གནས་མ་ལག་ཆོང་ཉེས་སྒྲུབ་གྲུ་ཤུང་ཉེས་ཟེར་གྱི
སྤྱི་དོན་རྒྱུང་རྒྱུང་བསྒྲུབ་ཉེས་དཔོན་པོ་ཤུང་ཉེས་ཟེར་གྱི
ད་རིག་མ་ཡག་མ་མེད་ཉེས་བླ་མ་ཤུང་ཉེས་ཟེར་གྱི
དེང་སང་བོད་སྐྱིད་ཉེས་ཉེས་བུ་ཕྱུག་ཤུང་ཉེས་ཟེར་གྱི་ཟེར་རྒྱུས།

(Sman bla skyabs 1996f)

In his final trip to Careful Village, "Careful Village's Thief" (Semchung déwee hkun ma, Sman bla skaybs 1996d), the villagers beseech him to help fight off a rash of thievery that has impoverished the community. They had previously sought the advice of another lama named Ra dzu na ma (ར་རྫུན་མ།), whose name spells out the Tibetan word *dzunma* (རྫུན་མ།), meaning "fake." The lama took monetary offerings from the community in return for his "services." In the end, it is revealed that the lama had been arrested for being a thief himself.

A studio audience laughs and applauds freely throughout the performances. They appreciate the village's humorous misunderstanding of the comedian-turned-holy-man, and the parodic reenactments of modified oral traditions allegedly orated on visits to the village. They laugh as the comedian speaks in a high pitch when voicing the speech of women and children, and when he punctuates the leader's speech with deep laughter. They applaud at witty turns of phrase, and the partner responds with his commentary as he reacts to the story being told in the present.

Zooming out from the performance itself and the recording's live studio audience, a still-larger audience listens eagerly at home on radio and audiocassette, which were the most important forms of mass media for Tibetan communities at that time. Since they historically experienced high rates of illiteracy, persisting into the 1990s (Fischer 2009, 16) and with few families owning television sets, the Chinese government invested early in the creation of Tibetan-language radio broadcast infrastructure as one key way to keep them informed about government policies (Zhou 2004, 89; Ji 2013; and Zhou 2007). The radio stations drew many of Amdo's best and brightest. Even at the height of the Cultural

Revolution, a teenaged Dondrup Jya was able to gain employment in one (Virtanen 2011, 38–39) despite the "deep freeze" (Hartley 2005) for Tibetophone media in the period more generally.

Despite radio's well-established place in Amdo's mass-media environment, personal radios and cassette players were rare even at the time that Menla Jyab wrote and performed the khashag series about "Careful Village" in the early and mid-1990s. "When I was a child," one Tibetan teacher shared, "you know, not many families had [cassette tape] recorders . . . So sometimes people listened to comedies by chance. If it played on the radio, they listened. But I think one family, they had a radio, uh, a recorder, and they had a cassette of the comedies . . . So people liked to listen to it" (personal communication, June 5, 2013, in English). Similar scenarios likely played out in Tibetan communities across Amdo, with listeners of all ages huddled around a radio or cassette player, perhaps the only one in the village, eagerly anticipating the next rollicking dialogue.

As this teacher's recollections suggest, the arrival of new technologies for recording, reproducing, and broadcasting sound media have spurred the widespread popularity of these comedic forms. No longer reliant on gathering audiences around the stage for an emergent and ephemeral performance, recordings allow enjoyment beyond the event itself. Listeners of the audio recordings can enjoy the exact same performance again and again. Over time, they may knowingly anticipate a favorite line or savor particularly witty expressions.

More than just laughter, however, Tibetans also find meaning and social critique in comedic dialogues. As one fan of Tibetan comedy put it, "These all have a common characteristic, and if you ask what that characteristic is, it's that they all give something to think about, and point the way for society's nomads. For example, they do zurza on bad activities" (personal communication, March 24, 2013). Other Tibetan consultants were similarly quick to place social critique and zurza at the center of these activities. In the "Careful Village" series and other comedies from the 1990s, the "bad activities" targeted frequently focus on the actions and attitudes perceived as being at odds with the modernizing project popular among Tibetan intellectuals in the 1990s.

At the end of the twentieth century, the Tibetan Plateau's most remote areas—many inhabited almost exclusively by Tibetans (Fischer 2008, 639)—were among the most impoverished in the nation, and "39 of Qinghai's 46 county-level jurisdictions had become officially classified as 'poverty stricken'" (Goodman 2004b, 379; Wang 2013). The percentage would have been even higher for Qinghai's Tibetan populations.[3] Horlemann (2002, 244) meanwhile recognized that Tibetan pastoralists were among the poorest in one of the poorest provinces in the People's Republic during this same period.

A variety of related problems accompanied, and in some cases compounded, this poverty. In education, for example, many village schools only offered the first few years of elementary school, after which students might need to board at a school in the township or county seat. This often required children to leave their family for weeks at a time, forcibly distanced from their native communities and lifeways. Schools that did exist were often poorly maintained (Kondro Tsering 2012) and suffered from a lack of qualified teachers, many of whom were abusive, gamblers, or drank excessively (Tsering Bum 2013; Rdo rje tshe brtan 2013). Combined with the government's lax enforcement of the existing policy mandating nine years of education, it should be no surprise that many parents often saw little benefit in putting their child through school.

This was particularly the case for girls, who were much less likely to attend school and much more likely to be illiterate (Fischer 2009, 19–20).[4] One comedy, for example, poignantly portrays and satirizes this common attitude when a father—having traveled from his distant village—tries to take his daughter out of the school where she is studying. Modeling the behavior and expectations of nomads talking with people in power, the father brings gifts and alcohol and offers to bribe him with further gifts of meat. His aim is to get the bride-price from selling his daughter's hand in marriage so that he can in turn pay the bride-price for his son to marry. Bribes of alcohol and meat may have worked with the school's previous headmaster, but this newly arrived principal is, well, more principled. He refuses to let the girl leave school. In short order, this khashag suggests concerns over the state of education, educators, and pastoral attitudes toward education. In the end, the girl is happy to continue her education.

The lack of qualified, skilled personnel and the infrastructure to facilitate access, meanwhile, dogged hospitals and other public services as well. During my fieldwork, for example, I often heard people question the usefulness of going to hospitals, even for quite serious medical conditions. One person told me of an elderly relative who went to a hospital for eye surgery and woke up with her eyelid literally stitched to her eye itself. Such narratives of either incompetence or malpractice were and remain unfortunately common along Qinghai's periphery, further underpinning the basic mistrust of Western medicine. In their place, rural communities often relied on "barefoot doctors,"[5] religious means of expiating sin, and Tibetan herbal medicine. When people did seek out doctors trained in Western medicine, language barriers often compounded the difficulty, as most institutional interactions were conducted in Chinese languages, a significant stumbling block for those who had never attended school.

On top of the matter of the human capacity to provide better services, the lack of modern infrastructure further complicated these issues. As late as the year 2000, for example, Horlemann (2002, 244–45) noted that, in Golok Tibetan Autonomous Prefecture, roads remained rudimentary at best, electricity and telecommunication facilities were available only in county seats and townships, and "one pastoralist . . . in [Gabde County] had to ride on horseback for two days to take his sick baby from his home to the hospital in [Gabde] County seat." One young Tibetan corroborated this, remembering that, for his pastoralist community in nearby county, "when I began school, Father sent me into the county seat on horseback, taking at least two days" (Chos bstan rgyal 2014). Infrastructure was also pressing need.

In hopes of improving economic outcomes for Tibetan pastoralists, the Chinese government implemented policies to decollectivize and privatize pastureland on the plateau and to sedentarize the grassland's inhabitants (Du 2012, 121; Sulek 2012). Grasslands that were once communally managed were divided among individual families based on family size, and (more recently) fenced in. These privatization movements have been known to cut across traditional "tribe" or "clan" boundaries, cleaving traditional social groups into separate administrative units. Doing so undermined traditional patterns of cultural authority and replacing it with the state and its legal structures.

The number of violent grassland disputes rose sharply as the rupture in traditional protocols for accessing and using prime land and water resources became an issue of chief importance. Indeed, Yeh argues that "contradictions between these socio-territorial identities and state territoriality precipitated boundary conflicts which might not otherwise have occurred, or which would have perhaps been easier to resolve" (2003, 520), while Dkon mchog dge legs (2012, 51–52) says, "Rangeland privatization intensifies conflicts between communities and creates small-scale conflicts, which were uncommon prior to privatization."

Admittedly, rangeland warfare was no new phenomenon. Feuds arising from access to pastureland, banditry, or love were not uncommon in Tibetan areas prior to the establishment of the People's Republic, and an unmediated conflict could fester into a multigeneration cycle of like-for-like reprisals (Ekvall 1964a, 1123). Nevertheless, scholarship suggests that the government's interventions during the post-Mao period appeared to be exacerbating the problem. With firearms unavailable in recent years, many wars were waged with knives and swords. More than a few of these conflicts plagued communities in the northeastern region of Amdo, and many Tibetans died or were injured before the communities resolved these issues. Given the range and severity of the concerns facing Tibetan society, it is unsurprising that Menla Jyab has placed a grassland dispute at the center of his dialogue (despite the rather depressing topic).

•

Winter sunlight streams through the floor-to-ceiling windows of a teahouse in the center of Ziling, making the seats uncomfortably warm until a hostess lowers the shades. Menla Jyab shakes my right hand with his left (he always keeps his right concealed to hide a childhood injury) and leans back comfortably in the deep leather chair across from me, wearing blue jeans, a black silk jacket with metallic buttons on the right in the classic Tibetan style, and glasses perched on his nose. His black hair, streaked with gray, is just long enough to tie at the back. A cowboy hat balances on the arm of his seat.

In our conversation, in between chain-smoking cigarettes and sips of *puer* tea, he discussed his views on the history of Tibetan comedic dialogues, his experiences as a performer, and his views on a number of his most famous scripts. He also spoke about growing up and starting school in a Tibetan pastoral area during the Cultural Revolution—providing him with a wealth of traditional knowledge that informs his comedic endeavors—and his life on stage. Throughout, he frequently diverted our conversation to the value of education and his concerns about the state of the Tibetan language, issues that he considered particularly important for Tibetan communities. But we began our conversation with his background.

To hear him tell it, Menla Jyab was born in 1963 in a pastoral community called Sumdo, located in Mangra County, Tsolho Tibetan Autonomous Prefecture, in Qinghai. Growing up in the chaotic years of the Cultural Revolution, he attended primary school in a tent at the age of seven. He was a good student, and he eventually matriculated at the renowned Tsolho Nationalities Normal School, which served as an incubator for several of the post-Mao period's most famous Tibetan intellectual and cultural talents. Then, in the 1980s, he joined the Qinghai Song and Dance Troupe and embarked on what would become a storied career as a comedian and public intellectual. Also publishing under the pseudonyms "Pleasure Bringing Snow Child" (Gangwu ga hjyel), and "Burning Pebble" (Nbarde)—the latter being his childhood nickname and a reference to the aforementioned injury (Anonymous 2010)—Menla Jyab developed a strong reputation as not only a comedian but also an accomplished poet and essayist.

Despite working as a lyricist, film actor, and more, Uncle Menla—as many in Amdo affectionately call him—owes much of his fame to the popularity of his work as a comedian. He wrote and published his first script, "The Artist" (Jyuhtselpa, Sman bla skyabs 1985), while still working in the song-and-dance troupe. Later, he spent two years studying acting at the Shanghai Theatre Academy between 1990 and 1992, where he honed his ability to combine his deep knowledge of Tibetan pastoral life and oral traditions with biting social critique of the "social ills" facing Tibetan regions and the formal arts of comedy. Since Menla Jyab's comedic performances densely interweave traditional verbal art, context-dependent witticisms, and satirical critique of trends in Tibetan society, people often suggest in reference to them that "every line has meaning."

As Menla Jyab sat chain-smoking across from me, our conversation moved from his background to his better-known performances. When we arrived at "Careful Village's Grassland Dispute" and the other comic dialogues in the series, I wanted first to ask about the fake lama. Without missing a beat, he replied, "So, primarily, at that time . . . these Tibetan problems couldn't be solved by China's laws. And Tibet's own, uh, common folk couldn't solve them alone. . . . if Alaks were pure of intention, the monasteries and all the Alaks could solve many of the people's problems, and especially grassland disputes . . . but they don't do it."

The "Tibetan problems" vary by dialogue, but a lama can take care of each of them. He can help mediate the divisive grassland disputes plaguing pastoral communities. He can also encourage people to attend (and even open) schools, change their attitudes toward marriage for love, and even get people to give up thieving. In many cases, lamas have done this, both before the 1990s and since.[6] But in Menla Jyab's estimation, they had used this tremendous charismatic authority all too infrequently.

He is not the first to place religious practitioners (and the public's faith in them) under a satirical lens. In the seventeenth century, the Amdo lama Shar Kalden Jyamtso composed songs of spiritual enlightenment chastising clerics for their impure ways (Sujata 2005; Makley 2007). Beyond this, Kapstein (2002, 103–10) and Dor zhi Gdong drug snyem blo (1997) have found further precedents elsewhere in the Tibetan written record,[7] while we have already seen above how the trickster Uncle Tonpa often targeted and impersonated clerics as well. More recently, Dondrup Jya famously lampooned fake monks in his short story "The Tulku," and author Tsering Döndrup (2019) placed the misbehavior of monks on display in his famous short story, "The Handsome Monk."

Art and reality are often intertwined, and people continue to impersonate monks to this day in order to swindle believers (see, for example,

Hu 2016). For Menla Jyab, the answer to the social problems facing Tibetan communities—to the grassland disputes, and to insularity and backwardness in a modernizing world, etc.—lies not in religion and religious institutions but in a modern, secular education. Importantly, Menla Jyab finds no place for the police and government in solving these problems. The only government representative in the series, the village leader, seeks the fake lama's higher authority to solve the village's problems, and statements across the four dialogues of the series suggest that even he feels his powers to be limited. Instead, a modern, secular education is the antidote, as Menla Jyab makes clear when he instructs the villages to build a school at the border between them. Education also features throughout the "Careful Village" series and across Menla Jyab's broader corpus.

"Careful Village's Grassland Dispute" concerns the effects of misplaced faith in religion and religious institutions; promoting modern, secular education; and violence hollowing out rural communities. Individually, any one of these khashag make a significant critique of the problems facing Tibetan society. Together, they align this performance and Menla Jyab's comedy more generally with a growing movement of "New Thinkers" (Samlo sarwa). Centering most famously around the controversial ideas of the author-intellectual Shokdung, whose sobriquet translates as "Morning Conch," the New Thinkers advocated for a Tibetan "May Fourth Movement" at the end of the twentieth century to parallel China's pathbreaking modernist movement nearly eighty years earlier (Hartley 2002; Yü 2013; Shokdung 2016). Like the Chinese May Fourth movement, the New Thinkers promoted a modern project defined by rupture with a seemingly "backward" and overly religious past through education, scientific advancement, marriage by choice, and rational human agency in a progressive and secular present.[8]

Even the name, "New Thinkers"—along with other discursive formations, like the New Youth (Nazhun Sarwa) web portal from comedian-intellectual Pakmo Drashe, and a "new generation" of poetry (Pema Bhum 2008)—draws parallels with the proliferation of groups and concepts labeled as "new" in China during the late nineteenth and early twentieth centuries, including Chen Duxiu's *New Youth* (Ch. Xin qingnian) magazine and Liang Qichao's "new people" (Ch. *xin min*) and "new prose style" (Ch. *xin wenti*, forwarded as a simpler, vernacular style of prose to replace classical prose forms) (Lee 2001, 31–32). However, unlike the May Fourth Movement's intellectuals, Tibet's New Thinkers distinguished themselves from their Chinese predecessors by avoiding calls for political change (Peacock 2019). Instead, they advocated a rupture with (primarily religious) traditions, "overturning old habits" (Shokdung 2008) that in their estimation were holding Tibetans back from engaging more fully in modern life.

The New Thinkers, however, were (and remain) a highly controversial group, and some Tibetans stridently opposed the perceived antireligious tone of their modernist intellectual cultural producers. Shokdung reportedly received death threats for his essays (Sonam Tsering 2016, x), while public intellectual Lobsang Yongdan, often known by his internet handle "Donkey Herder" (Bongdzi), argues that Menla Jyab, Shokdung, and other New Thinkers are little more than ethnic turncoats and mouthpieces for the ideology of the Chinese Communist Party. At the same time, however, by positing himself as a modern protagonist who acts as a false lama to cross boundaries and who uses his deceits for good, Menla Jyab also thematically links his comedies to Tibetan trickster tales, creating a space for traditional motifs in modern media.

That Menla Jyab has largely succeeded in walking the tightrope of satirizing religious practitioners without alienating audiences is a tremendous accomplishment and owes much to his ability to seamlessly combine humor and meaningful critique. Doing so rests heavily on his impressive ability to create and voice a variety of credible and intriguing characters. Indeed, the lines that win the biggest laughter and applause are often those in which he switches from his own natural speaking voice to imitate that of different community members: an elderly woman, a shy but respectful young man, a child, and, most prominently, the gravelly voice of the village leader, who punctuates his speech with a forceful, three-syllable laugh: "ha ha ha!" Menla Jyab then seamlessly weaves these characters' speech into his own conversation with Pakmo Drashe in the performance's present, reporting their words as part of his "conversational narrative" (Norrick 2000) retelling his travels to the village.

Such reported speech—in which speakers in the "narrative event" voice the words of characters in the "narrated event"—helps to create and identify each character's discursive "footings": a "participant's alignment, or set, or stance, or projected self," in which "a change of footing implies a change in the alignment we take up to ourselves and the others present as expressed in the way we manage the production or reception of an utterance" (Goffman 1981, 128).

Among the characters voiced in the "Careful Village" series, the leader, whose social status gives him authority to represent the people when talking to their chosen "lama," is the only villager to feature in more than one. Other characters emerge, speak a line or two, and then disappear as quickly as their words and are not enriched with psychological depth and motivations. They are primarily linguistic constructs that serve the needs of the narrative (Barthes 1970, 178–81; cf. Cashman 2008) and focus the audience's attention on themes and plot rather than on the characters themselves.[9]

Reporting these characters' speech, meanwhile, allows the storyteller to model a socially recognizable manner of speaking linked to the character or type of character being voiced (Volosinov 1973; Bakhtin 1981). Throughout the series, one notices that the speech and attitudes of the villagers appear fairly uniform, even though they sound different, are identified by different names, and are described as having unique physical characteristics. For example, villagers pepper their speech with oaths (*na*), as with the unnamed villager in the grassland dispute who is asked to only fight his maternal uncle:

MJ: Ah, speak up! Which is better: to enjoy your own life,
 or to destroy your own people?
PD: That's not like what a real thief would say. What did he
 [the man with the braided hair] say?
MJ: [in a different man's voice] **By my father's flesh,**
 how should I know? But it must be that: Living in shame
 for one's whole life is not equal to dying nobly for a
 single day.

སྨོན་བླ། ཨ་ཚིས་ཧོད། ཁྱི་ཚེ་ལོངས་སྒྱོད་བྱས་ན་ད་ག་མི་རིགས་ཆར་གཅོད་བྱས་ན་ད་ག་
ཕག་མོ། དེ་གཟོ་རྒྱན་མ་དོམ་ཟེག་གི་སྐད་ཆ་མི་རིག་གི་ཚེ་ཟེར་གི
སྨོན་བླ། ཨ་རྒྱའི་ཤ་གཅིག་ཤེས་ན། ད་ཚེ་གང་གི་ཧ་སྐྱལ་བྱེད་རོག་གོ་བསྟུས་ན་ཉིན་གཅིག་གི་
ཧ་བསད་བྱེད་དགོ་ནི་ལོས་ཡིན། (Sman bla skyabs 1996e)

In "Careful Village's Bride," an old woman villager identified as Aye Tsigtsema expresses her opposition to the proposed marriage between a village boy named Zalejya and an American woman, saying:

A tsi! Zalejya must have epilepsy! If I met someone like that [the foreign woman] alone in the fields, **by my mother's flesh**, I'd faint.

ཨ་ཙི་ཟ་ལེ་རྒྱལ་གཟའ་ཡིན་ནི་ལོས་ཡིན། དེ་བཟོ་དེ་མོ་ཟེག་ག་ཐང་ཟེག་ནས་ཐུག་བཏང་དས། **ཨ་མའི་ཤ** ཤུག་ཆད་མི་འགྲོ་ན། (Sman bla skyabs 1996c)

Menla Jyab and his speaking partner, by contrast, speak in their own voices in a plain and unadorned style, and the former swears only one oath: "by Picasso" (as in the contemporary painter Pablo Picasso). Audiences recognize these particular oaths as characteristic of pastoral communities.

In other instances, the villagers may also use humilifics—a practice in which speakers "downplay their own prestige by showing politeness and modesty and lowering their own status" (Tsering Samdrup and Suzuki 2019, 223; Beyer 1992, 210–12) common to Menla Jyab's home area. Placed on stage and in the mouths of pastoralists, the oath swearing and humilifics help to contrast their social voice with those of the comedian's own voice.

Standing in for the social backgrounds they are intended to represent, the behaviors and attitudes of rural characters contrast with the performers speaking in their own voices in the dialogue's present to construct two basic identities: the modern of the comedians, and the backward Other in the form of the villagers. For example, through voicing villagers in the "narrated event," in which he has already said that he has gone to the countryside, Menla Jyab indexes their rural background, which in turn suggests a relative lack of education. The performances, then, link modern ideas with urbanites like Menla Jyab (as himself) and his speaking partner. Backwards ideas, by contrast, are linked with the villagers.

In "Careful Village's Grassland Dispute," Menla Jyab places a variety of "social ills" on display for audiences, both in the studio and listening on at home. The most prominent two are the village's continued desire to wage deadly conflicts against fellow Tibetans, and their religious faith, which leads them to blindly follow the advice of a comedian. But in addition to these, audiences also see the village's mistrust of modern, state-run institutions like hospitals, and an inability to value a modern, secular education. In one part of the grassland dispute, the villagers try to clarify how it began and intensified. They are discussing how they slaughtered the other village's livestock when Pakmo Drashe says:

> PD: [addressing A again] Oh, I thought that he was talking about slaughtering people.
> MJ: [under his breath] Wouldn't that be a hospital [that slaughters people]?

ཕག་མོ། ཨོ། ང་བཟོས་ཀྱི་བཤའ་ཉེས་ན་འདོད་ལ།
སྨན་བླ། སྨན་ཁང་ཡིན་ས་ཡོད་ཀྱི་ར། (Sman bla skyabs 1996e)

The quick exchange alludes to a general distrust of hospitals in Tibetan regions, which were frequently poorly funded and staffed and led to poor health outcomes. Schools, meanwhile, often seemed like a waste of time for families that might need their children as labor just to make ends meet, but Menla Jyab has them build a school and encourages a young boy to pursue his education (turns 257 and 259). Voiced through his characters, the social issues examined in "Careful Village's Grassland Dispute" can be mapped to the following binary oppositions:

BACKWARD	MODERN
nomad/farmer	urban
grassland disputes	harmonious relations with neighbors
religious faith	agnosticism/rationalism
uneducated	educated

Reading across the four performances in the series, the juxtaposition of "backward" and "modern" social voices links to a broader "modernizing" project seeking to emphasize a temporal rupture with practices and attitudes viewed as best belonging in the past. Some of these seem unique to the Tibetan experience, as with the juxtaposition between bandits and thieves in "Careful Village's Thief," but others, like the preference for free-choice marriages over arranged ones, are common parts of modernist projects across China and around the world.[10]

BACKWARD	MODERN
lacking technology	having technology
gender inequality	gender equality
traditions	laws
bandits	thieves
arranged marriages	marriages for love
no foreigners	accepting of foreigners

In this way, Menla Jyab's use of reported speech becomes "a powerful linguistic apparatus to conquer alterity and thus to consolidate the modern self" (Inoue 2006, 50). He portrays the traditional subject as basically incapable of participating in modernity. Everything—from their faith in religion to their lack of technological literacy to their continued practice of traditional (rural) lifeways—denies the rural Other a "coeval" place in modern life (Noyes 2009, 240).[11]

These periodizations—modern and backward/traditional—are best understood as a part of the broader project of Tibetan modernity rather than as temporal categories (Makley 2013a, 193–94). As such, although the emphasis on technological development, gender equality, modern education, urbanization, and marriage for love may initially appear little different from the messages promoted in Chinese government propaganda, the "Careful Village" series and other comedic dialogues from this period also put different linguistic practices on display. Doing so subjects language and language use to satirical scrutiny. Again, the juxtaposition of characters and their social voices helps comedians to articulate and discursively construct new ideological positions through both *what* they say and also *how* they say it. This creates an additional set of critiques focusing on language that helps to shape the Amdo Tibetan project of modernity.

In the grassland dispute, and across the other dialogues in the series more generally, three linguistic practices stand out particularly clearly: oath swearing, oral tradition, and figurative language. All of these feature frequently in everyday Tibetan speech. Placed on stage, meanwhile, they simultaneously demonstrate Menla Jyab's impressive command of verbal art and deepen his satirical critique.

For example, Tibetans might swear oaths to emphasize the truth of their words, to make a promise, or to seal a deal with another party. Oaths operate on the principle that the spoken word ties to Tibetan "economies of fortune" (Da Col 2007) that have real-world effects on an individual and a community in this life, and potentially in future reincarnations.[12] Seen from this perspective, breaking one's word (literally "eating one's oaths") carries potentially grievous karmic consequences (Tshe brtan rgyal 2010, 196), and the swearer of too many oaths appears untrustworthy or rash.

Interestingly, fans with whom I spoke did not feel that oaths sworn on stage (or recounted in storytelling) put one's fortune on the line. Instead, in Menla Jyab's four trips to Careful Village, oath swearing draws a contrast between Menla Jyab's own speech and that of the characters he voices. In turn 195, for example, an unnamed villager tries to emphasize the depth of his commitment to his cause through swearing an oath, "by my father's flesh." With these three (Tibetan) syllables, Menla Jyab not only refers to these existing traditional ideologies but also links these ideologies to the villagers, whose oaths of flesh and blood mark them as nomads. As the series continues, villagers swear with increasing regularity. Menla Jyab, by contrast, swears only once when speaking as himself, and when he does, it is the entirely novel oath, "by Picasso" (as in the Spanish artist). When his partner comments on this, he says that he panicked and swore by the name of a famous painter. Without any way of understanding this oath, however, the village leader misses the reference, suggesting the community's insularity and lack of education.

The portrayal of oral traditions sends still more complex messages.

90 CHAPTER 3

Villagers may use proverbs or render their expression more eloquent through versification, as when the village leader describes the village's predicament using the following proverb drawn from the Tibetan epic of King Gesar:[13]

> A guys' fight is like an unbreakable stone,
> A girls' fight is like juniper that won't rot. (turn 61)

ཕོ་གྱོད་པ་བོད་བཞིག་རྒྱུ་མེད།།
མོ་གྱོད་ཤུག་པ་རུལ་རྒྱུ་མེད།། (Sman bla skyabs 1996e)

Like many other Tibetan proverbs, this is a short verse composed of two poetic lines. These lines are frequently parallel in structure, and the situations in described in each is meant to be paired and contrasted (Sørensen and Erhard 2013a).

But if proverbs and other rhetorical flourishes may traditionally sway a mediator (Pirie 2009), they sometimes confuse the audience. Menla Jyab rarely uses proverbs when speaking as himself, and oral traditions in these contexts are useful only to either dupe or with great modification. In resolving the grassland dispute, for example, Menla Jyab combines the mantra of the bodhisattva Yangjenma—*Om Swa Ra Swa Sti*—with his prophecy of the village's destruction. His purpose? To terrify the villagers into realizing that the dispute will be their own undoing. He relies on the villagers' inability to comprehend the chanting to dupe them into believing that a religious text—one that he appears to have made up on the spot—is in fact a prophetic one that applies to their situation. Mutually assured destruction, he seems to suggest, is the best way to secure a truce.

While Menla Jyab uses religious speech to dupe the village in this kha-shag, other oral traditions also feature throughout the series, including an entire dialogue centering on a wedding speech he made on a previous trip to the village. But it quickly becomes apparent that his speech is traditional only in the sense that audiences can recognize the meter, structure, and delivery as being inspired by Tibetan traditions. Instead Menla Jyab states at the outset that he has updated it:

The form of my wedding speech is fresh, to be in tune with the new era, and its meaning is easy to understand, as it's close to real life.

དའི་སྟོན་བཤད་རྣམ་པ་སོ་མ་ཡིན་ནས་དུས་རབས་གསར་བ་མཐུན་ནི་རེད། ནད་དོན་གོ་བ་བླངས་ན་དངོས་ཡོད་འཚོ་བ་ཉེ་ནི་རེད་ཡ། (Sman bla skyabs 1996f)

He then proceeds to demonstrate the extent of these changes by launching into the long speech. The opening stanza is a good example:

I will say, *ya*, now praise *e ma ho*, praise *e ma ho*, praise *e ma ho*.
Praise, praise, praise, praise the azure blue sky.
If you don't speak praises to the azure blue sky,
It is said that there is no place for satellites to orbit the earth,
And it is said that there's no place for these airplanes to fly
   in the sky.
And it is said that people won't know that this earth is round.
   (turn 21)

ཡ་ད་སྟོད་ཨེ་མ་ཧོ། བསྟོད་ཨེ་མ་ཧོ། བསྟོད་ཨེ་མ་ཧོ།
བསྟོད་བསྟོད་བསྟོད་ལ་དགུང་ཨ་སྔོན་བསྟོད།།
དགུང་ཨ་སྔོན་འདི་མ་བསྟོད་མ་བཟོད་ན།།
མེས་བཟོས་འཁོར་སྐར་ར་འཁོར་རེ་འདུག་ས་མེད་ཉིས་ཟེར་གི
ནམ་མཁའི་གནམ་གྲུ་འདིར་འཕུར་རེ་འགྲོ་ས་མེད་ཉིས་ཟེར་གི།
སའི་གོ་ལ་འདི་གོར་གོར་ཟིག་ཡིན་ནོ་ར་མི་ཤེས་ནི་ཟེར་གི་ཟེར་རྒྱུ།།
   (Sman bla skyabs 1996f)

In a traditional wedding speech, orators use the opening stanzas to invoke a host of Buddhist and autochthonous deities. These have now been replaced with discussions of modern technological wonders like satellites and aircraft. In other stanzas, Menla Jyab proceeds to promote free-choice marriage, criticize the behaviors of monks and leaders, and encourage better educational practices, among other topics.

He also makes more subtle changes. While a traditional wedding speech will open each stanza with phrases like "worship *om a hum*"

(མཆོད་ཨོ་ཨ་ཧོ།) that help to generate the auspicious circumstances of the wedding through the use of religious language, Menla Jyab uses the more innocuous—though still positive—"praise *e ma ho*" (བསྟོད་ཨེ་མ་ཧོ།). Such changes, when read alongside his above statement about intelligibility, effectively erase the traditional wedding speech's religious overtones. Like the grassland dispute mediation, Menla Jyab's speech marks religious and traditional texts as difficult to understand, and then changes one for his satirical purpose. Traditional verbal art, it seems, can only become appropriate for the modern world through the (parodic) interventions of the comedian-intellectual.

Just as comedians distinguish between "backward" and "modern" social positions, they also model the language practices of both the modern, educated, sophisticated, and urban selves of the comedians when they speak in their own voices as well as their discursively constructed opposite: the "backward," uneducated, unsophisticated rural speaker. Placed side by side for the audience's enjoyment and evaluation, this creates a second set of binaries that maps onto the first:

BACKWARD	MODERN
difficult to understand	easily understood
traditional genres	parody/comedy/khashag
verse	plain speech
monolingual	multilingual
vernacular	literary Tibetan register

It is difficult to overstate the significance of this linguistic critique. Although the government in China does support the very Tibetan-language media stations that aired these comedies, it also continues to promote a monoglot language ideology (Dong 2009) that places state-sponsored "universal speech" (Ch. *putonghua*) at its center and discursively casts minority languages and regional dialects as anti-modern "Others" (Tam 2016; Gunn 2005, 7; Li 2004, 103; Liu 2008,1). Through linking characters with specific speaking styles, comedians show traditional language practices to be sites of confusion and complexity and model a more simplified and direct alternative. In doing so, they add a linguistic element to their already penetrating social critique.[14] Interpreted through the satirical lens of zurza, this second set of binaries, modeled in comedic performance, suggests a set of language ideologies for a distinctly Tibetan engagement with modernity.

In China, where "the narrative of emancipatory modernity... has its power because it has elicited the commitment of both the Chinese state and the modern intelligentsia" (Duara 1995, 226), and where the Chinese Communist Party has placed considerable emphasis on modernization, the first set of social binaries described in relation to the "Careful Village" series would initially appear to share much in common with the sort of modernity frequently promoted by the Chinese state. Indeed, by privileging social issues like technological advancement, an antireligious secularism, and the rule of law over religion and tradition, Menla Jyab uses zurza to create a comedic performance that appears to conform to the "singular script" of Chinese modernity available to ethnic-minority cultural producers in China (Schein 1999, 387). But in extending his satirical critique to the creation of modern Tibetan-language practices, he refuses the state's script (without explicitly denying it) through providing new pathways for Tibetan modernity grounded primarily in linguistic practices.

•

Careful Village is a fictional place. The term *semchung* (སེམས་ཆུང་།), which may literally be translated as "small mind," implies timidity and, in certain contexts, meekness and cowardliness. The album title *Rudé tramo* (The colorful nomad camp) uses the word *tramo* (ཁྲ་མོ།), which can mean "pretty" in a slightly pejorative sense, or "colorful" in both a literal sense and, more appropriately in this situation, a connotative one. Put together with the name of the series, this suggests a pointed critique of the underlying malaise that led to the problems that the performers and many other Tibetan intellectuals feel their culture faces in the twenty-first century: that Tibetan society is increasingly insular, afraid of the outside world, infighting, fearful of thieves, and the like.

Internally, a number of lines and features of the comedies direct culturally fluent audiences to recognize them as not simply articulating local or even regional issues but promoting ones of concern to Tibetan people as a whole. One important way of discursively creating the massive scalar jump from village to entire translocal ethnic group is through references to conceptions of myth and history. At several points in the "Careful Village" dialogues, Menla Jyab and the characters he voices explicitly and discursively scale up from the village to the ethnic group. In "Careful Village's Grassland Dispute," for example, when his partner Pakmo Drashe realizes Menla Jyab has arranged for the villagers to fight only those opponents to whom they are related, the latter responds by saying:

> Didn't they all arise from the bodhisattva monkey and the rock ogress?
>
> ཚང་མ་སྤྲེའུ་བྱང་ཆུབ་སེམས་དཔའ་ར་བྲག་སྲིན་མོ་ནས་ཆད་ནི་རེད་མོ། (Sman bla skyabs 1996e)

This reference to the mythical progenitors of the Tibetan people rests on the tremendous "communicative economy" (Foley 1995) of Tibet's heavily referential language to discursively link the people of Careful Village to all other Tibetans. Audiences, in turn, recognize that the concerns being discussed confront not only the village but the ethnic group more generally.

This jump from village to ethnic group is achieved again in "Careful Village's Bride," when the villagers speak of their credentials to some American matchmakers, saying:

> We are descended from Lhalung Hualdor
>
> དེ་ག་ལྷ་ལུང་དཔལ་རྡོར་ཚང་གི་གདུང་རྒྱུད་ཡིན། (Sman bla skyabs 1996e)

This references Tibet's most famous assassin, a monk renowned for having slain the apostate King Langdarma in 842, before fleeing to Amdo.

In some cases, the reference might be a regional one, as some villages in Amdo trace their origins to Lhalung Hualdor, but this figure is also viewed as a Buddhist hero in almost all regions. Claiming common ancestry through both the historical hero Lhalung Hualdor, and mythical figures like the bodhisattva monkey and the rock ogress place Careful Village squarely within a much broader Tibetan cultural world.

If these examples reference culture, myth, and history to achieve a scalar jump, other performances do so through comparison with the world beyond the village. In "Careful Village's Thief," for example, the village leader says:

> As for where they went, they're *modern* thieves. They might have gone to India or China. But me, I don't speak anything but Tibetan. Where would I go to look for them?

དེ་གང་ད་བྱུད་ཐལ་ཟེར་རྒྱས་དེད་རབས་གི་རྐུན་མ་རེད་མོ། སྟོད་རྒྱ་གར་ར་སོང་གི། སྨད་རྒྱ་ནག
ག་སོང་ན། ང་བོད་སྐད་མིན་ཉེས་མི་ཤེས་ནི་ཟེག་གང་ད་བཙལ་གི་འགྲོ་རྒྱས། (Sman bla skyabs 1996d)

In choosing India and China, Menla Jyab sets Careful Village as a metaphor for the entirety of the Tibetan Plateau caught between the two countries. China and India, meanwhile, comprise different cultural systems and civilizations between which Tibetans have long felt caught. Significantly, he states this in linguistic terms, emphasizing that he will be inarticulate in these foreign lands, and therefore incapable of dealing with these modern thieves. In this way, "articulate ... individuals could become inarticulate and 'language-less' by moving from a space in which their linguistic resources were valued and recognized into one in which they didn't count as valuable and understandable" (Blommaert 2007, 2). By moving to other countries, and the other linguistic systems these countries represent, the village leader loses the authority of his position. He ceases to be the most-voiced villager in the "Careful Village" series and becomes distinctly voiceless.

Externally, both audiences and performers expect zurza (satire) and larjya (pride) as an integral part of a good khashag in Amdo. The combination of traditional verbal art, pride, and satire enables a comedy that might otherwise be treated as pure entertainment, or as a very localized phenomenon, to speak to broader social issues considered relevant to communities living on the Tibetan Plateau in post-Mao China. In the cases above, historical references then help audiences recognize that the dialogues describe not merely the unique issues facing a single village but rather those plaguing the whole plateau.

Mustering all his powers of satirical critique, his knowledge of traditional Tibetan verbal art, and his widely acknowledged ethnic pride, Menla Jyab places the entirety of contemporary (Amdo) Tibetan society under his critical lens. The social problems satirized, then, must be read accordingly. Thus, "Careful Village's Grassland Dispute," in which the village is at war with its neighbors, is an internal feud within the ethnic group. In describing the village's shortcomings and the difficulties it faces when confronted with such modern situations, the comedians expose problems they perceive to be facing contemporary Tibetan society, lampoon current attitudes, and (crucially) provide models for the resolution of such challenges of modernity, which are not limited to the village but face all Tibetan communities.

•

The four comedic dialogues about Careful Village remain extremely popular on the Tibetan Plateau to this day. People listen to them on long car rides, share favorite sections with each other on social media, and reference them in daily conversation. With a unique combination of humorous, conversational storytelling and socially meaningful critique—in short, their ability to "do zurza"—these khashag have had such a pervasive influence in Tibet that they have shaped attitudes and language practices both in Amdo and beyond. One consultant, for example, described how Tibetans invoke the name Zalejya—the young villager who wishes to marry a foreign woman in the second part of the series—to sarcastically draw attention to a companion's behavior: "For example, if I have a friend, and . . . if he likes a girl, I make a joke. . . . 'What's wrong? Don't be like Zalejya! You're not Zalejya, are you?'"

Menla Jyab uses zurza to access state media, and to share complex critiques about Tibetan engagement with modernity. His critiques tend to be indirect and rarely (if ever) mention socially identifiable individuals. In this way, his zurza remains similar to more conventional satirical fare legible to the state. But Menla Jyab's audiences, meanwhile, reuse favorite parts of his comedies to entertain and critique those around them, taking from the performances new rhetorical tools with which to educate (and lambaste the undesirable behavior of) others. Alongside Menla Jyab's generalized satire, then, the strain of person-specific but indirect critique seen in some oral traditions remains an important part of the Tibetan discursive repertoire.

And yet, Tibetan society does not stand still. New technologies, political and discursive environments, performers, and cultural trends have all emerged in the twenty-first century, reshaping the issues that cultural producers and audiences find important. Rather than replacing the modernist comedies of the 1990s, they create new layers on top of it that further complicate our understanding of Tibetan experience in contemporary China. Comedy and zurza continue to play an important role in this new environment, helping intellectuals articulate an evolving critique of the issues facing Tibetan communities.

4
Garchung
Televised Sketches and a Cultural Turn in the 2000s

Sounds of bleating sheep piped through the sound system turn the stage into a pastoral community. With a little imagination, you can almost see the grasslands unfolding ahead, dotted with white sheep and black yaks. An elderly-looking man wanders onto the stage wearing a nomad's felt raincoat. He takes off the coat and places it on the ground, briefly surveys the scene, and then strolls back off stage left. As soon as he exits, a tall Caucasian man and an Asian woman enter from the opposite end, speaking English. The foreigner says he is looking for black-necked cranes that only live on the Tibetan Plateau, and the guide thinks that "Uncle Horse Herder," a local herdsman, might know where to find them. At this, the herder walks onto the stage, shouting:

> *Aro!* This is my pasture. There's no passage! So, head off that way!

> ཨ་རོགས། འདི་ས་དབེའི་རྩྭ་ས་ཡིན། འགྲོ་ས་མེད། གན་པར་སོང་།

The audience laughs and claps at the obstinate herder, who they recognize being played by the star comedian Menla Jyab. This, the woman says, is Uncle Horse Herder, and she thinks that he might know more about the birds.

The woman, Hongmei, who turns out to be a Tibetan and a teacher at the local school, tries to speak with the herder and introduces the foreigner, Jersey, who gives a Tibetan greeting and bows awkwardly. The stunned herder responds, saying:

Look how human speech comes from his mouth.

ཁྱོད་ལྟོས། འདིའི་ཁ་ནང་ནས་མི་སྐད་བགགས་ནོ་ཨེ་རིག་གི།

More laughter.

The teacher tries to explain why she has brought the foreigner onto the horse herder's land. But she immediately runs into trouble, because the pastoralist seems largely incapable of understanding the young teacher, who mixes Chinese and Tibetan so often that her speech is almost unintelligible. For example, she says that the foreigner will bring *dollars*, which the herder mishears as *doleb* (stone slabs); she also says *meigor*, a combination of the standard Chinese *Meiguo* (America) and *gormo*, the Amdo Tibetan word for money. He not only fails to understand this term but mistakenly believes she is talking about a "beggar's money" because the first syllables of *mépo* (beggar) and *Meiguo* sound similar to his old ears. This makes no sense whatsoever to the herder. After all, what can "beggar's money" be? And regardless, none of this explains why the teacher has brought the man onto his land. When the teacher tells him the foreigner is looking for birds, he is even more confused.

All of them know that the black-necked cranes live on this land, but the horse herder seems disinclined to allow the pair onto it. He lies, saying that the birds have left and that the foreigner should do the same. Frustrated, the teacher pulls him aside and, running around like a terrier to face the nomad, who is trying to turn his back to her, she argues:

This is an excellent opportunity! The god of wealth has arrived at our door. You might need help with money in the future.

ཇི་ཅུཨེ་(机会)་དགའ་གཟིག་རེད་མོ། ཚའི་ཤེན་ཡེ(财神爷)་བཟོ་སྟོ་ཁར་ཐོན་བཏང་ནི་རེད། གཞུག་ནས་སྟོར་མོ་བཟོ་དགོས་ནི་ཐང་།

Far from impressed with the young woman's reasoning, Uncle Horse Herder responds, saying:

Dear Teacher, you seem like the reincarnation of one who's died a pauper.

དགེ་རྒན་ལོ་ལོ། ཁྱེད་འདི་སྟོང་མོ་མེད་ལ་ཤི་སོང་ནི་ཞིག་གི་རྣམ་ཤེས་ཡིན་ས་རེད།

There's raucous laughter this time.

Then the foreigner begins to speak. In Tibetan! "What if I look from far away?" he asks. The herder is stunned, and the camera cuts to a member of the studio audience, who leans on his neighbor, mouth agape; the herder is clearly not alone. "It's like he's speaking Tibetan," the herder says. The foreigner insists that he won't cause a problem, and he and the teacher try to convince the herder. With the foreigner speaking Tibetan, the horse herder is willing to listen and to share a bit of his knowledge, but he still denies the presence of the cranes.

When confronted with his deception, he reveals that his opposition is cultural:

> Small Treasure Lake is not some meaningless puddle. It is Gesar's [wife] Drukmo's mirror. The slender-winged white crane [on the shore of the lake] is the Tibetans' spirit bird. It is Drukmo's soul bird.

མཚོ་ཆུང་གཏེར་བུ་ཟེར་ན་གན་རང་ང་ནང་དོན་མེད་ཉེས་ཆུ་འཁྱིལ་ཞིག་མ་རེད། གན་སྒྲིང་སེང་ལྷམ་འབྲུ་མོའི་དོ་བཀྲ་རེད། དེ་ཁ་གི་ཁྱུང་ཁྱུང་དཀར་མོ་གཤོག་ཡག་མ། བོད་ཁ་བ་ཅན་གྱི་ལྷ་བྱ་རེད། སྒྲིང་སེང་ལྷམ་འབྲུག་མོའི་བླ་བྱ་རེད། ཨོ་ཡ།

Later, he takes the teacher aside to let her know that the birds, the lake, and the village's fortune are inextricably linked:

> Small Treasure Lake is our village's bucket of fortune. The birds on the shore are like the butter on its rim. It is said that during the years when the birds are many, the elders live longer and livestock prosper; when there are no birds there, then everything is doomed.

མཚོ་ཆུང་ནོར་བུ་ཟེར་གོ་ནི་གནའ་དུ་ཚའི་སྟེ་བ་གི་གཡང་གི་རྫོ་ཞབས་ཡིན་ནི་རེད། མཚོ་ཁ་བུ་ཚའི་རི་ཁ་གི་མར་འདུ་འདུ་བོ་རེད། བྱ་མང་གི་ལོ་དེར་ལོ་ལོན་གི་ཚེ་ཐག་རིང་ད་ཕུགས་རོག་གི་འཕེལ་ཁ་དར་ར། བྱ་མེད་དུས་ད་བུ་ཚང་གོ་ནི་ཡིན་བསོད་ནམས་ཟད་གོ་ནི་ཡིན་ཟེར་ནི་རེད།

With these exchanges, the herder thereby forces the conversation to remain firmly within Tibetan ways of understanding their world, with concerns of individual and village fortune paramount. He also compares the cranes to butter on the rim of a bucket, referencing a practice reserved for auspicious occasions, like weddings and New Year festivities. Linking local geographies to the Tibetan epic of King Gesar, meanwhile, is a common way communities place themselves on the Tibetan cultural map. By focusing on cultural rather than economic arguments, the horse herder justifies his decision to deny access to the lake. And with good reason: Although many birds live at the lake at the moment, things were not always thus. Previously an outsider had looked in the lake, and it coincided with a string of disasters for the village. The horse herder is unwilling to take any chances, what with the community's fortune on the line.

But what if the foreigner was a Buddhist? After all, Hongmei reasons, there are Buddhists all over the world these days. So, she asks the foreigner about his religion. Jersey says he is atheist. Knowing that this answer is no good, she lies and tells the horse herder that Jersey believes in Tibetan Buddhism. The foreigner, however, seals his own fate by contradicting the teacher, saying that it is better to tell the truth and that he doesn't believe in religion (literally saying he "has no faith"). The teacher is visibly frustrated at this, and the horse herder incredulously asks:

Where on earth are there people who don't have a religion?

འཛིག་རྟེན་ན་དད་པ་མེད་ནིའི་མྱི་ར་ཡོད་ནི་ཨེ་རེད།

This situation appears to be one that he simply cannot fathom. Can the foreigner come back from this?

Next, things turn downright dangerous when the herder learns that the foreigner is from England, reminding the herder of the Younghusband expedition of 1904 in which a detachment of British soldiers defeated the Tibetan army (a staple of Maoist-era propaganda). The young "Brit" says, "It wasn't me! That's history!" But the herder mistakes "history" (ལོ་རྒྱུས།, locally pronounced *lorjee*) for the similar-sounding personal name Dorje (རྡོ་རྗེ།). In the Amdo dialect, everything but the initial consonant of these two words sounds similar, and the horse herder thinks the foreigner is trying to shift the blame. Even after clarifying the mistake, the herder remains unconvinced:

Well, that's just what your chances of seeing the cranes are: history!

དའི་མཚོ་ཆུང་ནོར་བུའི་ཁ་གི་ཁྱུང་ཁྱུང་ཚོར་ལྷ་རྒྱུའི་གོ་སྐབས་འགྱུར་སོང་ནི་རེད། ལོ་རྒྱུས་རེད།

In a last-ditch attempt to help the foreigner achieve his goal (and possibly secure donations for the school in the process), the teacher and the foreign researcher try further arguments to convince the herder. Focusing on ecological conservation and the scientific study of the black-necked cranes, they argue for the benefits of allowing further research. But the herder is again confused when the teacher uses the standard Chinese term *shengtai baohu* for ecological conservation, Only after the *foreigner* clarifies with the correct Tibetan term (yes, you read that correctly!) does the meaning become clear. Again, however, the herder is unimpressed. By limiting access to his land, he believes that he has been engaged in ecological conservation for years already. The teacher offers to take a picture on the foreigner's behalf and to boost the potential tourism money that could come from spreading news about the cranes. None of this sways the herder's opinion. In the end, he trudges off alone in the direction from which he had come, leaving the teacher and the foreigner shrugging helplessly.

"Gesar's Horse Herder" (Gesar htardzi) is the performance that initially inspired my interest in Tibetan comedy. From the first time I saw it, I felt that it spoke to important concerns facing Tibetan communities in the twenty-first century about the present and future of the language, culture, and environments. Conversations with performers and fans further solidified this impression when they regularly cited it as a favorite in relation to contemporary debates over language practice. More importantly, the comedy demonstrates just how significantly the satirical critique of Tibetan comedy—and the broader twenty-first-century intellectual project in Amdo—had begun to change. It begins with the more visual medium itself, which hints at the very real technological and infrastructural changes to Tibetan communities in this period.

•

Sitting in the tiny back room of a small music shop selling mandolins and VCDs (video compact discs, which served as the primary medium through which people enjoyed audiovisual material during my fieldwork), I am chatting with a well-known actor and singer, who also happens to be the proprietor of the shop. With his hair cut short and wearing baggy jeans, a long-sleeve T-shirt, and a string of large prayer beads around his neck, he does not look like the long-haired, robe-wearing, and usually poor pastoralists he normally portrays on stage and film. Before I can even ask a question or set up my recorder, he immediately launches into a long disclaimer about his lack of education, his background as a singer, and his inability to speak authoritatively about comedy.

When I finally do manage to get a question in, I ask about his experience performing khashag. After all, I have heard fans use khashag to refer to both comedic dialogues and the sketches for which he is best known. It quickly becomes clear to me that I have put my foot in my mouth. The comedian vigorously corrects me and says that he does not do khashag. He primarily performs *garchung* (sketches, གར་ཆུང་།). "What's called *garchung*," he says, "is played with [physical] performance, they say it's like that. This thing called a *khashag*, the two of us stand up and I speak to you, and you speak to me. That's called *khashag*" (pers. comm., August 23, 2013).

It is one of those fortuitous fieldwork faux pas in which an errant word provides valuable new perspectives. Over time, I heard other comedians make a similar distinction between khashag and either garchung or *zhadgar* (comedic plays). One comedian, for example, agreed with the premise and expanded on it, saying:

Well, in general, in the 1980s and 1990s I mostly did dialogues, and, uh, in terms of the artistic forms, if you divide it into dialogues and sketches, comedic dialogues were mostly written during the 1980s and 1990s. At that time, there really wasn't much to prepare. At that time, it wasn't visual. They didn't record images, and it was primarily recording sound. When they recorded, after I'd finished writing the script, I'd hold the script, and uh, the microphone, and I could hold it and it was all right to say it like this.

Sketches weren't like this. Most comedic dialogues were like this. And when the later garchung arrived, uh, [we had to] memorize the script, and then find the cast, and they had to memorize, and then the directing process—it's called *daoyan*, right? This process was involved, and then we finally [performed] it. It was like that.

Not limited to the names of the genres, the verbs used in conjunction with performance further reflect the difference between the two forms: a sketch, for example, is *htsé wa* (played, རྩེད་པ།) or *trabhtun ye wa* (performed, འཁྲབ་སྟོན་བྱེད་པ།), while a khashag dialogue is *shed pa* (spoken, བཤད་པ།).

To Amdo's comedians, this distinction between khashag comedic dialogues and garchung sketches recognizes that the newer, more visual, garchung required different artistic, material, and technological capacities. These terminological distinctions also hint at the different technological, artistic, and thematic properties of the form. While 1990s comic dialogues were primarily disseminated on radio broadcasts and audio cassettes, new garchung reached audiences through state television station and, later, on VCDs and the internet.

These sketches are also stylistically and thematically different from the comic dialogues of the 1990s, in that they satirize a host of new issues, a testament to how rapidly conditions have changed in the Amdo's intellectual sphere. For example, whereas comedic dialogues and other cultural production in the 1990s satirized "social issues" associated with modernization, the comedies and other cultural production in the twenty-first century engage in what I call a "cultural turn." Similar to what Ptackova (2019, 420) has termed "traditionalization," defined as the (re)invention of tradition to distinguish Tibetan identity from the

Han, this cultural turn focuses on issues like language, tradition, ritual, and environment, in support of a growing Tibetan nationalism. After all, vernacular and traditional practices are often "valorized when the nation is project" (Ortiz 1996, 37).[1]

With the switch to a more visual medium and performance genre, some new stars emerged, finding that the style better suited their talents for physical comedy. Shidé Nyima and Soktruk Sherab, for example, both gained popularity and fame thanks primarily to their skills, especially with physical comedy. Many of these performers have gone on to feature in television shows and film, like the 2009 hit miniseries *The Pig's Head Soothsayer* (Mohtun phamgo), featuring Shidé Nyima, and the 2008 series *Yesterday's Story* (Khasang gi tamjyul), in which Soktruk Sherab took a star turn. Other established comedians, like Pakmo Drashe, who voiced the "Careful Village" series alongside Menla Jyab, gradually faded from the comedic scene. Some of Amdo's comedic stars also seamlessly transitioned to this new style. For example, Menla Jyab's fame and popularity grew with the transition to this more visual comedy.

•

At the close of the 1990s, as comedians and other intellectuals promoted a Tibetan May Fourth Movement, Qinghai—including the Amdo heartland—had the worst economy in the entire country. Other regions of China's ethnically diverse western regions lagged similarly behind the metropolises in the well-developed coastal regions. Then, in 2000, the Chinese government initiated the "Great Open the West Campaign." This far-reaching project dominated state policy in the first decades of the twenty-first century, with massive investments in infrastructure, afforestation programs, transportation, a natural gas pipeline (Goodman 2004a), and particularly education (Clothey and McKinlay 2012). It also included encouraging the migration of non-Tibetan populations into traditionally Tibetan regions (see, for example, Yeh 2013b) and an extensive "ecological migration" program, in which Tibetan pastoralists were moved off the grassland in the name of protecting it, also subsidized by the state in the name of environmental conservation (Ptackova 2013).

While the Great Open the West Campaign transformed the economic, social, and infrastructural landscape of the Tibetan Plateau, the Chinese government also ratified the UNESCO Convention for the Safeguarding of the Intangible Cultural Heritage in 2004 and began to undertake a broad campaign to identify and protect intangible traditions throughout the country. Leaders and culture brokers specifically targeted minority practices for heritage recognition, and by 2009 (the second year of official listing), Tibetan traditions comprised three of China's twenty-nine successful applications to the UNESCO list, a representation far outstripping the region's proportion of the total populace of the country. This official and broad-ranging support for traditional practices and knowledge, also seen as a way to boost local economies, suddenly authorized new discourses on state media and rendered new narratives about the values of tradition "tellable"—the qualities in a narrative and in a context that make it worth telling (Sacks 1992)—for a Tibetan audience in ways that they had not been in previous decades.

Contemporaneous to these many government-led initiatives, a host of international NGOs supported cultural preservation projects alongside those relating to running water and solar cooker distribution. Infrastructure investments also brought an influx of government money to the region, while the brisk and lucrative interregional trade in caterpillar fungus further supported local economies in this period and enriched some of the region's rural inhabitants. Unprecedented amounts of disposable income, increased settlement in urban or periurban environments, infrastructural improvements (including lined electricity), and the new availability of electronic devices and other media technologies all helped to encourage the Tibetan Plateau's increasing integration with China's market economy.

Expanded television ownership also made new, more visual forms of cultural production possible. But getting seen on television was no easier than getting heard on radio broadcasts, and the state's gatekeepers continued to strictly monitor the messages shared through these media. Many of the most famous performances ended up initially airing on the annual New Year's Eve variety gala, the Losar Gongtsog. This spectacle aired on local television stations and featured emcees (broadcasters from the various television stations around the plateau) introducing songs, dances, greetings from other areas, and, of course, comedies. Still to this day, the show's producers scrutinize each word of these events to ensure that they strike the correct political tone. In many cases politics weigh more heavily than entertainment value. With these strict controls on performance, Amdo's comedians' ability to use language artfully, humorously, and meaningfully—in short, their ability to mobilize zurza as a "cultural resource" to "solve problems"—remains a key discursive tool for comedians to turn humor into meaningful and tellable performance. Again Menla Jyab's satirical critique derives its power primarily through the juxtaposition and comparison of various characters, like the foreigner Jersey, the teacher Hongmei, and the obstinate pastoralist, Uncle Horse Herder.

In this regard, one reason for the incredible popularity of "Gesar's Horse Herder" is the stunning presence of the Tibetan-speaking foreigner. For some audience members, this might have been the first time they saw a Caucasian person speaking their language. Interestingly, however, "Gesar's Horse Herder" is not the only performance to use foreign characters, though it is perhaps the most famous. In one part of the "Careful Village" series, a villager wants to marry a foreign woman who, coincidentally, has also come to the Tibetan Plateau to research birds. Foreign characters provide a valuable break in everyday life and allow comedians to openly discuss behaviors and social issues that might otherwise be taken for granted. The unique combination of (assumed) wealth and high prestige on the one hand and cultural and linguistic semicompetence on the other provides fertile ground for both humorous misunderstandings and biting satirical critique. In "Gesar's Horse Herder," for example, the presence and actions of the "Englishman" Jersey allows the audience to compare and contrast his actions and ideas with those of the two Tibetan characters. In particular, his words and activities point the satirical spotlight directly at Hongmei.

For all the modern social capital we can assume from her position—a high level of schooling leading to a job as a teacher, knowledge of multiple languages, access to the latest fashions, and more—Teacher Hongmei is not to be emulated. Instead, her name, clothing, attitudes, and behavior all index distance from Tibetan culture. One comedian even derisively asserted that the teacher, "has become Han," (རྒྱ་ལོག་སོང་གཟིག) in a tone that made quite that this was not intended as a compliment. In particular, the teacher falls short in three areas that emerge as central components of the twenty-first century cultural turn and of the of satirist-comedian's new critique: knowledge of traditional culture, knowledge of traditional environments, and linguistic (in)competence.

Most obvious of these are the instances in which Hongmei mixes Chinese words into her Tibetan speech. In fact, she borrows Chinese words several times, including the following:

1) **The god of wealth** has arrived at our door.
   财神爷བཟང་སློ་ཁར་ཐོན་བཏང་ནི་རེད།
2) He says that I need to **translate**
   ངས་翻译་བྱེད་དགོས་ནི་རེད་བཟེས།
3) There's no **relation**
   关系་བདག་གོ་ཅང་ར་མེད་གི
4) That's **about** it.
   ད་大概་དེ་མོ་གཟིག་རེད།

Each time she borrows Chinese terms, Hongmei's inability to communicate with the horse herder becomes more evident. By the end, the foreign visitor even corrects her Tibetan on two separate occasions. In the first, he corrects her use of the Chinese term *dagai* (roughly or approximately), while in the second and more pronounced instance, the foreigner teaches the teacher how to say the Tibetan term for ecological conservation:

> HONGMEI: *Shengtai baohu* is everyone's responsibility.
> UNCLE HORSE HERDER: I didn't understand a word you said.
> Hongmei: (in English to Jersey) I'm sorry, what is "ecology" in Tibetan?
> JERSEY: *Hjyekham.*
> HONGMEI: (to herself) *Hjyekham, hjyekham.* (then to Uncle Horse Herder) Ecological conservation is everyone's responsibility.

HONGMEI: 生态保护ནི་ཡོང་རྟོགས་ཀྱི་ལས་འགན་རེད་ཟེར་གི་རེ།
UNCLE HORSE HERDER: ད་ཁྱིའི་དེ་ར་ཅང་མ་གོ་ཐལ།
HONGMEI: I'm sorry, what is "ecology" in Tibetan?
JERSEY: སྐྱེ་ཁམས།
HONGMEI: སྐྱེ་ཁམས། སྐྱེ་ཁམས། སྐྱེ་ཁམས་སྲུང་སྐྱོབ་ཞང་ས་བྱེད་དགོས་ནི་རེད་བཟེས་ཡ།

In this exchange, Hongmei's baffling inability to produce pure Tibetan creates a sentence that is so incomprehensible to the horse herder that it alienates her from her interlocutors, suggests her cultural distance from Tibetan traditions, and weakens her own negotiating stance. This impression is furthered when the horse herder says that he hadn't understood her at all. With this, the situation has become so egregious and untenable that Hongmei is practically incapable of interacting with the tradition-associated horse herder.

If Hongmei's linguistic practices impede clear communication, her cultural attitudes further alienate the very nomad she is trying to persuade. At a key moment, the teacher argues that even she knows of the existence of cranes on the elderly nomad's land and that gaining recognition for them could bring economic benefits to the community. Menla Jyab's character, however, immediately retorts:

> In my opinion, there is a lot that you don't know.
>
> ངས་བསམ་ན་ཁྱོས་ཤེས་ཀྱི་མེད་ནི་མང་གི

Hongmei is right, but so is the horse herder. The elusive, black-necked cranes *do* live on his land, and the community probably *could* benefit from allowing tourists to see them. But in solely emphasizing economic concerns, the teacher betrays her disregard of traditional cultural practice. By contrast, the herder's decision not to allow the foreigner on his land shows that he cares about more than money. He bases his decision on a more complex historical and cultural logic, insisting that Tibetan ways of knowing their world should have a place in his conversations.

Tibetan audiences also realize that the horse herder has good reasons for refusing to allow the foreigner—and particularly an admitted atheist—onto his land. In calling his own character "Gesar's horse herder" and discussing how the lake in question is "Drukmo's mirror" (referring to Gesar's wife), Menla Jyab creates a metonymic link (Foley 1995, 5–11) to a much larger cultural tradition of associating individual locations with Gesar's exploits, and the even broader tradition of associating remarkable handprints and footprints on rocks with the presence of great religious figures.

Tibetans traditionally also view themselves as living alongside a variety of more-than-human beings, including both animals and a variety of autochthonous numina the interactions of which have the power to affect people's lives for good or for ill. Grasslands and water sources are potentially dangerous, liminal spaces. A nap on the grassland can lead to encounters with deities (as in the case of inspired performers of the Gesar epic), and a poorly placed bowel movement can cause illness. Lakes and rivers are often home to *lu*, a class of autochthonous numina that live in lakes, control wealth, and can cause human illness. The plateau's human inhabitants must navigate these spaces with care to avoid upsetting the delicate balance that has allowed human life to flourish.

In the sketch, the tradition-oriented horse herder explains that the lake and its cranes are the source of the village's fortune, and as such, they must be protected and managed—and the horse herder intends to do exactly this. In doing so, he is clearly unwilling to risk another change to the region's precarious fortune. This is more than mere lip service, as the herder underlines in speaking about how another outsider had previously upset this delicate balance by looking in the lake. In the teacher's opinion, cultural concerns should have no bearing on the overwhelming economic issues facing Tibetan communities in the present. But in doing so, she comes off distinctly second best, and only emphasizes the significant cultural disconnect between the modern teacher and the traditional herder.

In addition to providing a defense of Tibet's traditional cultural knowledge, the herder also uses his discussion on fortune to link Tibetan ideas of the environment to an area of contemporary political concern.

Gaeerang (2017, 15) shows how the contemporaneous emergence of environmental policy and a conservation-linked Buddhist revival have led Tibetans in the twenty-first century to embrace environmental conservation. Menla Jyab's herder avoids explicit Buddhist reference but provides traditional perspectives of the environment as a space filled with both human and nonhuman agents that shape individual and communal fortune. In his eyes, he *has* been protecting the environment through limiting human access to his land. The foreigner and the teacher, meanwhile, speak from a position in which environmental knowledge is based in modern, "scientific" ideas of space and environment. In refusing the outsiders' perspective, Menla Jyab simultaneously promotes environmental conservation as a *Tibetan* value, and provides a rebuke of narratives that that overlook indigenous environmental knowledge and instead center Western scientific practices.

From language practices to traditional knowledge systems to ideas about the natural environment, the interactions between different characters in "Gesar's Horse Herder" develop a satirical critique that privileges the tradition-oriented characters and gives them the upper hand over the more modern ones. The critiques about Tibetan language and culture resonate so strongly not least because they provide an uncomfortable mirror through which many Tibetans see their own attitudes (and those of their family and friends) satirically distorted back at them. The teacher Hongmei's mixing of Chinese and Tibetan, for example, mirrors the everyday speech of many Tibetans across Amdo. In particular, they regularly use standard Chinese terms like *dianshi* for "television" and *dianhua* for "telephone." Beyond emergent technologies, they may also use Chinese numbers when sharing a phone number, or use Chinese names of policies and official positions. Beginning in the early 2000s, however, popular attitudes toward this sort of mixing began to change, with sketch comedies and other cultural production discouraging the use of these Chinese terms. Instead, comedians and intellectuals promoted "pure" Tibetan, characterized by the absence of terminology borrowed from Chinese languages.

In many ways, this response has precedent in Tibetan history. Tibetan culture has historically placed tremendous emphasis on the work of translation, dating back at least to the creation of the writing system and the introduction of Buddhism to the region. To accommodate Buddhism, and to translate the Buddhist canon into Tibetan, generations of translators received royal patronage. Beyond religious translation efforts, political encounters with Uyghurs, Mongols, and other cultures have all left their mark on the Tibetan language, which has changed over time as a result of these many influences. In some cases, Tibetans have borrowed words directly from other languages, but it has often involved a preference for nativizing and translating outside terms. Similarly, in the post-Mao period, Tibetan discouraged borrowing in favor of calques (Shakya 1994; Makley 2013b) and neologisms (Tournadre 2003). For example, *lokled* (བློག་ཀླད།), the accepted Tibetan word for "computer" (literally "electric brain") is a calque formed by translating the separate components of the Chinese term *diannao* 电脑. In other cases, Tibetan neologisms like *khapar* (ཁ་པར།) for "telephone" or *lungtrin* (རླུང་འཕྲིན།) for "radio" (literally "wind message") are promoted. In each situation, these practices link to a growing purist language movement.

Interestingly, some speakers, and this includes comedians, show less resistance to borrowing from English, suggesting that the purist movement is, strictly speaking, a Sinophobic one (Billé 2015) instead of a more generally xenophobic one (Thomas 1991), and purists remain interested primarily in resisting the encroachment of borrowed terms from state-supported Putonghua, the language of power to Amdo Tibetan's language of solidarity (Hill and Hill 1980).[2] This decentralized, grassroots (Roche and Lugyal Bum 2018) movement also benefits from the support of both secular and religious intellectuals, who further promoted it through social media and in essays, poems, memes, and songs (Roche 2020), as well as by word of mouth.

Not limited to issues of language, the teacher Hongmei's lack of cultural competence also speaks to growing intergenerational and geographical rupture in the transmission of traditional cultural knowledge. With new sedentarization and urbanization policies moving pastoralists into fixed dwellings—often in the name of the environmental protection and better grassland management—traditional ways of living in and moving through the natural world changed almost overnight. The public education system, too, contributed to this rupture, with many students spending weeks and months away from their homes in boarding schools, either in the nearest townships or sometimes in coastal metropolises. How can young people, meanwhile, be expected to learn Tibetan language, values, and expressive traditions when they are so removed from the elders and the geographies that long served as the primary sites for cultural transmission?

With increasingly obvious gaps emerging in young people's linguistic and cultural knowledge, many cultural producers quickly embraced Tibetan traditions that had previously appeared as sources of shame. In the People's Republic's participation in international projects of safeguarding intangible cultural heritage, meanwhile, Amdo Tibetan intellectuals found the space to express concerns about the perceived precarity of traditional cultural knowledge in the early years of the twenty-first century. In a keynote at the 2014 Himalayan Studies Conference, Tibetologist Françoise Robin (2014b) noticed the beginnings of this cultural turn in literature and poetry of the early 2000s. Like comedy, the poetry and films Robin examined in that talk began to reclaim once-denigrated pastoral imagery as a sign of national Tibetan identity. As a poet himself, Menla Jyab will certainly have been aware of these developments, and his comedies reflect and contribute to this growing discourse in Amdo's intellectual community. "Gesar's Horse Herder" is just one example.

•

For many years after it initially aired, Tibetans most frequently watched "Gesar's Horse Herder" as part of a VCD album entitled *My Golden Homeland* (Sermdok gi phasa) (Sman bla skyabs 2006b). This was also how I first experienced the sketch as well. Available in media shops around Amdo, it featured ten of Menla Jyab's most famous sketches from this period. Together they help to better understand this cultural turn. Indeed, while "Gesar's Horse Herder" seems to break with the social critique comedies from the 1990s, some of the sketches on the album continued the trend of satirizing the behavior of herders, as with "At Ease Hotel" (Semde dronkang) in which a student and a pastoralist share a hotel room. The student toys with the older man, who is anything but "at ease" in the urban environment. He has in fact arranged to meet the student (though they had never met) but instead views everyone as a potential threat. Everything works out in the end, but the older man's discomfort in the urban setting makes him the clear target of the performance's satire.

In another performance from the album, some nomads look out of touch in modern situations, but the reasons for their incompetence has changed. In "Sending a Message" (Hked tongwa), for example, a rural couple visits a Tibetan radio station to send a message home but appears similarly incapable in the urban world. They ask the station to provide a *mowa* (divination specialist) to help guide their decisions, but more tellingly, they also struggle to say their own address without resorting to Chinese terms for their county and work team.

Sometimes both herder and urbanite look bad, as in "Twenty Cents" (Zurnyi)—described in the introduction—in which a pastoralist is confused about why he should have to pay to use a public restroom (as is common in China) when he could just urinate on the side of the building. The attendant, however, insists that he pay the paltry ¥.2 fee to use the restroom or face a ¥100 fine for public urination. The herder appears comically out of touch, and the attendant comes across as shamefully attached to silly rules. Finally, in "Door-to-Door Sales" (Gotsong) a pair of Tibetan-speaking salesmen from Ziling trying to bilk a nomadic simpleton into selling his high-quality robe in exchange for a cheap knockoff leather jacket. From the very first interaction, however, the salesmen have difficulty with the herder. The salesmen speak Tibetan poorly and seem afraid that he might become violent with them. Later, an additional herder comes in to help, and after a series of hilarious mishaps and miscommunications, the pastoralists finally get the better of the urban city slickers.

Not all comedies pit urban and rural characters against each other. In "Cordless Phone" (Hkumé khapar) two old rivals—one formerly wealthy man whose family fell on hard times during the Maoist period and one former servant whose family is now relatively well off—meet at a teacher's home to await telephone calls from their children in the city. (Before the advent of mobile phones, many rural communities had only a few landline telephones, where people would gather to wait for prearranged calls.) With the teacher's daughter—played by Menla Jyab's own daughter—writing her homework and minding the fort, the two old men trade barbs and try to get the upper hand by correcting their opponent's use of Chinese terms. In particular, each tries to correct the other's habit of referring to a telephone with the Chinese *dianhua* instead of the Tibetan *khapar* and other small linguistic errors when referring to modern institutions and devices. As the rivals' grown children each call home, it becomes clear that they have fallen in love with each other and intend to marry, much to their fathers' consternation and the audience's enjoyment.

If 1990s comedies about Menla Jyab's trips to Careful Village seemed to discursively create a set of binaries to produce a Tibetan social modernity rooted in urban, rational, and secular thought, the satirical critique in "Gesar's Horse Herder" suggests the emergence of a new set of binaries for which the previous moral geography is less important. Instead, these are based in attitudes toward tradition and language practice. They appear to invert the 1990s critique through portraying the rural characters more positively than the modern urbanites without fully displacing it. The other performances from the album support this, and show that, rather than replacing the social critiques of the 1990s, "Gesar's Horse Herder" layers a new, cultural critique atop them, rooted in a language of Tibetanness rather than the moral geography of social modernity.

UN-TIBETAN	TIBETAN
mixed language	linguistic purity
environmental exploitation	environmental conservation
loss of traditional culture	cultural preservation

While all the issues are treated separately here, it is worth noting that, for Tibetans, they are often interlinked, with their threats generally coming from the same developments. In conversation again with Menla Jyab, I remarked on the fact that he frequently plays the part of an old man or a pastoralist in his garchung and never the urbanites.

"So why is it that I usually perform old man after old man? I'm talking about traditional culture. . . . The old man stands in for an ethnicity's traditional culture, and yet in his heart, he feels that all these new things have arrived like the flowing of water. Now culture—like Tibetan speech and writing—faces the greatest danger, and if conditions keep going like this, there will be great danger."

Language, culture, and environment are generally inseparable in Menla Jyab's eyes. The danger that these three things face is taken as a threat to the continued existence of the Tibetan ethnic group.

In reclaiming Tibet's previously maligned language and culture, comedians from Amdo support the increasingly important intellectual project of Tibetan cultural nationalism through reappropriating new, politically acceptable discourses. Like Han Chinese cultural nationalism, which "takes advantage of the official discourse and seeks to impose its will on the Party-state by contesting the meaning of the same signifiers" (Guo 2004, 1), ethnic-minority communities use emerging national and transnational discourses promoting the safeguarding of cultural heritage, as well as constitutional guarantees for minority languages, to advocate for their own cultural nationalisms. Though not essential to Tibetan cultural nationalism, zurza provided a valuable tool for comedians and other cultural producers to reappropriate state discourse and access state media to articulate their own nationalist critique of Tibetan society.

While others have recognized Tibetan nationalism as focusing primarily on religious terms (Kolås 1996), however, Menla Jyab and other comedians carefully avoid positive portrayals of institutional Buddhism. Instead, the tradition-oriented protagonist in "Gesar's Horse Herder" models a secular and cultural nationalism based primarily in topics of language and culture. The pastoralist also, meanwhile, creates a (limited) space for indigenous cosmologies and environmental knowledge in this cultural nationalism through his understandings of the natural environment, but he continues to keep religion at arm's length by avoiding any explicit mention of folk religious practices related to the autochthonous creatures inhabiting the Tibetan world.

•

Getting stiffly off the bus in a dusty county town, I search the crowd of onlookers. The friend I am supposed to be meeting hasn't arrived, but the town is a small one, so I shoulder my large backpack and walk along the main road. As I pass the gate of a hospital of Tibetan medicine, one man turns to his friend and says, "It looks like Mr. Stuff's back is full of stuff!" It is not the first time someone has looked at my large hiking backpack and referenced the line from "Gesar's Horse Herder," in which the herder plays on the homophony between the English name Jersey and the Tibetan word *jyurdzee* (རྫར་རྫས, translated here as "stuff"). It won't be the last. "Gesar's Horse Herder" is so influential that it shapes and constrains popular attitudes, behaviors, and even speech practices by providing (humorous) scripts for Tibetans to address the changing conditions of life in contemporary China.

The influence extends well beyond jokes about the foreigners in their midst. Sitting on a cloudy grassland one late summer in Malho County, one young man, a recent university graduate, opined on the changes he had noticed in Tibetan attitudes toward language and the role that comedians have played in shaping them:

> As in the past, if I tell you what it was like, when you went to school and came back or worked in an office, a person like this, no matter what, if they spoke a few words of Chinese, this was excellent. And, among nomads, if you could speak Chinese, it was evaluated as being really, uh, sort of great. And so, in the past, if you could speak some Chinese [with your] Tibetan, they had the idea that "oh, he's really an impressive person."
>
> However, these days, this perception is changing. This change has been influenced by comedies. If you ask what they do, these days, for example, if you go to school, when you come back, if you don't know how to speak pure Tibetan when speaking Tibetan, and if you're speaking Chinese, that's not good. They say that in [these] comedies, right? So, they say it's not good if you add Chinese to your Tibetan. That's not what a good person does. Khashag [in the colloquial sense of both comic dialogues and sketches] say this quite clearly. Herders know this. Moreover, [they say], "Oh, when speak-

ing Tibetan, you speak pure Tibetan, and when speaking Chinese, you speak pure Chinese." They also say it should be like this, right? So Menla Jyab and Jamyang Lodree have spoken about this [habit of] speaking of Chinese in their Tibetan. (pers. comm., August 31, 2013)

This perspective, framing pure Tibetan language as the linguistic habit of a "good" person, speaks to the extent and significance of this cultural turn in twenty-first century Amdo, while the reference to Menla Jyab and the late Jamyang Lodree—standing in for their comedic performances more generally—addresses the importance of satirical comedy in modeling particular linguistic and cultural attitudes and shaping the attitudes and behaviors of Tibetan audiences.

Performed in 2007, "Gesar's Horse Herder" carefully curates the encounter between the teacher Hongmei, the foreigner Jersey, and the sketch's title character to help articulate this important change from a social critique of Tibetan backwardness to a cultural one. Like the comic dialogues of the 1990s, performances such as this are instant classics. Unlike "Careful Village's Grassland Dispute" and other comedies of the 1990s, however, it is the modern teacher who features as the target of satirical critique, coming off distinctly worse in the encounter with the incorrigible Uncle Horse Herder. This radical shift from a social critique to a cultural one stands out as one of the most significant developments in early twenty-first century cultural production from Amdo. The cultural nationalism that emerges during this decade does not dissipate in the years to come. Instead, it moves online, intensifies, and becomes more frustrated. With this change, new forms of satirical cultural production emerge to articulate this critique digitally.

5

Zheematam
Tibetan Hip-Hop in the Digital World

In November 2014, I received a message from the well-known comedian and actor Shidé Nyima asking if I could meet him at a teahouse in Ziling. When I arrived, I vaguely registered that he had selected a spot near the premises of the Qinghai Tibetan broadcasting station but did not initially think much about the location. I realized its significance when he sat down with a producer from the television station. Over a cup of tea, he explained that he was preparing a script for the upcoming Losar Gongtsog variety show. The program, modeled on CCTV's internationally popular *Chunwan*, would welcome the Tibetan lunar new year with singing, dances, and comedy. He wanted the script to include a foreign character. Was I in? I agreed on the spot, and was told that we would begin rehearsing in a few weeks.

At first, we simply met as a cast and read the script, memorizing our lines, and focusing on transitions. In the following weeks, we added movement while rehearsing daily in the banquet hall of the hotel across the street from the television station. It had been fitted with a small stage, and we worked out the gestures and actions there. In between practices, we shared meals with the dance troupe contracted to perform for the event. As the show drew near, the headline acts started to appear. I watched as the others in my group got excited when famous singers began dropping in. Not the biggest names in the Tibetan musical world, mind you, but celebrities nonetheless. The excitement was palpable.

Then a new album from Dekyi Tsering dropped, featuring a combination of rap and more saccharine pop songs. It was like color coming into a black-and-white world, and it soon threatened to overwhelm everything else—both online and off—in this small but vibrant corner of the Tibetan Plateau. The music video for the hit single "Vowels and Consonants" (Yangsel) provided the first sign of things to come. It seemed to be everywhere on my WeChat timeline, while my friends watched it on repeat and discussed it at length.

The music video begins with the artist standing in front of a classroom, playing a substitute teacher telling the class that he is filling in, before beginning what would seem to be a boring lecture about "the value of language." As the teacher turns his back to the class and begins writing on the board, students begin to zone out and chat with one another, and one boy quietly slips a pair of large headphones over his ears, whereupon a beat fades in, softly at first but then growing in volume. The teacher seems to become aware and taps his finger on the board to the beat a few times before suddenly turning around and rapping. The young boy with the headphones gapes in amazement.

The teacher raps about Tibetan history and the founding of the writing system, then starts listing the consonants; the boy finishes for him with his hand raised. The boy and the teacher go back and forth about Tibetan grammar, culture, and history, and in the end the class is asked:

> Do you have the courage to sound the unprecedented sweet call of the blue cuckoo?
> [the students respond] We do! We do!
> Do you have the courage to sound the unprecedented dragon's roar that welcomes the spring?
> [the students respond] We do! We do!
> Do you have the courage to sound the bell of the unprecedented new era?
> [the students respond] We do! We do!

དགེ་རྒན། ཁྱར་མེད་ཁ་བྱུག་སྟོན་མོའི་གསུང་སྟུན་ཞིག་སྒྲོག་པའི་སྒྲོབས་པ་ཨེ་ཡོད།
སློབ་མ་ཚོ། ཡོད་ཡོད།
དགེ་རྒན། ཁྱར་མེད་དཔྱིད་དཔལ་བསུ་བའི་འབྱུག་སྒ་ཞིག་སྒྲོག་པའི་སྒྲོབས་པ་ཨེ་ཡོད།
སློབ་མ་ཚོ། ཡོད་ཡོད།
དགེ་རྒན། ཁྱར་མེད་དུས་རབས་གསར་པའི་ཅོད་བརྡ་ཞིག་སྒྲོག་པའི་སྒྲོབས་པ་ཨེ་ཡོད།
སློབ་མ་ཚོ། ཡོད་ཡོད།

With comedies already identifying language as an area of intellectual concern in the early 2000s and song lyrics defending the importance of maintaining Tibetan language and culture, already a popular topic, "Vowels and Consonants" tapped into this. But while the lyrics were far from revolutionary, both the video and song seemed to create a compelling break with the Tibetan music scene that had come before, through a unique combination of energy, novelty, visual storytelling, and reasonably high production values that set them apart. Whereas many other music videos at that time featured singers walking through empty grasslands, the one for "Vowels and Consonants" seemed to tell a story and possessed the highest production values of any I had seen to date.

"Vowels and Consonants" was not the first Tibetan rap song produced within the People's Republic of China. As early as 2009, the same artist performed a popular song called "Father" (Apha). The famous singer Sher bstan dabbled with rap interspersed in some of his songs around the same time. Outside of China meanwhile, the popular Shaphaley (who takes his stage name from the title of his most famous song, and the name of stuffed fried bread) has pioneered Tibetan hip-hop in exile. But these initial attempts are only drops in the bucket compared to the torrent of new songs and artists who began performing in and after 2014 and whose songs reach ever larger audiences, thanks to the widespread adoption of smartphones and other digital technologies.

Most Tibetans in Amdo refer to this new performance style as either *zheematam* (གཞས་མ་གཏམ།, literally "neither verse nor speech") or with the Chinese word *shuochang* (speaking singing).[1] Though their work is less humorous than the sketches and comic dialogues of preceding decades, the performers still see themselves as "doing zurza" and providing a new generation of artists with opportunities to rework oral traditions and emerging cultural practices—in conjunction with modern concerns about linguistic and cultural loss—into new and emerging art forms. In doing so, their work builds on the trends of previous generations and articulates a new set of concerns, all during a period of increasing restrictions in Tibet's cultural sphere.

•

Little over a year after Menla Jyab's "Gesar's Horse Herder" aired, demonstrations erupted in Lhasa and rapidly spread across the Tibetan Plateau, including Amdo. The government's response was swift and repressive (see Makley 2018 for a firsthand account from Rebgong). For many, these events in the lead-up to the 2008 Beijing Olympics mark a radical change both in Tibet and across China. The Olympics offered global affirmation, while the contemporaneous global financial crisis affected the country's economic miracle less than it did many Western democracies. In response, Chinese officials began to develop an assertiveness that podcast host and China watcher Kaiser Kuo (2017) called "the new truculence" and became more confident in the view that China's authoritarian "consultative democracy" (see, for example, Ma 2015) and managed market economy provided a superior form of national development. The first decade of China's twenty-first century really ended in 2008.

In Amdo, 2008 marked several significant cultural and political shifts linked to—but also sometimes distinct from—these national and international developments. In 2009, a number of Tibetans began self-immolating to express their dissatisfactions on several fronts, and for a significant portion of my fieldwork, news of yet another self-immolation—often reaching me through informal networks or my daily Google alerts, rather than official media—punctuated my morning coffee. In testimonials left behind, these people often spoke not about separatism but about preserving and developing Tibetan language and culture (Barnett 2012, 54). At the time of writing this monograph, over 160 Tibetans, most of them from Amdo, have ended their lives in this fashion.

At the same time, the state began rapidly expanding into ever more intimate domains of everyday life: language, traditions, and lived spaces. The government's participation in UNESCO's intangible cultural heritage regime has seen traditional practices identified for protection—thereby bringing vernacular practices under the purview of the state—while officials have simultaneously encouraged the Sinicization of religions, as part of their promotion of a harmonious society (Brown and O'Brien 2020, 273). Some traditions, like the bardic retelling the Tibetan epic of King Gesar, have flourished with state recognition as an "intangible cultural heritage" and the ensuing support that that recognition brought. Others, like the Shépa speech tradition in Choné, have suffered in spite of such recognition, as linguistic and cultural competences shift (Bendi Tso 2023, 1). Language, in particular, has come under increasing scrutiny, with new education policies advocating for more standard Chinese language instruction within Amdo's bilingual education policies. This short list is representative, but not exhaustive, of the expansion of state space in the twenty-first century in Amdo and around the People's Republic.

The government has also emphasized increased market participation, further integrating Tibetan communities into China's market economy (Yeh 2013). This led to a range of Tibetan enterprises emerging during this period: from shops run by Buddhist monasteries (Caple 2019) to NGOs that rebranded themselves as social enterprises to new, Tibetan-owned technology and film companies. In hopes of capitalizing on the growing presence of digital technologies, the government has also worked with private companies, providing grants and loans for the development of Tibetan-language digital platforms, including e-commerce platforms, educational technology platforms based on the Blackboard Learning management system, and the Tibetan-language search engine Yongzin (in 2016). The computing company Lobzang, meanwhile, has forged a business out of creating Tibetan-language hardware and software to aid in learning.

The collection and sale of caterpillar fungus continued to sustain local incomes into this period, and many families earned unprecedented amounts of disposable income just at a time when DSLR cameras, smartphones, and other devices become part of everyday life. Tibetans were especially eager to purchase Apple's iPhone, because early iterations of the device supported Tibetan-language input without significant tinkering. With the advent of smartphones, the Chinese omni-app, Weixin (WeChat) has become one of the dominant ways of the interacting with others across China, and Tibetans are no different. People send notes, voice messages, and an ever-increasing number of stickers in individual conversations and group chats, and share media (blog posts, images, videos, and more) on their timelines. For some groups that do not have their own writing system, or for speech communities with low literacy rates, WeChat has become a valuable tool for communicating and language maintenance at a time when many are dispersed across the country as students and migrant laborers (Yulha Lhawa 2019, 564).

As larger amounts of Tibetan life have moved online, and companies (often with state support) have created Tibetan-language technologies to support them, residents of Amdo have incorporated digital technologies into their efforts to promote and preserve their language and culture. Shortly after arriving in Amdo in 2010, one friend confided that after the demonstrations of 2008, he would only listen to Tibetan singers who perform in Tibetan. In 2012, a budding filmmaker garnered local and international attention for his debut documentary, *Valley of Heroes* (Khashem Gyal 2012; see also Robin 2014b), which purported to examine language attitudes in one part of Amdo as a stark statement about the state of Tibetan-language education in the region. On WeChat, I saw intellectuals admonish others to speak "pure Tibetan," meaning that they should not borrow Chinese terms.

To further support people's ability to speak pure Tibetan in a time of rapid change, the abbot of northern Sichuan's massive monastic center at Serta Larung Gar, Khenpo Tsultrim Lodree, began an influential project to create highly popular picture dictionaries with new words for emerging technologies. During my fieldwork, these volumes seemed omnipresent in schools, homes, and bookstores throughout Amdo. Not merely "virtual" activism, online expressions also intertwine with offline actions. In 2010, many across the Amdo region started to express concerns over what they considered to be the marginalization of the Tibetan language within the state's education system, and this boiled over into student protests.

Though expressing many of the same concerns about the future of Tibetan language and culture, sketch comedy and comedic dialogues have been one of the major losers in this digital turn. Just as I began to study comedies, I found many established performers nearing retirement age and few young people interested in taking their place (including many self-professed fans). One comedian opined that this was because young people were generally unable to write scripts, lacking the requisite life experience and skills in verbal arts.

All of this may be true, but this only tells part of the story. Instead, many of the young Tibetans I knew were more interested in music and film, both of which seemed to present fewer barriers to entry in the years after 2008 and allowed performers to remain somewhat on the peripheries of state space. Just about every Tibetan can sing to some extent (there is even a popular aphorism about it), and music is a highly effective vehicle for expressing and circulating popular ideas. Film, meanwhile, seemed to be a new frontier, with directors like the late Pema Tsetan and Zonthar Gyal earning honors at international film festivals.

To compound this, only the late comedian Jamyang Lodree seemed interested in training younger performers. He regularly shared his scripts, and in the years immediately preceding his sudden passing in 2019, he held free training workshops for aspiring comedic performers. Amdo's premier filmmakers, by contrast, also have developed a reputation for fostering young talent, and such born-digital cultural production benefited from both the cachet of new media and the opportunity to work with artistic forms that balanced the emerging and traditional.

Beyond film, the affordability of new technologies and emergence of social media also enabled new forms of cultural production to emerge. An active blogosphere has provided a space for literate Tibetans to contest a movement of Buddhist ethical reforms called "the New Ten Virtues" (Gayley 2016) or to vent frustrations about the government's new bilingual education laws (Dak Lhagyal 2019). On social media, meanwhile, people share video clips of movies and TV series with humorously dubbed conversations, perhaps the most popular of which is a scene from *Braveheart* in which Mel Gibson and his band are discussing digging caterpillar fungus instead of the English army.

Music, in particular, has taken a leading role in promoting the sort of Tibetan nationalism popular in Amdo (Lama Jabb 2011), with modern music production in Amdo generally divided into the categories of "pop music" or the tradition-inspired genre called *dunglen*, in which musicians (individually or in groups) sing while playing either a mandolin or a rapidly plucked, stringed instrument called a *dranyen*. Music videos, meanwhile, create unique opportunities to mix lyrics with a visual language of common Tibetan identity (Warner 2013, 545). In this period of intense, "disempowered" cultural, political, and technological development (Fischer 2013), rap emerged as a way for young cultural producers to express themselves and reach audiences.

In many ways, Tibetan rap in Amdo reflects both the national and international development of the genre. Emerging from the cumulative "politics and aesthetics" of African American experience (Rabaka 2013, 285), rap has grown into a global phenomenon, blending the unique sense of spoken delivery and authenticity with local poetics and cultural features everywhere it goes. Hip-hop's popularity stems at least partly from how it provides youthful musicians with the opportunity to create an "in-your-face rebellious youth style that challenges class inequalities wherever it expresses itself on the globe" (Osumare 2007, 71). And yet the focus on resistance risks obscuring the much richer and more complex landscape that rap inhabits. With reference to hip-hop in the Middle East, for example, Almeida (2017, 6) noticed that the rap is also part of the music industry and may be co-opted by industry and government for its own goals.

In China, where the state's control over channels for publishing and disseminating music requires that rap demonstrate *zheng nengliang* (positive energy), artists deploy local concepts to balance these demands with ideas of hip-hop authenticity (Sullivan and Zhao 2021, 275). This does not, however, stop hip-hop artists from engaging in strong social commentary. Liu (2014, 283) noticed how Chinese rap songs sung in regional languages help to articulate subnational identities as part of a "larger countermovement promoting the use of local language in local media to assert the identity of a local community."

Similarly, Tibetan hip-hop emerges in a cultural space characterized by international and national trends. Han rap group Higher Brothers, for example, performs nationalistic hip-hop that is popular even with some Tibetans (Su 2019). The government also often produces rap videos to accompany and promote its "five-year plans" both domestically and abroad. But Tibetan artists, as we shall see, also mix local ideologies of verbal art—including zurza—and global hip-hop to create something uniquely Tibetan.[2] Doing so recognizes that both traditional and newer expressions of Tibetanness are "equally Tibetan and essential for their generation in the future" (Warner 2019, 30). But in this art, the aesthetic of zurza changes yet again, becoming less about humor (though some work is still funny and playful) and more about inversion, indirection, and critique. The critiques point to failings of both the state and previous generations of Tibetan intellectuals.

•

Drone footage shows a Tibetan village. Judging from the stone architecture, it is in the eastern region of Kham. Next a Tibetan dranyen player begins to strum a folk tune popular from Central Tibet. Singers sing about Tibet as a happy place, where barley grows. Images cut to the rapper Uncle Buddhist, dreadlocked and wearing baggy clothes, standing in the middle of a town square, then dancers in traditional dress, suggesting a festival—in fact, the famous Tsampa Festival in Yushu Tibetan Autonomous Prefecture, in which participants throw freshly ground roast barley flour at each other.

Then the music stops, and the video cuts to an old man standing on a mountaintop, orating about the origins of the staple food tsampa in the Amdo dialect while throwing roast barley flour atop an open flame as part of a fumigation offering. The speech narrates the history of the food as Tibetans memorialize it, with barley first planted in the fields along the Yarlung River in Central Tibet, representing the initial introduction of agriculture, and then expressing a wish that Tibetans never lose the ability to make their staple food. As the orator finishes with the classic "*zerjyu ré*," which ends segments of oratory in Amdo, with a louder, higher, drawn-out *ré*, Uncle Buddhist starts rapping, building off all that has come before. His lyrics speak of barley as a key staple that has spread throughout the plateau and become central to the Tibetan identity:

> The green grain of the fields in the Yarlung Valley don't have wings, but still have wings.
> The white wings reach to all the territories surrounded by snow
> Like a golden belt that ties all regions.
> The winged barley grains rise from the sun's lap, and [they are] prayer beads of letters.
> They help to write the light of this nationality's history on the roof of the world, spreading to the four directions from Tsethang Gongpo mountain.
> Black-haired tsampa-eating Tibetans!
> The winged barley grain is the Snowland's dream and a deity for the Tibetan people of the Snowland.
> Those winged barley grains are the messenger of the gods.
> It is a light for of white-minded [virtuous] people.
> The places where the winged barley grain flies, the honey-white tsampa's flavor spreads, and the red-faced people flourish.
> The places where the winged barley falls, honey-white tsampa's flavor subdues, and turns people's minds to the virtuous dharma.

ཡར་ཀླུངས་བོ་ཐང་ཞིང་གི་ནས་འབྲུ་སྔོན་མོར་གཤོག་པ་མེད་དོ་གཤོག་པ་ཡོད།
འདབ་གཤོག་དཀར་པོ་གངས་ཀྱི་ར་བས་བསྐོར་བའི་ཡུལ་གྲུ་ཀུན་ལ་བརྒྱངས་ཏེ།
ཆོལ་ཁ་ཡོངས་ལ་སེར་པོ་གསེར་གྱི་སྐེད་རགས་བཅིངས།
ནས་འབྲུ་གཤོག་ཐོགས་དེ་ཚོ་ཉི་མའི་པང་ནས་ཕྱིར་བའི་ཡི་གེ་ཕྲེང་བ་སྟེ།
རྕེད་ཐང་གོང་པོ་རི་ནས་ཕྱོགས་བཞིར་མཆེད་པའི་མི་རིགས་འདི་ཡི་ཤེས་རིག་འོད་ཀྱི་ལོ་རྒྱུས་
    འཛམ་བུ་གླིང་གི་གཙུག་ཏུ་འབྲི་རོགས་མཛད།
མགོ་ནག་རྩམ་ཟན་བོད་པ་ཚོ།
ནས་འབྲུ་གཤོག་ཐོགས་གངས་ཀྱི་རྨི་ལམ་ཡིན་ལ།
གངས་ཅན་བོད་མིའི་ལྷ་སྐལ་ཡིན། ནས་འབྲུ་གཤོག་ཐོགས་ལྷ་ཡི་ཕོ་ཉ་ཡིན་ལ།
མི་སེམས་དཀར་པོའི་འོད་སྣང་ཡིན།
ནས་འབྲུ་གཤོག་ཐོགས་འཕུར་བའི་ས་ལ་སྦྲང་དཀར་རྩམ་པའི་དྲི་ཞིམ་མཆེད་ཅིང་སྨུག་པོ་མི་
    ཡི་རིགས་རྒྱུད་འཕེལ།

ནས་འབྲུ་གཏོགས་ཐོགས་བབས་པའི་ས་ལ་སྦྱངད་དཀར་རྩམ་པ་དྲི་ཞིམ་ཐུལ་ཞིང་མི་སེམས་
དཀར་པོ་ཆེས་ལ་ཕྱོགས།

 This describes the opening to Uncle Buddhist's electrifying hit "Tsampa" and its accompanying music video. The rapper, whose real name is Ludrub Jyamtso, is one of the new stars in the Tibetan hip-hop scene, thanks in part to his 2016 album *City Tibetans* (Drongchyer wodpa). Musically, traditional instruments form the melody of the song, with an electric bass and drum line coming in at different points. The traditional instruments play a Central Tibetan folk song, as singers also add their lyrics. Visually, the opening scenes feature a Khampa village and dancers, as well as the elder from Amdo making an offering on the mountain. Throughout, the video jumps between images of the rapper on mountaintops and participating in the festival more generally. Together, the mountaintop speech from Amdo, the dance and tsampa festival from Kham, and the Central Tibetan background music from Ü-Tsang combine to articulate musically and visually the classic emic division of the Tibetan world into three ethnolinguistic regions. These then set the stage for Uncle Buddhist's lyrical intervention.

 Lyrically, the song uses free verse, as opposed to the seven- or eight-syllable meters most common to Tibetan folk and popular music traditions. In the region's context, this sort of free verse is often associated with the poetry of modernists like Dondrup Jya. Like many modernist poets, however, his works often draw significantly on Tibetan poetic traditions (Lama Jabb 2015, 12–13). Similarly, many rap songs employ formulae and parallelism common in traditional expressive arts. In "Tsampa" for example, Uncle Buddhist refers to Tibetans as *gonak tsamzan* (black-haired tsampa eaters). In Tibetan oral and literary traditions, the first two syllables frequently combine with *Bod* (Tibetan), with the latter coming either before or after *gonak*, depending on poet-speaker's needs and preferences, to make a convenient three-syllable noun phrase that slots easily into the seven- and eight-syllable meters of folk songs and other oral traditions. Other phrases like "honey-white tsampa" and "green barley grain" both use four-syllable phrases and create valuable images of auspiciousness. Interestingly, Tibetan rap—and "Tsampa" is a good example of this—also largely avoids the rhyming patterns that often characterizes global versions. Rhyme appears to be important primarily insofar as it results from the creation of parallel lines.

The content of the lyrics is also redolent with meaning. The song's title, "Tsampa," refers both to the staple breakfast and travel food made by mixing barley flour, butter, hard cheese, and some hot liquid (preferably milk tea or butter tea) into a dough, and also to the roasted barley flour that is its main ingredient. The song and video both use both auditory and visual means to reinforce a nationalist message about Tibetans, who have long referred to themselves with the epithet "tsampa eaters." It is a self-identification so powerful that the sign for "Tibetan" in Tibetan Sign Language is the act of kneading tsampa in a small bowl (Hofer 2017, 122). Scholar Tsering Shakya (1993), meanwhile, used the term in the title of an article examining contemporary Tibetan identity. Uncle Buddhist's song builds on this practice of mixing tsampa to visually and auditorily link Tibetans from each of the three major regions around the habit of making and eating tsampa.

The use of the staple food, with reference to the fields in which Tibetans say it was first grown, draws upon a practice common in Tibetan popular music of the time in which lyrics help discursively create a shared identity through images of history, culture, and territory (Lama Jabb 2011, 1). In fact, "Tsampa"—and indeed much of the burgeoning genre of Tibetan rap more generally—employs many of the same discursive strategies as other forms of popular media to meld the expressive possibilities of new media with emerging concerns about the state of Tibetan language and traditions. In doing so, it creates a sort of "hidden transcript" (Scott 1990). This is not unique to hip-hop from Tibet (see, for example, Lamotte 2014, 689), but the potential social and political consequences that Tibetan cultural producers face, makes this sort of subtle messaging essential (Morcom 2018, 140).

The second verse of the rap takes this still further by linking tsampa to the unity and vitality of the Tibetan people:

If green barley is a single grain, then I and we are as well.
Black-haired, tsampa-eating Tibetans transmit tradition to the future.
When home is far away, you are distant from the yellow yak butter, and each day the purity of yogurt becomes more and more difficult to taste.
Although with each day, the body's clothing changes, the mouth's tongue falls dumb, and the mind becomes more and more unable to cope.
I want to say, "Don't forget the green barley's origins, but keep it in mind!"
I want to say, "Don't forget the kindness of the honey-white tsampa, but keep it in mind!"

ནས་འབྲུ་སྔོན་མོ་རྡོག་གཅིག་ཡིན་ན་ཆོག་པའི་ང་དང་ང་དག་ཀྱང་།
མགོ་ནག་རྩམ་ཟན་གདངས་ཅན་བོད་མིའི་རྒྱུད་པའི་རྒྱུད་པ་ཕྱི་མ་སྟེ།
ཕ་ཡུལ་ཁ་ཐག་བགྱེད་ཅིང་འབྲི་མར་སེར་པོར་རྒྱུད་ཐག་རིང་ལ་འོ་ཞོ་སྔུད་མེད་སྒྱུང་བ་ཉིན་རེ་
བཞིན་དུ་རེ་དཀའ་རེ་དཀའ་ཡིན་ན་ཡང་།
ལུས་ཀྱི་ཆ་ལུགས་བརྗེས་ཤིང་དག་གི་སྒྲ་སྟེ་སྨུག་ལ་སེམས་པས་རང་ཚུགས་མ་ཐུབ་པ་ཉིན་རེ་
བཞིན་དུ་རེ་བྱ་རེ་བྱ་ཡིན་ན་ཡང་།
ནས་འབྲུ་སྔོན་མོའི་བྱུང་བ་མ་བརྗེད་ཡིད་ལ་ཟུངས་དང་ཟེར་ན་འདོད།
སྦྲང་དཀར་རྩམ་པའི་བཀའ་དྲིན་མ་བརྗེད་ཡིད་ལ་ཟུངས་དང་ཟེར་ན་འདོད།

The vision of a changing society in which foodways—and, by extension, their very identities as Tibetan—as people move and become physically distanced from the grassland is a key theme in Uncle Buddhist's work. Having grown up in urban environments and only learned Tibetan as an adult, the rapper feels this issue most keenly. But this has all given him a unique perspective on the difficulties these communities face in transmitting language and culture in the twenty-first century.

Some of these concerns are further reflected in his hit "City Tibetans," which has gained popularity and notoriety for its dark video. In Tibet, you may well be watching the video on your smartphone. You open it in a browser window, and as it begins to play, you immediately see a red moon; in Tibetan Buddhism, the blood moon is an auspicious time when the merit earned from good deeds will be multiplied. Next, a group of young men, drinks in hand stumble through the streets of a town—seemingly one of Amdo's county towns. Then suddenly, the rapper sees figures standing in red-lit doorways wielding torches and wearing masks associated with religious cham dances and with Tibetan opera. His friends just walk by, seemingly oblivious, but the man seems to feel he is being stalked by these figures. The rap begins unaccompanied in a soft, raspy, singing voice.:

> In the east of the world,
> In the Himalayas,
> The Tubo kings—seven *tri* kings, six *lek* kings, and eight *dé* kings[3]—
> Ruled the Tibetan lands for generations.
> Thonmi invented the Tibetan script.
> The light of wisdom shines through this land.
> This early history is glorious.
> The recent history is unspeakable.
> The current situation is unspeakable

> ས་འཛམ་བུ་གླིང་གི་ཤར་ཕྱོགས༎
> རི་བོ་ཧི་མ་ལ་ཡའི་ནང་རོལ་དུ༎
> འདི་ན་གནམ་གྱི་ཁྲི་བདུན་བར་གྱི་ལེགས་དྲུག་ས་ཡི་སྡེ་བརྒྱད་ལ་ཡ༎
> རྒྱལ་རབས་དང་རྒྱལ་རབས་བུས་བོད་ཁམས་བསྐྱངས་བཞག༎
> ཐོན་སྨྲོན་དཔོན་ཐོན་མིས་ཡི་གེ་གསར་བཟོ་མཛད་བཞག༎
> སྔོངས་འདི་ལ་ཤེས་རིག་གི་འོད་འཕྲོ༎
> འདི་སྔོན་བྱུང་གི་ལོ་རྒྱུས་རོ་མཚར་ཆེ་ཡ༎
> ད་ལྟའི་ལོ་རྒྱུས་བཤད་སྤོབས་མེད༎
> ད་ལྟའི་གནས་བབས་བཤད་སྤོབས་མེད༎

These opening lines appear to follow a similar pattern to the beginning of "Tsampa," using phrases referencing the Himalaya Mountains and Tibetan history to frame and locate the remainder of the rap and its critique geographically in Tibetan regions. But "City Tibetans" quickly moves from broader framing into critique when contrasting the present situation with Tibet's glorious past, adding a temporal frame that invites the audience to share a view of the present as a period of intense cultural and social change. Back on screen, the rapper walks forward. His friends are no longer with him, and a backlit door appears in the road in front of him with masked figures standing on either side.

> A fame-destroyer first, and a disgrace second.
> A fame-destroyer first, and a disgrace second,
>   but today I sing forcefully for you.
> Strong barley wine makes one a crazy drunk.
> When drunk, I'm a madman.

> སྨྱོ་སྟོད་པོ་གཅིག་དང་ཞབས་འདྲེན་གཉིས།
> སྨྱོ་སྟོད་པོ་གཅིག་དང་ཞབས་འདྲེན་གཉིས།
> དེ་རིང་ང་ཡིས་ཁྱེད་ཚོར་སྟོབས་ཀྱིས་ལེན།།
> ནས་ཆང་བཟི་ཁ་བཙན་པོ་བཟི་བར་བྱུར་ན་སྨྱོས།།
> བཟི་བར་བྱུར་ན་ཆང་འཐུང་སྨྱོན་པ་ཡིན།།

The rapper walks through the door, suddenly transported from the dark city streets to a pristine, sunlit, and open grassland, rapidly intones:

> Sick body, sick body, sick voice, sick voice, sick mind, sick mind.
>   This is us!
> Wandering souled red-faced Tibetans,
> Wandering souled red-faced Tibetans. Us!
> Tibetan boys and girls like me! They can't speak Tibetan and
>   don't wear Tibetan clothes, but if you trace their heritage,
>   they are Tibetan.

> ལུས་ནད་པ། ལུས་ནད་པ་གདངས་ནད་པ་གདངས་ནད་པ། ཡིད་ནད་པ་ཡིད་ནད་པ་ང་ཚོ།། །
> བླ་འཁྱམས་པའི་གདོང་དམར་པོའི་བོད་པ།།
> བླ་འཁྱམས་པའི་གདོང་དམར་པོའི་བོད་པ།།
> འདི་ང་དང་ང་འདྲའི་བོད་པའི་གཅེས་ཕྲུག་གཅེས་མ། བོད་སྐད་མི་ཤེས། བོད་ལུ་མི་གོན། པ་བརྒྱུད
>   དེད་ན་བོད་ཡིན།།

Here, the rapper's critique becomes clearer: many Tibetans no longer wear traditional clothes or speak Tibetan. Powerfully visually contrasting the benighted and drunken city with the sun-soaked countryside, Uncle Buddhist identifies urbanization as one of the key sources for this loss of linguistic and cultural capacity. Distanced from the grasslands and divorced from the sites of language and culture, people in cities have become ill in body, speech, and mind.

Uncle Buddhist's critique that urban Tibetans are both physically removed from Tibetan spaces and psychologically distant from their language and culture derives substantial power not least because it links to popular narratives already circulating among communities in Amdo. Comedies like "Gesar's Horse Herder" (examined in chapter 4) had already identified the urban-rural divide as a potential threat to the transmission of Tibetan linguistic and cultural knowledge as early as 2007. Simultaneously, throughout my time in Amdo, I heard people share narratives about how one Tibetan intellectual sent his child to middle school in the countryside (rather than in Xining, where they might receive a "better" but Chinese-only education). Many people praised his decision to jeopardize his child's economic future in favor of a cultural one. Nevertheless, the narrative stands out, and bears repeating by Tibetans, because it appears to buck the broader trend of families making the opposite decision when presented with the opportunity to send their children to schools in Chinese cities. Others tell of a Tibetan child growing up in the city, who said that her relatives "smelled" when they visited from the countryside. In the 2015 sketch I performed, one of the cast had grown up entirely in the city. Unable to either read or effectively speak in Tibetan, he wrote his lines in Chinese characters to mimic the sounds of the Tibetan he was to speak. His character was labeled as "Korean" to further explain some of his linguistic deficiencies. I could go on. Uncle Buddhist's rap suggests that this trend has only intensified in recent years.

However, instead of blaming the cities themselves or the policies that encourage urbanization, Uncle Buddhist takes it upon himself to address these issues in his own life. Sitting astride (and sometimes riding) a horse while men around him ride their motorcycles over the grassland, he further emphasizes this agency in his refrain:

From this day forward,
until the day of my death,
I won't stay silent but speak my pain.
A mouth is for eating as well as speaking.

དེ་རིང་ཉི་མའི་ཞབས་ཆད་འདི་ནས།
ང་མི་ཤི་ཉི་མའི་ཆུན་ཆད་བར་དུ།
ཁ་ཁ་རོག་མི་འདུག་ན་སྲུག་བཤད་ཀྱང་བཤད།
ཁ་ཟ་སྲུད་ཡིན་ལ་བཤད་སྲུད་ཀྱང་ཡིན།

The promise begins softly but increases in power and intensity with each line until he is practically shouting the final one, leading into an impassioned plea:

Brothers and sisters, listen to me!
I'll admit my own faults.
My father tongue and writing are stumbling.
I'm the descendant of the Tibetans. Nope.
It's shameful that I don't understand regional traditions.
This is a stain! This is a failure! Is it not, my friend?

གྲོགས་པོ་གྲོགས་མོ་གསོན་ཅིག་རྣ་བ་བླགས་ཏེ་ང་ལ་ཉོན།
ངས་རང་སྐྱོན་ང་རང་གིས་བཤད།
ཕ་སྐད་ཡི་གི་ཀུ་ཅེ་གོམ་ཅེ་ཡིན།
གདོང་དམར་ཆང་གི་རྒྱུད་ཆང་གི་རྒྱུད་པ་ཡིན་མ་རེད།
ཡུལ་སྲོལ་གོམས་གཤིས་ཆ་ལ་ཆོལ་དེ་ལ་ཚ་རེད།
འདི་སྐྱིག་རྟོད་རེད་འདི་ཕམ་ཁ་རེད་མ་རེད་གྲོགས་པོ།

Other popular songs from Amdo's musicians in the twenty-first century also do considerable work to valorize the Tibetan language and support its use, often even describing it as the soul of the people (Roche 2020). But Uncle Buddhist goes further, criticizing the linguistic incompetence of urban Tibetans like himself. In the lines above, he switches to imperatives and begins to link linguistic and cultural incompetence with "shame" and "failure" as Tibetans. It is a shortcoming suggested also by the song's ungrammatical title (which would normally require a genitive particle).

Having grown up in an urban environment himself, Uncle Buddhist calls "City Tibetans" his favorite from the debut album of the same name, saying, "I feel that it really portrays my innermost feelings; it conveys all the things that I think about. I portray the things that I have gone through by making fun of myself, and in this way, it can be a warning for today's young people. It is about what I experienced growing up. I wrote down my very own thoughts, and that is what I wanted to convey" (High Peaks Pure Earth, 2020). These thoughts are specific about the behaviors being criticized, but the broad thrust of the rap means that "City Tibetans" does zurza by engaging in the sort of generic critique common to cultural production across the post-Mao period.

•

But this is only one mode of zurza that hip-hop artists deploy. Jason J, meanwhile, uses a complex array of traditional imagery and direct quotations in a more traditional style of zurza in his hit song "Alalamo." I met Jason J in the summer of 2017, a little over six months after its release. He was studying tourism management at a university in Ziling. He had secured a day off from his internship at a hotel to perform at an English school's summer party, at the request of one of his university teachers. I was also in attendance. The school's owner was a friend, and I knew that my presence as a Caucasian foreigner would be seen to somehow underline the school's credentials. The summer party was held a little bit outside of town, a picnic in the countryside as a reward for everyone's hard work. The outskirts of Ziling and smaller urban areas of Qinghai have many such small businesses that rent out their land and provide the food for precisely these sorts of gatherings.

After eating, people began to sing and dance. The children sang English songs that they had prepared for the day. I struggled through a few bars of one of my standby songs, and Jason J and another singer, also invited guests, performed as well. Technical difficulties prevented him from singing his signature hit that day, but I recognized him from the music video, as I had played it many times for my daughter back home. He also recognized me from the sketch I had done a few years earlier. We eventually decided to sit down soon for a recorded conversation away from the distractions and obligations of the picnic. A few days later, we sat in a Starbucks in the center of Ziling and chatted about his life and work to that point, focusing particularly on his hit single "Alalamo."

As the video begins, the sun is setting over a city skyline, through which a meandering river runs. Soft, slow synthesized music plays for about fifteen seconds before Jason J appears and begins his rap. With a measured, almost monotone delivery, he begins his free-verse poem by addressing his intended audience, and describing the purpose of his song:

> Youths, who are striving after the ideals they have heard from me and those like me, as for the song I'm singing now, I've loved, suffered, and even cried for your youth and mine. But I haven't ever given up on the path of my heart, and I've never bowed my head.

> ང་དང་ང་འདྲ་བའི་ཁོ་ཡི་ཁ་ནས་ཐོས་པའི་ཕུགས་བསམ་ཇེར་བ་ཞིག་གི་ཆེད་དུ་འབད་བརྩོན་བྱེད་བཞིན་པའི་ན་གཞོན་ཚོ། ད་ནི་བླངས་བའི་གླུ་གཞས་འདི་ནི་ཁྱེད་དང་ང་ཡི་ལང་ཚོའི་ཆེད་དགའ་མྱོང་། སྡུག་མྱོང་། མཆན་ན་དུ་ཡང་མྱོང་། འོན་ཀྱང་སེམས་ནང་གི་ལམ་དེའི་ཆེད་དུ་ཡིད་སེམས་ཕས་མ་མྱོང་། མགོ་བོ་སྒུར་མ་མྱོང་།

The Tibetan word *langtsho* (ལང་ཚོ) used in the lyrics refers to the qualities of youth and youthful vigor. It is the promise that each generation possesses. The remainder of the verse describes how, despite others giving up on these hopes and dreams, he will not. He will continue pursuing them. He will not bow *his* head.

With the refrain, Jason J's collaborator, Suozha (short for Sonam Tashi), appears in black jeans and a black shirt and leather jacket, singing the refrain in a high falsetto: *Ala, a la la mo, tha la la mo zer la a la len go* (ཨ་ལ། ཨ་ལ་ལ་མོ། ཐ་ལ་ལ་མོ་ཟེར་ལ་ཨ་ལ་ལེན་གོ). Though these vocables have no English translation, they are deeply resonant for Tibetan audiences, who will recognize in them the syllables used in the first lines of sung arias from the Tibetan epic of King Gesar.

In the second verse, Jason J further defines his vision of the future for

Tibet's youth, using the imperatives "look!" and "listen!" to address his audience directly. His vocal pitch rises, and his pace quickens ever so slightly, a climax in intensity both to the lyrics and their delivery:

> We are arising from a single line. We are the inheritors of ancestral heritage and our parents' hopes for the future. Ancestral heritage! Parents' hopes! And so, we can never stop moving forward. He's Amdo. I'm from Kham. She's from Ü-Tsang. No! No! We're all a single family. Though unrelated by flesh and blood, we are successors of a single ancestor.

> ང་ཚོ་ནི་རིགས་རྒྱུད་གཅིག་ལས་ཆད་པའི་གདོང་རྒྱུད་ཡིན། མེས་པོའི་ཤུལ་བཞག་རྒྱུད་འཛིན་ ཨ་མཁན་དང་ཕ་མའི་མ་འོངས་པའི་རེ་བ་ཡིན། མེས་པོའི་ཤུལ་བཞག་ཕ་མའི་རེ་བ། དེ་དང་དེའི་ཆེད་ མདུན་བསྐྱོད་ཀྱི་གོམ་པ་ནམ་ཡང་རྒྱུན་མ་ཆད། ཁོ་ནི་ཨ་མདོ་རེད། ང་ནི་ཁམས་པ་རེད། མོ་ནི་ དབུས་གཙང་རེད། མ་རེད་མ་རེད་ང་ཚོ་ཚང་མ་ཁྱིམ་ཚང་གཅིག་པ་རེད། ཤ་དང་ཁྲག་གི་འབྲེལ་བ་ མེད་ཀྱང་མེས་པོ་གཅིག་གི་རྒྱུད་འཛིན་ཡིན།།

Up to this point, the song is unremarkable beyond its infectious and easily remembered refrain. For the music video, the performers deliver their lines from various urban vantages: inside a many-windowed building, overlooking the Pearl of the Orient Tower in Ziling, etc. The beat is little other than rim shots and high hats, the melody made up of synthesized music. It is as if the entire song is constructed to direct audiences to the lyrics. The rapper said as much during our conversation, arguing, "My lyrical style really focuses on the colloquial. It has a lot of colloquial speech. When others listen to it, oh, they understand the lyrics. Why is this? In most Tibetan music, poets write the lyrics, and the people don't understand them. I don't write lyrics that the people can't understand." After this, he went on to liken lyrics by poets to traditional poems full of obscure metaphors, which he considers to be at odds with hip-hop.

At this point, we might notice immediately resonances with cultural producers from earlier periods. In the 1980s comic script "Studying Tibetan," speakers opined that the ability of the "the people" or "the masses" to understand the Communist Party's policies. In one of the 1990s "Careful Village" performances, Menla Jyab justifies his modernization of a traditional wedding speech on the grounds that it will be easier to understand. In the 2008 garchung "Gesar's Horse Herder," the teacher Hongmei's mixing of Tibetan and Chinese makes it difficult for her to communicate with the title character. More than just the content of his lyrics, Jason J's concerns about being understood link his work stylistically to the broader trends of the post-Mao cultural world in Amdo.

Since they can be understood, his messages about language, cultural heritage, and ethnicity can reach their target audiences. Valuable? Yes. But this should not be enough to make the song stand out from the many other popular Tibetan songs promoting these views. Jason J then proceeded to explicitly link hip-hop and zurza, the first of my interlocutors to do so. This is what makes his lyrics stand out. He illustrates this with the first two lines of the third verse, pointing out that they reference two famous modernist poems by the iconoclast Dondrup Jya (introduced in chapter 2):

I haven't seen the waterfall-like youth,
I haven't seen the wildly beating heart.

ཐབ་ཆུ་བཞིན་གྱི་ལང་ཚོའི་རྣམ་པ་དེ་ངས་མ་མཐོང་།
དྲག་ཏུ་མཆོང་ལྡིང་བྱེད་བཞིན་པའི་སྙིང་དེ་ངས་མ་མཐོང་།

In the first of these lines, the rapper invokes and inverts the language Dondrup Jya's seminal poem, "The Waterfall of Youth." Regularly recited at Tibetan cultural events and memorized in some schools, the poem remains one of the most iconic and recognizable contemporary Tibetan poems. The second line is a reference to another of Dondrup Jya's poems, entitled "There Is a Wildly Beating Living Heart Here." Both poems are renowned for constructing a vision of Tibet's modern present and future through radically breaking with its past (Shakya 2001, 37). With tremendous communicative economy, the mere mention of these poems metonymically refers to the broader Tibetan modernist movement, of which Dondrup Jya remains one of the most iconic figures. Through inverting the titles into negatives, the artist "does zurza" on the modernist view, saying that he hasn't seen the future that these poems promise.

Instead of directly stating his opposition to the modernist perspective, Jason J inverts the poem titles to create an indirect critique of the broader epistemic positions for which they stand. At the same time, the reference to the titles is far more person-specific than the literary or comedic critiques of the first few decades of the post-Mao period. Traditional zurza builds on and inverts the words of others to articulate humorous critiques (as seen in chapter 1), and Jason J's use of a more specific one here suggests the persistence of a folk understanding of zurza in Amdo, rooted in both indirection and targeting specific and identifiable people and ideas rather than generalized behaviors.

Instead of the failed promise of a radical break with traditions, Jason J uses the lines immediately following to encourage Tibetans to learn and pass on their linguistic and cultural traditions in the modern era.

> Brothers and sisters!
> Cherish well our brilliant ancestors' glory,
> diligently study their completely beautiful cultural heritage,
> listen to the heartfelt advice I am singing and keep it in mind.

> ནུ་བྲ་ཚོ།
> འདི་དུ་འཁོར་བའི་མེས་པོའི་གཟི་བརྗིད་ལེགས་པོར་གཅེས།
> རབ་ཏུ་མཛེས་པའི་ཤུལ་བཞག་རིག་གནས་ཧུར་གྱིས་སྦྱོང་།
> ཁོ་བོས་བླངས་པའི་སྙིང་གཏམ་དངར་པོ་དེ་རྣ་བས་ཉན་ཏེ་སེམས་ལ་ཉེར་དང་།

The remainder of the final verse references uniquely Tibetan ways of understanding and engaging with the world. His statements about auspiciousness and fortune reference traditional routes of creating auspicious circumstances through speech. Phrases like "*Kisoso*! May the gods be victorious," meanwhile, recall mountaintop rituals for local deities who protect the village from misfortune; the words of the refrain repeated again and again return the listener to the Gesar epic—ritual and narrative. The forms that Jason J proffers cover the range of the Tibetan expressive traditions to include ways of being and knowing the world. Importantly—and perhaps prudently, given the restrictions on religious expression in popular media—it would seem to include vernacular religious traditions outside of institutional religion but also only tangential to the state's heritage regime.[4]

In promoting the protection of traditions and advocating for ethnic unity (based around the traditional chol kha sum idea of the three ethnolinguistic regions of Amdo, Kham, and Ü-Tsang), "Alalamo" promotes similar goals as Uncle Buddhist's hits "Tsampa" and "City Tibetans." Jason J's indirect (but clear) critique of the modernity promoted by Tibetan cultural producers in previous decades of the post-Mao era is more than a mere hidden transcript. If it is resistant, it is resistant not to the state but to the earlier generation of producers and their overwhelming focus on modernization.

•

Jason J and Uncle Buddhist are a study in contrast. Unlike Uncle Buddhist, whose urban upbringing and elite education at the Contemporary Music Academy in Beijing have influenced his development as an artist, Jason J grew up in the pastoral areas of Tsekhog (Ch. Zeku) County, studied hospitality management in university, and is a self-taught rap artist. Whereas Uncle Buddhist only learned Tibetan for his album, Jason J grew up in a Tibetan-speaking environment and received a bilingual education in a prefecture renowned for its emphasis on Tibetan-language cultural production. This contrast extends even to their appearances, with Jason J's slight frame and short hair making him less conspicuous than the dreadlocked Uncle Buddhist. These contrasts appear in their music too: Uncle Buddhist delivers his lines with force, sometimes racing from one to the next, whereas Jason J takes his time. The latter's music videos are less cinematic than Uncle Buddhist's multimedia storytelling, and his lyrics use zurza to critique previous generations of Tibetan intellectuals, while Uncle Buddhist's form more of a hidden transcript resistant to state discourses.

But despite their myriad differences, both converge in using hip-hop to promote ethnic unity as well as the protection and maintenance of Tibetan languages and traditions in the twenty-first century. Their explicit and implicit reference to the traditional chol kha sum encourages

Tibetan audiences to unite around the shared identity of the *Bod pa* (Tibetan people) as an internally diverse but still unified group. Their passionate defense of Tibetan language and culture in the face of significant political and economic headwinds presents a clarion call for the region's youth to learn their native tongues and to maintain traditional cultural knowledge.

In doing so, they align themselves with issues that have become increasingly prominent in Amdo's twenty-first-century cultural production, and especially in music. Uncle Buddhist's "City Tibetans" takes this issue up explicitly from his own perspective as a Tibetan who has grown up in an urban environment in which a Chinese language—whether Putonghua standard Chinese, Sichuanese, some version of the Qinghai dialect, or the Beijing dialect—is the primary medium of everyday interaction outside the home. At the end of the song, he repeats several times the promise to not stay silent, fading gradually into silence. The emphasis on maintaining cultural traditions in "Alalamo" and on foodways in "Tsampa," meanwhile, emphasizes the need to continue practicing the most quotidian of traditions at a moment of tremendous change. Importantly, these are often neither institutional religious practices nor those officially recognized as intangible cultural heritage. In doing so, Jason J, Uncle Buddhist, and other Tibetan rappers use this new art form as a form of grassroots language planning (Moriarty and Pietikäinen 2011, 372–75) and as way to support revitalization (Cru 2018, 3) of Tibetan language and culture.

Like the comedies in previous decades that used it to shape popular attitudes, zurza serves as one essential ingredient that helps to simultaneously access new media and authorize a trenchant form of critique. Rap artists in Amdo use it to localize this new art form, and to shape popular attitudes toward Tibetan language and culture. Zurza, then, not only makes content meaningful but also continues to serve as an indigenous resource for cultural localization and innovation in Tibet. But it also changes—or perhaps *is changed*—at least partly thanks to contact with various media and ideologies, each carrying with them new meanings and expressive expectations.

In the hip-hop examined here, artists still say they are "doing zurza," but it ceases to be as humorous or playful. Instead, it uses indirection to articulate an (at times) almost angry cultural nationalism directed both at the current conditions of Tibetan life and of the intellectual foundations of Tibetan modernism. The example of Jason J, however, demonstrates that this inversion and indirection also ensures that zurza provides a resource of constant revision and renewal of Tibetan culture in the face of increasing political and economic headwinds.

Conclusion
The Irrepressible Trickster

In late 2019, concerns about a mystery illness emanating from Wuhan gradually morphed into a full-blown pandemic reaching all corners of the globe: COVID-19 needs no introduction. As the movement of goods and people around the world ground to a halt, increasing amounts of human interaction and creativity moved online and into digital spaces. Tibetan interactions were no different, with China's zero-COVID policy limiting travel even within the country more seriously than was done in many parts of the rest of the world. There was, in fact, no guarantee that a person would be allowed out of their homes even just to buy necessities. People might find that one day they could do their shopping in the local market, and the next a neighbor's positive test might result in their entire apartment complex going into lockdown, with little indication of when they might be able to leave. Everything from education to traditional performances moved into online spaces as people turned to digital spaces to transmit culture and maintain bonds of sociality at a distance.

Comedians and other cultural producers quickly rose to meet shared challenge by creating new works to entertain online audiences and (sometimes) to assist in efforts to fight the new virus.[1] Namlha Bum (mentioned in chapter 1), sometimes called "Daddy Cheche" after one of his most famous roles, starred in a series of short videos in which he selfishly bumbles about town, overlooking many of the new regulations of the COVID-19 era in the process. The series, entitled "Daddy Cheche's

Shorts on Pandemic Precautions," includes over ten videos, acting as public service announcements for Tibetans in Amdo.

The videos, most of which come in at under two minutes in length, each place a single practice on display. In one, the comedian blithely walks into a market without a mask, oblivious to the fact that everyone has their face covered. Guards turn him away at the door. In another video, Daddy Cheche sets about cleaning his apartment, but his mask-wearing wife corrects him for not using alcohol to sterilize surfaces. In a third, he gets bored of quarantine after traveling and is caught going about town when he should still be at home. While the topics may differ, each video also shares a common structure: a humorous illustration of an activity, plus an intertitle in Tibetan and Chinese stating explicitly how Namlha Bum's character has transgressed the appropriate practice. The video then ends with a statement from the performer—as himself, sitting at a computer—about the correct behavior.

The videos, created in 2020 with the support of the government of the Tsholho Tibetan Autonomous Prefecture, were then broadcast on the prefecture's television station and shared online.[2] Video effects like speeding up time, along with extradiegetic soundtracks (like an a cappella version of the Super Mario Brothers theme song or the one for the famous "Pig's Head Soothsayer" miniseries), help to generate some extra humor and entertainment value. Using the tried and tested techniques of indirection and sarcasm—that is to say, using zurza—Daddy Cheche's misdeeds illustrate the correct behaviors by negative example. The use of zurza again allowed a Tibetan presence in yet another form of cultural production and at the height of the pandemic.

A host of other short videos—ranging between one and twenty minutes in length—have also appeared in recent years, some with a similar aesthetic, others more akin to filmed garchung. Most are scripted. Many appear to be privately produced, while others have government backing. Like the comedies of previous decades, these satirize a range of behaviors, including distracted driving, public drunkenness, and gambling, among others. They also benefit from reaching audiences apart from the New Year's variety show. Now comedians and other creators can respond to events in real time.

Alongside these short videos, streaming and video-sharing platforms like TikTok and Kuaishou—already on the rise before the pandemic—have emerged as popular ways for people to reach audiences across previously unthinkable distances in real time. Expressive practices that had only recently begun circulating beyond their communities with the advent of audiovisual media—cassettes tapes, VCDs, and DVDs—now reach audiences around the world with the same immediacy of the oral performance (connectivity permitting). Pastoralists stream their morning routine as they roast barley or churn butter, bards stream as they perform the Tibetan epic, singers duel opponents from the comfort of their own homes. In many cases, they may perform for hundreds or even thousands at the same time.

Such platforms, however, have their limitations. For users of Kuaishou, which Tibetans call Jyoktrin, Tibetan script is not supported and Tibetan-language videos are subject to increased scrutiny. While WeChat permits Tibetan-language posts, most are limited to a relatively select group of followers. The restrictions on language are a sign of the times, and the degree to which the space for minority-language cultural production has become constricted in recent decades. At the same time, it persists, often in humorous form, because of its ability to be perceived as bringing zheng nengliang—and streamers may explicitly label their videos and channels as such—and because of tangential links to ongoing government projects of cultural heritage safeguarding. In doing so, such new forms of communication link tradition bearers with audiences in new ways, and potentially provide tools for Tibetans to overcome problems of distance, formalized education, and urbanization that seem to take many away from the communities that have sustained their culture.

The increasing numbers of platforms and expressive forms available to Tibetan cultural producers, alongside the residual presence of favorite works from decades past, makes the present moment (indeed, the twenty-first century more generally) an era of aggregation. Consumers can listen to their favorites from the "Careful Village" series, followed immediately by streaming a video "Gesar's Horse Herder" and then a rap video. The specific, temporal, and contextual critiques of the different works collapse into a single logic of Tibetan cultural survival: their shared interests in modernizing communities through language.

•

A decade earlier, in the fall of 2009, I arrived on the Tibetan Plateau to conduct my first fieldwork with the goal of researching first horse race festivals and then Tibetan trickster tales. Despite finding many sanitized versions of favorite episodes in published collections or available as illustrated children's books, I only ever heard a few oral retellings of such trickster narratives that year. Those stories I *did* hear were confided, with furtive and almost embarrassed looks. These were old stories, a little bit dirty, and not really appropriate for repeating. Beyond trickster tales, in fact, I was left with the impression that the relating of Tibetan folktales in general had largely ceased. As potential narrators found their audiences more enamored with modern media, including both Chinese film and television, folktales now lived primarily in collections compiled, edited (excised of any salacious or unwholesome material), and published alongside other works of "folk literature."

Student autobiographies from across the Tibetan Plateau reinforced my sense of the decreasing place of folktales in rural life, with many devoting an entire chapter to the sudden appearance of television and how it changed the fabric of their lives. Even elders, they claim, began to feel that the old stories were unimpressive: how can cultural heroes like Uncle Tonpa or King Gesar possibly compete with the likes of film star Jackie Chan or mythical hero Sun Wukong, the Monkey King in *Journey to the West* (Kondro Tsering 2012, 96)?

These recollections found parallels in nostalgic films and television series that began appearing around that time. The hit miniseries *Yesterday's Story* (Rdo grags, 2008), with its catchy theme song and powerful plot, depicts a pastoralist encampment undergoing the changes of the early post-Mao era—moving from tents to fixed dwellings, the influx of modern technologies and other vices—through the experiences of Grandpa Nyima and his family. Grandpa Nyima, a patriarch whose stories had once made him the center of his small encampment, watches helplessly as his family abandons traditional lifeways in favor of modern alternatives. Around the same time, the award-winning film *The Silent Holy Stones* (Lhangjag gi mani donbum) (Pad ma tshe brtan, 2005) shows a young monk who seems more interested in television than in his studies (perhaps understandably). This reaches its visual and narrative climax in a scene in which he joyfully dons a plastic mask of Sun Wukong at a party. Doing so visually emphasizes the intense changes brought on by mass television ownership and, by extension, technology.

In some cases, cultural producers sought to keep folktales and traditional knowledge alive in the minds of Tibetan audiences through retelling and reimagining folktales in new media; *The Pig's Head Soothsayer* (Mohtun phamgo), the highly popular miniseries of the popular folktale, provides one standout example. In the 2014 feature-length film *Uncle Tonpa* (Aku Tonpa), meanwhile, director Lujya Rati takes considerable artistic license to create a narrative that links some of the trickster's tamer exploits into a single narrative. In addition to and beyond these reimaginations of folktales, this book has shown that cultural producers have also sought inspiration in zurza (rather than in any particular narrative or tradition) to tell stories about contemporary Tibetan life in new genres and media. The works studied here provide a representative, rather than exhaustive, look at post-Mao cultural production in Amdo. The focus specifically on secular cultural production necessarily overlooks the important place of religion in Tibetan identity both historically and into the present day, but it is done primarily to highlight the continued role of zurza.

If folklore is the stories people tell themselves about themselves, then post-Mao Tibetan cultural production in Amdo has seemed to create modern stories that these producers were telling themselves about their contemporary lives. Though these stories can be attributed to specific individuals, in many cases, Tibetans across Amdo (and beyond) quote them in daily conversation, incorporating them into their own conceptions of their modern selves. They describe anxieties over the state of the language, culture, and environment in Tibetan communities, and provide new "equipment for living" in a rapidly changing world.

Using zurza, the texts profiled across the pages of this monograph serve as new trickster tales for a modern Tibetan society. Zurza invites audiences to engage with these new narratives of modern life along traditional lines, and to consider how works might entertain, engage in critique, and proffer some sort of (sometimes implicit) resolution. Menla Jyab's pretending to be a lama to dupe the people of Careful Village is a staple of Uncle Tonpa stories, and also models the solution to a significant problem. Uncle Horse Herder's use of folk wisdom and traditional reasoning to protect local interests against higher-status outsiders also invites audiences to consider the behavior and attitudes of the teacher Hongmei. Less directly, the speakers in Dondrup Jya's "Speaking Tibetan" scheme about how to deal with the language tricks of a superior, and twenty-first-century rappers seek to shape public opinion by satirizing behaviors deemed inappropriate or incongruous. The solutions modeled all offer ways for communities to make *Tibetan* futures out of their present conditions. Tricksters are, after all, healing characters (Jung 1968), and cultural healing is often what is needed in societies that have had languages and cultures threatened by a dominating, external force (Squint 2012, 108).

I *had* found tricksters after all, just not the tales I had expected. Instead of traditional narrative, I had found comedy and hip-hop. Instead of Uncle Tonpa, I had met Uncle Menla, Uncle Buddhist, and several other comedians, rappers, and authors. These cultural producers also live betwixt and between. Like tricksters, they cross physical and social boundaries (Hyde 1998) with ease, and model pathways for cultural healing. Keenly observant comedians and other cultural producers, keeping one foot in the city and the other in their home communities, have found the emergence of these new technologies to provide valuable spaces to engage in meaningful work. Uncle Buddhist, who grew up in the city not learning Tibetan well, is now a famous Tibetan rapper. Menla Jyab, Dondrup Jya, and Jason J, meanwhile, left the countryside for education and employment but later became central to the Tibetan cultural world through their influential work. I had gotten a similar sense from Alai, an internationally renowned Sinophone Tibetan author (who is almost universally disliked by Tibetan readers), whose most famous works often include some reference to Uncle Tonpa.

Sitting on the geographic and social margins of society—and always "the Other" in relation to the dominant society by virtue of being minoritized—these cultural producers bring the trickster to life every day. Both in their work and their lives, Menla Jyab and others model for their audiences—readers, listeners, and viewers—new ways of trickster-living and linguistic and cultural healing in a modernizing society.

The trickster ethos that these cultural producers embody and employ is also evident in the boundary-crossing behaviors of many of the Tibetans I met who navigate their lives in contemporary Amdo, including those who have chosen to work within the government. Those in positions of power advocate for their ethnic group. Though things might have changed in recent years, as the focus on party orthodoxy has grown, I have often been struck by the ways that many who work in government have found to practice Buddhism, advocate for Tibetan culture, and access valuable resources, even under the watchful eye of the state. Take, for example, the police officer I met in Golok, who circumambulated the holy mountain of Amye Machen—a grueling multiday hike in the best of weather—as if it were an extreme sport; he also had the six-syllable mantra *Om Mani Padme Hum* tattooed in large writing across his chest. According to him, this work was little more than a way to pay the bills— that is, render unto the party that which is owed to the party.

I met many young Tibetans who also seemed to take similar boundary-crossing positions. With families pressuring them to join the Communist Party and seek the financial stability of government employment, these young people navigate a complex set of incentives and desires. In many cases, however, those working in government have served as some of the staunchest advocates I have met for safeguarding Tibetan traditions or building new educational opportunities for youth (as described in Makley 2018). Often, they also praise the government for the tremendous investments of human and financial capital that it has made on the Tibetan Plateau. Though this praise runs counter to many of the narratives to which we are most accustomed in the Euro-American West, they seem heartfelt (at least in context), as it seemed to provide resources for them to work within the system to carve out Tibetan cultural futures, and the work is ongoing.

•

I left Amdo in 2015, returning for short trips each year prior to 2019. Since leaving, I often struggled to describe to people outside of China—including but not limited to academics, activists and members of the exile community—the very complex calculus of internal motivations, social pressures, and external incentives that seemed to shape the decision-making processes of the Tibetans I met. At conferences, workshops, and in casual conversations, my descriptions were frequently met with some variation of the response: "They're brainwashed" or "They have no choice." Others reflexively seemed to blame every problem on "the Chinese." I cannot accept these assumptions—at least not when formulated in this way.

Tibetans in the People's Republic undoubtedly live in and navigate a highly constrained environment, in which they must carefully monitor what they say and do (and, as I have shown in this book, *how* they say and do them). But ignoring the creative ways that Tibetans have maintained and even revolutionized their culture—both from within the state system and in resistance to it—denies them agency and treats them only as victims. I have shown how zurza—the Tibetan arts of indirection, sarcasm, and satire—provided cultural producers with a powerful way of actively localizing new expressive resources, accessing state media to do this work, and ensuring Tibetan physical and cultural presence in some of the harshest of times. Across decades and media, the texts examined in this book record some of the ways that Tibetans have used zurza to foreground issues seen as particularly pressing for their communities in spite of the tremendously asymmetric power of the Chinese state.

Zurza sits in conversation with discourses of ethnic pride, modernity, and linguistic identity, helping to advance some of the most important intellectual and cultural debates of the post-Mao era. The specific practices and forms that Tibetan intellectuals and cultural producers in Amdo use for sarcastically expressing ethnic pride and supporting ethnic development are unique to their circumstances and constrained by the requirements of their positions—but they do this nonetheless. Rather than "collusion," "collaboration," with the state, or outright resistance to it, these people were strategically considering how to improve their own lives and those of their fellow Tibetans.

This environment is also dynamic. Each of the decades profiled in this book shows how cultural producers work in response to Tibet's evolving political, intellectual, and media environments. This dynamism continues today, as I noticed in short fieldwork trips between 2016 and 2018. In 2016, on my first return to China, Ziling had not one but two Starbucks coffee shops (there had been none when I left the year before). In 2017, a viral social media post about changes to the implementation of China's bilingual education policy (Dak Lhagyal 2019) resurfaced old debates and anxieties about the present and future of the Tibetan language. By 2018, urban Tibetans in Ziling no longer did circle dances in the city's central square due to a new regulation aimed at curbing noise pollution, and some (even retired) officials confided that they would no longer circumambulate religious sites. These signs hinted at the rapidly changing material and political conditions over the last few years.

With zurza providing an important, traditional resource for cultural producers to draw on, the ongoing existence and popularity of the expressive forms studied in this book—comedic dialogues, sketches, hip-hop, and others—tell a story of Tibetan cultural resilience and survival in post-Mao China. They create and maintain spaces for Tibetan language and culture in state media and in daily life, all despite the disruptions experienced by communities across Amdo. The future of Tibetan media and expressive cultures are very much up in the air at the moment. Whatever form it takes, however, and whatever issues it engages, zurza and Tibetan trickster energy will almost certainly have a role to play if Tibetanness is to survive in and beyond modern media.

Glossary

All terms below are Tibetan unless otherwise noted.

Ache Lhamo ཨ་ལྕེ་ལྷ་མོ། • a form of Tibetan opera from Ü-Tsang, often featuring some satirical performance

"Alalamo" ཨ་ལ་ལ་མོ། • a song by the hip-hop artist Jason J

Amdo ཨ་མདོ། • an ethnolinguistic region

Amhkel ཨམ་སྐད། • the dialects of Tibetan spoken in Amdo

Arik Lenpa ཨ་རིག་ལེན་པ། • a popular buffoon from Amdo Tibetan oral traditions

Bod (T) བོད། / **Zangzu** (Ch.) 藏族 • the name Tibetans now use for the Tibetan ethnic group, pronounced *wod* or *wol* in Amdo

Bongdzi བོང་རྫི། • literally "donkey herder," the internet handle of controversial public intellectual Lobsang Yongdan

chol kha sum ཆོལ་ཁ་གསུམ། • the Tibetan concept that divides the plateau into three major ethnolinguistic regions: Amdo (northeastern Tibet), Kham (eastern Tibet), and Ü-Tsang (Central Tibet)

Dekyi Tsering བདེ་སྐྱིད་ཚེ་རིང་། • a Tibetan rapper

Dohmad མདོ་སྨད། • the traditional name for Amdo

Dohtod མདོ་སྟོད། • the traditional name for Kham

dokwa བཏགས་པ། • extemporaneously composed poems people share back and forth in order to belittle each other's appearance or behavior; written as *btags pa*, and also pronounced regionally as *daksa*, *dakree*, and *dokra*.

Dondrup Jya དོན་གྲུབ་རྒྱལ། • 1953–85, author and cofounder of modern Tibetan literature

dongchong xiacao (Ch.) 冬虫夏草 • *see* yartsa gunbu

dranyen སྒྲ་སྙན། • a Tibetan stringed instrument plucked like a lute

Drijya Yangkho འབྲི་བརྒྱ་གཡང་ཁོ། • a character in the "caterpillar fungus" comedic sketch

Drowa zangmo འགྲོ་བ་བཟང་མོ། • a classic Tibetan opera

Drukmo འབྲུག་མོ། • King Gesar's wife in the Tibetan epic, often treated as the paragon of virtue and womanly beauty

Dubhe བདུད་བྱེ། • 1968–2016, a popular singer of Tibetan dunglen music

dunglen རྡུང་ལེན། • a style of music, particularly popular in Amdo, in which a single singer or group of singers plucks either a traditional dranyen or a mandolin while singing

fengci (Ch.) 讽刺 • satire

Gansu (Ch.) 甘肃 • a province in Northwest China

garchung (T) གར་ཆུང་། / **xiaopin** (Ch.) 小品 • literally "small plays," one of the terms most frequently used for Tibetan sketch comedies in the twenty-first century

Gesar གེ་སར། • the hero of the Tibetan national epic

géwa དགེ་བ། • the Tibetan term for the Buddhist concept of "virtue" or good action

Golok (T) མགོ་ལོག / **Guoluo** (Ch.) 果洛 • a Tibetan autonomous prefecture in the southern part of Tsongon (Qinghai)

Gomang (T) མགོ་མང་། / **Guomaying** (Ch.) 过马营 • a town in Mangra County, in Amdo

Goméla (T) སྒོ་མེ་ལ། / **Laji Shan** (Ch.) 垃圾山 • a mountain pass west of Ziling

Gonpo Dorje jamchod མགོན་པོ་རྡོ་རྗེའི་ཇ་མཆོད། • "Gonpo Dorje's Tea Prayer," an early script sometimes argued as the first Tibetan khashag

gormo སྒོར་མོ། • the Amdo Tibetan word for money

Guide (Ch.) 贵德 • *see* Trika

Guinan (Ch.) 贵南 • *see* Mangra

Gungthang Tenpa Dronme གུང་ཐང་བསྟན་པའི་སྒྲོན་མེ། • 1762–1823, the author of "Gonpo Dorje's Tea Prayer," sometimes called the first Tibetan comedic dialogue

Guoluo (Ch.) 果洛 • *see* Golok

Guomaying (Ch.) 过马营 • *see* Gomang

gushi (Ch.) 故事 • stories

Hainan (Ch.) 海南 • *see* Tsolho
Han (Ch.) 汉 • the majority ethnic group in China
He Chi (Ch.) 何迟 • 1922–92, a Manchu performer of xiangsheng who was criticized for the performance "Buying Monkeys"
Henan (Ch.) 河南 • *see* Malho
Hou Baolin (Ch.) 侯宝林 • 1917–93, a renowned performer of Chinese xiangsheng
Hu Yaobang (Ch.) 胡耀邦 • 1915–89, the former general secretary of the Chinese Communist Party from 1982 to 1987
Hui (Ch.) 回 • the largest Muslim minority group in China

Jamyang Lodree འཇམ་དབྱངས་བློ་གྲོས། • 1974–2019, a popular comedian from Golok in Amdo
Jigme Rigpai Lodro འཇིགས་མེད་རིག་པའི་བློ་གྲོས། • 1910–85, the sixth incarnation of Tsetan Shabdrung
jyala རྒྱ་ལྭ། • modern clothing like jeans and T-shirts, literally "Han clothing"
Jyanang རྒྱ་ནང་། • "Inner China," referring primarily to the developed coastal regions
Jyoktrin (T) མགྱོགས་འཕྲིན། / **Kuaishou** (Ch.) 快手 • a social media application for sharing videos and streaming popular with Tibetans
jyutselpa སྒྱུ་རྩལ་པ། • an artist

katsom ཀ་རྩོམ། • a thirty-line Tibetan poem in which the first syllable of the first line is the first letter of the Tibetan syllabary, and each successive line starts with the ensuing letters
khabde ཁ་བདེ། • wit or eloquence, literally "good mouth"
Kham ཁམས། • one of the three ethnolinguistic regions of Tibet recognized in the chol kha sum, comprising Yushu Tibetan Autonomous Prefecture in Qinghai, most of Ganze Tibetan Autonomous Prefecture in western Sichuan, Diqing Tibetan Autonomous Prefecture in the northwesternmost part of Yunnan, and the eastern portions of the Tibet Autonomous Region
khamtshar ཁ་མཚར། • witticisms and speech practices marked by an emphasis on quick-witted banter, literally "amazing mouth" (in some locations, it can also be used interchangeably with *kure* to say "I'm just kidding")
khashag ཁ་བཤགས། • staged and scripted comedic dialogues
khatak ཁ་བཏགས། • silk scarves that Tibetans frequently offer to guests, newlyweds, and important people

156 GLOSSARY

khel ཁིད། • a traditional genre of riddle lore in which speakers indirectly and metaphorically describe an object or concept for others to guess

Khenpo Tsultrim Lodree མཁན་པོ་ཚུལ་ཁྲིམས་བློ་གྲོས། • b. 1962, the abbot of Serta Larung Gar monastic college

Kuaishou (Ch.) 快手 • *see* Jyoktrin

Kumbum སྐུ་འབུམ། • a monastery in Amdo near Ziling City

kure གུ་རེ། • joke; often takes the verb *tsé* (to play)

labjyagpa ལབ་རྒྱག་པ། • "boasting" or "bullshitting," a form of Tibetan speech in which speakers make outlandish statements, sometimes competing to be more ridiculous than what came before

Labrang བླ་བྲང་། • a monastery in Gansu

Laji Shan (Ch.) 垃圾山 • *see* Goméla

lama བླ་མ། • a holy man or guru. In Amdo, lamas mediate disputes, perform religious services for the community, and are traditionally afforded unquestioning respect.

Langdarma གླང་དར་མ། • r. 841–42, the common name for the last king of the Tsanpo dynasty in Tibet

larjya ལ་རྒྱ། • a Tibetan concept meaning "pride," "dignity," or "honor" that became especially important to Amdo Tibetan intellectual conversations and cultural production in the early years of the post-Mao period

laye ལ་ཡེ། • a traditional love-song genre popular in Amdo

Lhalung Hualdor ལྷ་ལུང་དཔལ་རྡོར། • the commonly used name for the monk who assassinated King Landarma in 842, often said to have spent the remainder of his life in Amdo

Lobzang Dorje བློ་བཟང་རྡོ་རྗེ། • the former director and performer in the Eastern Lhasa Propaganda Team, popularly called "King Zangmo"

lomtun བློ་མཐུན། • comrade

Losar Gongtsog ལོ་སར་དགོང་ཚོགས། • a major television program that airs annually on the eve of the Tibetan New Year

lu ཀླུ། • autochthonous numina in the Tibetan lakes and waterways that are sometimes thought to control wealth and cause human illness

Ludrub Jyamtso ཀླུ་སྒྲུབ་རྒྱ་མཚོ། • a rapper who performs under the name "Uncle Buddhist"

Lujya Rati ཀླུ་རྒྱལ་རྡོ་རྗེ། • a filmmaker from Amdo and director of a feature-length film about Uncle Tonpa

lungta རླུང་རྟ། • small, square pieces of colorful paper with a prayer printed on them that may be thrown into the air (in Amdo, this word may also refer to a person's luck)

lushag གླུ་བགས། • a genre of Tibetan antiphonal folksong

Ma Sanli (Ch.) 马三立 • 1914–2003, a Hui performer of xiangsheng who was criticized for the performance "Buying Monkeys"
Malho (T) མེ་ཧོ། / **Henan** (Ch.) 河南 • a Mongolian autonomous county where the Mongolian population speaks Amdo Tibetan
Mangra (T) མང་ར། / **Guinan** (Ch.) 贵南 • a county in Tsongon
Menla Jyab སྨན་བླ་སྐྱབས། • b. 1963, a famous comedian from Amdo
mirik gi larjya མི་རིགས་ཀྱི་ལར་རྒྱ། • "ethnic" or "national" pride; see larjya
minzu shibie (Ch.) 民族识别 • the nationwide project to identify the ethnic minority groups in the country

na མནའ། • "oaths"
nahtam གནའ་གཏམ། • "folktales" in Amdo, literally "old speech"
Namlha Bum གནམ་ལྷ་འབུམ། • a comedian from Amdo
ndroghkel འབྲོག་སྐད། • nomad dialects
ngen pa ངན་པ། • a bad person

Pema Tsetan པད་མ་ཚེ་བརྟན། • 1969–2023, a famed Tibetan author and filmmaker from Amdo
phalké ཕལ་སྐད། • a form of Tibetan writing using "vernacular" language
Phuntsog Tashi ཕུན་ཚོགས་བཀྲ་ཤིས། • a Tibetan comedian from Lhasa
Putonghua (Ch.) 普通话 • standard Chinese, the national language of the People's Republic of China, literally "universal speech"

Qinghai (Ch.) 青海 • *see* Tsongon

Rebgong རེབ་གོང་། • a county and region in Amdo roughly equivalent to Tongren County in Huangnan Tibetan Autonomous Prefecture
ronghkel རོང་སྐད། • a farming dialect
Ruyong Riglo རུ་ཡོང་རིག་ལོ། • a character in the "caterpillar fungus" comedic sketch

Samlo sarwa བསམ་བློ་གསར་པ། • New Thinkers
Secretary Wangchen དབང་ཆེན་ཧྲུའུ་ཅི། • a character in the "Studying Tibetan" comedic dialogue

Shar Kalden Jyamtso བཤར་སྐལ་ལྡན་རྒྱ་མཚོ། • 1607–77, a renowned monk and vernacular poet from Amdo

shengtai baohu (Ch.) 生态保护 • ecological conservation

Shidé Nyima ཞི་བདེ་ཉི་མ། • b. 1966, a popular comedian, poet, actor, and filmmaker

Shokdung ཞོགས་དུང་། • b. 1963, a prominent public intellectual from Amdo during the late twentieth and early twenty-first centuries

shtemdree རྟེན་འབྲེལ། • an omen, interdependence, material prosperity, or dependent origination

shuochang (Ch.) 说唱 • rap music, literally "speaking and singing"

Sichuan (Ch.) 四川 • a province in Southwestern China

Sokdzong སོག་རྫོང་། • a popular name for Malho County, literally "Mongolian County"

Soktruk Sherab སོག་ཕྲུག་ཤེས་རབ། • a popular actor and comedian from Amdo

sonam བསོད་ནམས། • merit

ta dadpa ཐ་དད་པ། • the category of transitive or agentive verbs verbs that take a subject marker

tamhwé གཏམ་དཔེ། • versified aphorisms and proverbs; used in Amdo

tamshel • གཏམ་བཤད། • a genre of versified Tibetan speeches

Tri Ralpachen ཁྲི་རལ་པ་ཅན། • c. 805–c. 838, one of the three dharma kings of Tibet

Trika (T) ཁྲི་ཀ། / **Guide** (Ch.) 贵德 • a county in Tsongon

tsampa རྩམ་པ། • both a flour made from roasted barley and the staple Tibetan meal made from mixing the barley flour with butter, water or tea, cheese, and sometimes other ingredients, like sugar; also the title of a song in chapter 5

Tsekhog (T) རྩེ་ཁོག / **Zeku** (Ch.) 泽库 • a county in Malho Tibetan Autonomous Prefecture in Qinghai

Tsering Döndrup ཚེ་རིང་དོན་གྲུབ། • b. 1961, a Tibetan author from Amdo

tséwa རྩེད་བ། • literally "to play"

Tsolho (T) མཚོ་ལྷོ། / **Hainan** (Ch.) 海南 • a Tibetan autonomous prefecture south of Qinghai Lake

Tsongon (T) མཚོ་སྔོན། / **Qinghai** (Ch.) 青海 • a province in Northwest China

Tsongonpo མཚོ་སྔོན་པོ། • Qinghai Lake; also the title of a poem by Dondrup Jya that is regarded by some as a Tibetan national anthem

tulku སྤྲུལ་སྐུ། • a reincarnate lama; also the name of a famous satirical short story by Dondrup Jya

Ü-Tsang དབུས་གཙང་། • one of the three major ethnolinguistic regions of Tibet mentioned in the chol kha sum formulation, often glossed simply as "Central Tibet"

Weixin (Ch.) 微信 • a popular Chinese social media application, commonly known as WeChat

xiangsheng (Ch.) 相声 • the Han tradition of staged and scripted comic dialogues from northern China, commonly translated as "crosstalk" or "face and mouth routines"

xiaopin (Ch.) 小品 • *see* garchung

Xin qingnian (Ch.) 新青年 • *New Youth*, a magazine of the May Fourth Movement

xin min (Ch.) 新民 • new people, a discursive formation from Chinese scholars in the late nineteenth and early twentieth centuries

xin wenti (Ch.) 新文体 • new prose style, a form of writing promoted by Chinese scholars in the late nineteenth and early twentieth centuries

Xining (Ch.) 西宁 • *see* Ziling

Yangjenma དབྱངས་ཅན་མ། • the boddhisattva associated with music and the arts

Yangsel དབྱངས་གསལ། • "Vowels and consonants," the title of a popular rap song

yartsa gunbu (T) དབྱར་རྩྭ་དགུན་འབུ། / **dongchong xiacao** (Ch.) 冬虫夏草 • caterpillar fungus (*Ophiocordyceps sinensis*)

Zalejya ཟ་ལེ་རྒྱལ། • a fictional character from "Careful Village's Bride"

Zangzu (Ch.) 藏族 • *see* Bod

Zeku (Ch.) 泽库 • *see* Tsekhog

zerjyu ré ཟེར་རྒྱུ་རེད། • a phrase appended at the ends of stanzas in traditional oratory

zhadgar བཞད་གར། • a humorous play; used interchangeably with garchung

zheematam གཞས་མ་གཏམ། • rap music, literally "neither verse nor speech"

zheng nengliang (Ch.) 正能量 • positive energy

Ziling (T) / **Xining** (Ch.) 西宁 • capital city of Tsongon (Qinghai)

Zonthar Gyal ཟོན་ཐར་རྒྱལ། • b. 1974, a Tibetan filmmaker from Amdo

zurza ཟུར་ཟ། • the Tibetan practice of critique targeting an individual or a type of social figure through indirection and humor, literally "eating the side." Sometimes glossed in English as "satire" and "sarcasm," the concept emerges in post-Mao Amdo as a key feature of some of the most popular forms of cultural production.

Notes

Introduction

1. See Rea (2015) for more on humor's quotidian subversion of grand narrative.

2. For more on the politics of ethnic identification in Tibetan groups who are now considered Tibetan, see Kolås and Thowsen (2005, 39–41) and Upton (2000). Sometimes more political than scientific, many of those now classified as Tibetan speak what Roche and Suzuki (2018) call minority Tibetan languages, some of which are classified as non-Tibetic. Groups like the Prmi, meanwhile, are classified as Tibetan in Sichuan but are given their own ethnic classification status in Yunnan (Harrell 1996, 279).

3. For more on the Hui, see Gladney (1987a, 1987b, 1996, 2004, 120–75 and 282–311), Hillman (2004), and Cooke (2008a, 2008b).

4. For further reading on the Tu, see Limusishiden and Jugui (2010), Limusishiden and Stuart (1995, 2010), Limusishiden (2011), Stuart and Limusishiden (1994), Limusishiden and Roche (2017), Roche (2011, 2014), Roche and Wen (2013), Wang, Zhu, and Stuart (1995), Zhu and Stuart (1996), Slater (2003), Wen (2010), and Zhu, Qi, and Stuart (1997).

5. For some resources on the Salars, see Dwyer (2007), Ma and Stuart (1996), Ma, Ma, and Ma (1993), and Goodman (2008).

6. See, for example, Roche (2016), Khan (1996), Diemberger (2007), Bulag (2000, 2003), and Wallenböck (2016).

7. See also Pema Bhum's 2001 memoir.

1. Dokwa

1. For more on the harvesting and sale of caterpillar fungus, see Sulek (2019).

2. My thanks to Tsering Samdrup, both for assistance with some of the earth-

ier translations in this chapter and for pointing out how these names also can tell much about the characters and their social histories.

3. For more on Tibetan proverbs more generally, see Tournadre and Robin (2006), Sørenson and Erhard (2013a, 2013b), Lhamo Pemba (1996), and Pirie (2006, 2009, 2012, 2013). For a discussion of the social uses of proverbs, particularly in mediating conflict in Amdo, see Pirie (2009, 2013).

4. This includes wedding speeches and "praises of place," as well as a variety of smaller speeches. For more on Tibetan oratory, see Thurston (2012, 2019), Thurston and Caixiangduojie (2016), Tshe dbang rdo rje, Anton-Luca, and Stuart (2009), and Blo brtan rdo rje and Stuart (2008).

5. For more or riddles and tongue twisters in Amdo, see Blo brtan rdo rje, Stuart, and Roche (2009).

6. These sung traditions have regionally specific tunes that differentiate the genres. There are also other conventions associated with these forms. For example, throughout most of Amdo, it is taboo to sing love songs in front of opposite-gender relatives, but in at least one area of Tsekhog County, Huangnan Tibetan Autonomous Prefecture, boys may sing them in the presence of their grandmothers. In one village in Rebgong, meanwhile, villagers cover their faces so as to perform them alongside villagers of the opposite sex during the Luroo harvest festival. For more, see Rossi (1992) and Anton-Luca (2002).

7. Also known as a padmaraga sapphire, these are pink stones.

8. I have slightly amended this from the original, to conform with spellings used in this book and those that I have seen used most frequently. This includes rendering the English name as Uncle Tonpa (instead of Uncle Dunba, which is closer to the Amdo dialect pronunciation), and ཨ་ཁུ་སྟོན་པ། instead of ཨ་ཁུ་བསྟན་པ།.

9. It is worth pointing out that Tibet was not quite as isolated as this may portray. Tuttle (2005) shows the important role Tibetan Buddhist leaders played in helping to shape modern China. This is indicative of the long-standing political and cultural exchange between Han and Tibetan communities that predates the establishment of the People's Republic. Additionally, Tibetan culture owes much to Indian, Nepali, and Mongolian influences as well. Others have pointed out how some of the hallmarks of modernity, including an emphasis on scientific examination and rational human agency, also began to appear in Tibetan communities much earlier than the twentieth century (Gyatso 2011, 8–9).

10. McDougall notes that there are multiple published versions of the "Talks," and that at least some contain edited or alternative versions. For this selected

passage, McDougall's translation omits the phrase "No, satire is always necessary" and includes a note that some versions add it (McDougall 1980, 81 n235).

2. Khashag

1. This script uses some unorthodox spellings for Amdo dialect colloquialisms. I have kept the spellings in the written script that I have.

2. *Shuji* and *mishu* are both commonly translated as "secretary" but refer to two very different positions within China's government. The former refers to the highest-ranking official—the party secretary—of a given area. The latter is more akin to the Western term in that it refers to the *shuji*'s personal secretary, who also is his protégé, which can be a significant inroad to advancement in the government (Li 2015).

3. This represents an indigenously Tibetan way of organizing cultural knowledge. The five greater cultures or sciences are "arts and crafts," medicine, grammar, logic, and Buddhist doctrinal studies. The five lesser sciences are poetry, synonymy, rhetoric, drama, and astronomy.

4. This refers to traditional Tibetan woodblock-printed books, which are read horizontally on the long side.

5. All of the quotations in this section taken from the edition in Dondrup Jya's collected works (see Don grub rgyal [1980] 1997).

6. Bud Abbott and Lou Costello, known primarily by their surnames, were an American comedic duo active between 1935 and 1957. Working across radio, television, and film, they were among the most famous such performers of the period. See Miller (2000, 5–28) for an introduction to the pair, with a particular emphasis on their horror-comedies.

7. See Don grub rgyal (1997) for the original text.

8. See Don grub rgyal ([1984] 1997) for the original text.

9. Virtanen (2008, 243; 2011, 51) very briefly discusses this performance but spends a much greater portion of her studies on his stories and poetry. This omission is not limited to the Western Tibetological field. Sprel nag pa rig 'dzin grags ldan's (2009) edited volume of studies related to Dondrup Jya includes thirty essays dedicated to the author's literature, but not one discusses "Studying Tibetan." These examples comprise only a fraction of those on Dondrup Jya, but they should be enough to illustrate the tendency to overlook "Studying Tibetan" when examining his opus.

10. Link (2010, 58) argues that the term *crosstalk*, most commonly used to

translate the Chinese *xiangsheng* (literally "face and voice") (as in Thurston 2013 and Link 1984), is in fact a mistranslation, and that "the term might best be rendered as "comedians' routines." That said, "crosstalk," as a descriptive of the major dynamic of the art, may be a more commonly used term in popular discourse. Chinese historians date the term *xiangsheng* to the Qing dynasty (Sun 2007, 2). For more on the history of *xiangsheng* in general, see Wang, Wang, and Teng (2011). For Western studies of *xiangsheng* since 1949, see Link (1984), Moser (1990), Kaikkonen (1990), and Link (2010).

11. Mao originally proposed this in the 1949 talks at the Yan'an Forum on Literature and Art. For more, see Denton (2003, 463–69).

12. Importantly, this is not unique to Tibetan communities. You (2012), for example, notices how new *gushi* (stories) in the 1960s incorporated both traditional and novel storytelling strategies to meet the political and ideological needs of China's socialist education.

13. As used in Western China more generally and among Tibetans specifically, "Inner China" (Jyanang in Tibetan) refers to China's more developed coastal areas. It frequently applies also to landlocked provinces in central China like Shaanxi.

14. Hou Baolin (1917–93) was one of the most famous performers of *xiangsheng*. Link (1984, 88), for example, calls Hou "China's premier xiangsheng performer," and Tsau (1980, 47) and Moser (1990, 47) call him the genre's star performer. Hou has also been prolific in documenting the art of crosstalk (see Hou and Xue 1981, Hou 1980, and Hou et al. 2011).

15. The year 1861 agrees with Moser (2018), who traces the genre's origins to the mourning period after the death of the Xianfeng emperor. Many Chinese sources on the history of *xiangsheng* "crosstalks," however, often credit the earlier Zhang Sanlu with the founding of the form during the reign of the Qing dynasty's Daoguang emperor (1820–50) (see Wang, Wang, and Teng 1995, 70; and Kaikkonen 1990, 66). Tsau (1980, 33), meanwhile, traces the origins to much earlier Tang dynasty "adjutant plays" (Ch. *canjun xi*).

16. Goldstein (1998, 38), for example, points out that 'Bras spungs monastery in Lhasa had only 547 monks in 1995 despite reportedly boasting ten thousand in 1959. He also notes that the maximum number of monks allowed at the monastery as of that publication was six hundred.

17. A careful and diachronic study of education in Tibetan areas of China over the last few decades is beyond the scope of this study. There is, however, a sizable corpus of literature on Tibetan education in this period. For more, see

Bass (1998, 2008), Clothey and McKinlay (2012), Postiglione (1992, 1999, 2006, 2008); Seeberg (2008), and Wang and Phillion (2009). For more on minority education in China more generally, see Hansen (1999).

18. Shakya also wrote, "One of the phrases that dominated Tibetan literature between 1980 and 1987 was *mi rigs kyi la rgya*" (2008, 77), written in this book as *mirik gi larjya*.

19. Dondrup Jya is not the first author to write in Tibetan vernacular; some famous religious leaders historically used limited amounts in their writings (see Mog chung phur kho 2010). But the vast majority of Tibetan writers often use a distinct literary register.

20. The Four Modernizations sought to focus national development efforts in the areas of agriculture, industry, defense, and science and technology.

21. For more research on the form and usage of such paroemias, see Sørenson and Erhard (2013a and 2013b). Collections of Tibetan proverbs are legion; see Tournadre and Robin (2006) for one such collection.

3. *Khashag* on Air

1. A full translation of this performance is available as part of an article I published in *CHINOPERL: Journal of Chinese Oral and Performance Literature* (see Thurston 2013).

2. Tri Ralpachen was one of the three dharma kings of Tibet, and the penultimate king of the Tibetan Empire.

3. Zenz (2014, 129) cited the percentage of urban-based Tibetans as 8.6 percent according to the 2000 census, thus suggesting that 91.4 percent would be considered rural at that time.

4. Fischer (2009, 16) reported illiteracy rates over 40 percent in Qinghai and over 70 percent in the Tibet Autonomous Region into the 1990s, and numbers were higher for women than men.

5. Facing tremendous struggles with ensuring adequate healthcare in rural areas, "barefoot doctors" were a group of minimally trained medical practitioners who served their communities. For an introduction to this system and its history, see Zhang and Unschuld (2008).

6. The tenth Panchen Lama famously championed Tibetan education in the early years of the post-Mao period. Meanwhile, in Rarjya County, Golok Tibetan Autonomous Prefecture, the lama Jigme Jyamtsen established a school that remains one of the best-known private educational institutions in Amdo.

7. For more on Tibetan tricksters, see Dkon mchog dge legs, Dpal ldan bkra shis, and Stuart (1999), Orofino (2011), Aris (1987), and Rwa se dkon mchog rgya mtsho (1996). For an important, albeit sanitized, collection of Uncle Tonpa tales collected and printed in China, see Sichuan Sheng Minjian Wenyi Yanjiu Hui (1980). For more on Uncle Tonpa's more ribald exploits, see Rinjing Dorje (1997) and Aris (1987, 143–44).

8. This is not to say that Tibet lacked a scientific tradition prior to this period. In fact, rational, scientific critiques can be found in Tibet before the twentieth century (see, for example, Gyatso 2011 and Lobsang Yongdan 2011).

9. The focus on plot at the expense of character development is similar to a number of well-known and well-researched folklore genres, including legend (Briggs 1988; Dégh 2001), anecdote (Cashman 2008; Mullen 1978, 113–29), and others.

10. Han Chinese authors criticized arranged marriage as a cruel institution during the May Fourth Movement. Taking its cue from that, the Chinese Communist Party also made marriage a key to its modernizing program, portraying arranged marriages as backward, feudalist, or unmodern. Beyond China, meanwhile, scholars have also emphasized the importance of free-choice marriages and romantic love in early modernizing movements in Nigeria (Griswold 2000) and Nepal (Ahearn 2003, 2004). Though the practice of arranged marriage continues even into the twenty-first century (Thurston and Tsering Samdrup 2012, 55), it is central to the modernist Tibetan critique of tradition, and comedy is one important way these ideas were disseminated to the broader population.

11. For similar observations beyond Tibet include, see Noyes (2009, 240).

12. The term *economies of fortune* is an umbrella term for a variety of overlapping and mutually influencing fortune-related forces in the Tibetan worldview—including, but not limited to *shtemdree* (sometimes written as *tendrel* and translated variously as "omen" [Ekvall 1964b], "interdependence" [Kunsang 2003, 1080], "blessing, in the sense of material prosperity" [Clarke 1990], or "dependent origination"), *géwa* (virtue), *sonam* (merit), and *lungta* (luck). For more on the importance of fortune in Tibetan communities in Amdo, see Sa mtsho skyid and Roche (2011).

13. The Gesar epic is one important source of proverb-lore in China. The proverb featured here comes from the popular *Hor gling g.yul 'gyed* episode of the epic, in which the heroic king defeats neighboring Hor and its demonic king (see Gcod pa don grub and Chab 'gag rta mgrin 2000).

14. These hygienic language practices have proven to be an essential part of the modern project alongside social critiques, parallel other modernist interventions across Asia, including in Mongolia (Billé 2010), Japan (Heinrich 2012; Inoue 2006), and China. In each case, specific language practices become a conduit for promoting engagement with modernity. In China, meanwhile, many Qing-dynasty and May Fourth Movement intellectuals advanced vernacularization—promoting a more vernacular form of writing in place of Classical Chinese—to help create a discursive break between the premodern and the modern in a "new" China (Tong 2010; Lee 2005). After the establishment of the People's Republic in 1949, the new government implemented further interventions in both writing and speaking the Chinese language as essential part of state-promoted modernization. New, "simplified" (Ch. *jianti*) characters replaced traditional (Ch. *fanti*) ones, with the aim of improving literacy communication (Chen 2004, 154–56), *pinyin* romanization was promoted to improve learning (DeFrancis 1984, 251), and the state created a "common speech" language around which the unified Chinese nation would progress. This is not a new situation, and is further explicated in Moser's (2016) book, *A Billion Voices: China's Search for a Common Language.*

4. Garchung

1. Garchung's development as a distinct performance style, with its own stars, parallels that of Han Chinese *xiaopin* skits popularized most famously by Zhao Benshan (Mu 2004; Gao and Pugsley 2008). Importantly, like garchung, xiaopin also address a different constellation of issues (Du 1998). However, unlike the Han Chinese media environment, in which crosstalk continues to be popular even after the advent of the more visual sketches, Tibetan garchung largely displaced khashag dialogues.

2. See Thurston (2018c) for a fuller discussion of the Tibetan language purism movement.

5. Zheematam

1. Historically, the term *shuochang* can refer to a number of traditional prosimetric genres in China that bridge the oral and literary divide. See Børdahl (2003, 4) for more on this interplay between written and oral, and "tell-sing literature" (*shuochang wenxue*).

2. In this way, we see similarities to how Hoklo rappers in Taiwan link rap to a traditional form of narrative singing (Schweig 2014).

3. The phrase in the Tibetan presents a traditional way of metonymically referring to the dynasty of Tubo kingdoms by the syllables that several of them shared in their names: seven whose names share *khri*, six whose names share *legs*, and eight whose names share *sde*.

4. For example, although fumigation offerings may be a part of a number of practices now listed on UNESCO's list of the intangible cultural heritage of humanity, the practice itself and the prayers spoken on a daily basis to propitiate local deities do not receive such valuation.

Conclusion

1. Bai's (2020) study of Mongolian fiddle stories demonstrates that this is not limited to the Tibetan context.

2. It is still possible to view some of these videos online. As of March 7, 2023, the Yongzin search engine, for example, kept archives of several videos, including the mask-wearing video described here (https://video.yongzin.com/v_show/playVideo.do?videoid=40288cc17aec7f23017ba5577eb836ad). The specific offices credited in the videos include the Propaganda Bureau; the Bureau of sports, Culture, Tourism, and Broadcasting; the television station, and the prefectural song and dance troupe.

3. Sun Wukong is a character from the famous Chinese tale *Xi you ji* (Journey to the west). This tale has been the subject of numerous movies and television series and has tended to reach Tibetan audiences primarily through these television series, sometimes translated into Tibetan. See Robin (2008) for further discussion of *The Silent Holy Stones*.

References

Abrahams, Roger D. 1962. "Playing the Dozens." *Journal of American Folklore*, 75:209–20.

Abu-Lughod, Lila. 1999. "The Interpretation of Culture(s) after Television." In *The Fate of "Culture,"* edited by Sherry B. Ortner, 110–35. Berkeley: University of California Press.

Adams, Vincanne. 1996. "Karaoke as Modern Lhasa, Tibet: Western Encounters with Cultural Politics." *Cultural Anthropology* 11 (4): 510–46.

Ahearn, Laura M. 2003. "Writing Desire in Nepali Love Letters." *Language and Communication* 23 (2): 107–22.

———. 2004. "Literacy, Power, and Agency: Love Letters and Development in Nepal." *Language and Education* 18 (4): 305–16. https://doi.org/10.1080/09500780408666883.

Almeida, Cristina Moreno. 2017. *Rap Beyond Resistance: Staging Power in Contemporary Morocco*. London: Palgrave Macmillan.

Anagnost, Ann. 1997. National Past-Times: Narrative, Representation, and Power in Modern China. Durham, NC: Duke University Press.

Anonymous. 1990. "6.9 Quake in China Kills 109." *Los Angeles Times*, April 27, 1990. http://articles.latimes.com/1990-04-27/news/mn-349_1_quakes-kills-china.

Anonymous. 2010. "Sgyu rtsal pa Sman bla skyabs kyi ched las thad kyi bcar 'dri'i lan སྒྱུ་རྩལ་པ་སྨན་བླ་སྐྱབས་ཀྱི་ཆེད་ལས་ཐད་ཀྱི་བཅར་འདྲིའི་ལན།" (Interview responses on the artist Sman bla skyabs's Specialty). *Na gzhon gsar ba* (New youth), May 25. http://www.tbnewyouth.com/article/interview/20100525615.html.

Anton-Luca, Alexandru. 2002. "Glu and Laye in A Mdo: An Introduction to Contemporary Tibetan Folk Songs." In *A Mdo Tibetans in Transition: Society and Culture in the Post-Mao Era*, edited by Toni Huber, 173–96. Leiden: Brill.

———. 2006. "Teaching THDL Extended Wylie." http://www.thlib.org/reference/transliteration/teachingewts.pdf.

Aris, Michael. 1987. "'The Boneless Tongue': Alternative Voices from Bhutan in the Context of Lamaist Societies." *Past and Present* 115 (1): 131–64.

Avorgbedor, Daniel K. 1994. "Freedom to Sing, License to Insult: The Influence of Haló Performance on Social Violence among the Anlo Ewe." *Oral Tradition* 9 (1): 83–112. http://journal.oraltradition.org/files/articles/9i/4_avorgbedor.pdf.

———. 1999. "The Turner-Schechner Model of Performance as Social Drama: A Re-Examination in the Light of Anlo-Ewe *Haló*." *Research in African Literatures* 30 (4): 144–55.

———. 2001 "'It's a Great Song!' *Haló* Performance as Literary Production." *Research in African Literatures* 32 (2): 17–43.

Babcock-Abrahams, Barbara. 1975. "'A Tolerated Margin of Mess': The Trickster and His Tales Reconsidered." *Journal of the Folklore Institute* 11 (2): 147–86.

Backhaus, Peter. 2007. *Linguistic Landscapes: A Comparative Study of Urban Multilingualism in Tokyo*. Multilingual Matters 136. Buffalo, NY: Multilingual Matters.

Bai, Geguntuul Hongye. 2020. "Fighting COVID-19 with Mongolian Fiddle Stories." *Multilingua* 39 (5): 577–86.

Bakhtin, Mikhail M. 1981. *The Dialogic Imagination: Four Essays by M. M. Bakhtin*. Edited by Michael Holquist and Caryl Emerson. Austin: University of Texas Press.

Ballinger, Franchot. 2006. *Living Sideways: Tricksters in American Oral Indian Traditions*. Norman: University of Oklahoma Press.

Bamo Qubumo. 2001. "Traditional Nuosu Origin Narratives: A Case of Ritualized Epos in *Bimo* Incantation Scriptures." *Oral Tradition* 16 (2): 453–79. http://oraltradition.org.

———. 2008. "Zai kou tou chuantong yu shu xie wenhua zhi jian de shishi yanshu ren—jiyu ge'an yanjiu de minzu zhi xiezuo 在口头传统与书写文化之间的史诗演述人——基于个案研究的民族之写作" (Epic performers between orality and literacy: A case study on ethnographic writings). *Beijing Shifan Daxue xue bao (shehui kexue ban)* (Journal of Beijing Normal University [social sciences edition]) 2008 (1): 74–84.

Bangsbo, Ellen. 2008. "Schooling for Knowledge and Cultural Survival: Tibetan Community Schools in Nomadic Herding Areas." *Educational Review* 60 (1): 69–84.

Barandiaran, Asier. 2009. "The Creation of Basque Oral Poetry by Four American Bertsolaris." *Oral Tradition* 24 (1): 161–204.

Barnett, Robbie. 2012. "Political Self-Immolation in Tibet: Causes and Influences." *Revue d'etudes tibétaines*, no. 25 (December), 41–64.

Barthes, Roland. 1970. *S/Z*. Paris: Seuil.

———. 1977. "The Death of Author." In *Image, Music, Text*, translated by Stephen Heath, 142–48. New York: Hill and Wang.

Bass, Catriona. 1998. *Education in Tibet, Policy and Practice Since 1950*. London: Zed Books.

———. 2008. "Tibetan Primary Curriculum and Its Role in Nation Building." *Educational Review* 60 (1): 39–50.

Basso, Keith. 1979. *Portraits of "the Whiteman": Linguistic Play and Cultural Symbols among the Western Apache*. Cambridge: Cambridge University Press.

Bauer, Ken. 2005. "Development and the Enclosure Movement in Pastoral Tibet since the 1980s." *Nomadic Peoples* 9 (1–2): 53–81.

Bauman, Richard. 1977. *Verbal Art as Performance*. Prospect Heights, IL: Waveland Press.

———. 2004. *A World of Others' Words: Cross Cultural Perspectives on Intertextuality*. Malden, MA: Blackwell.

Ben-Amos, Dan. 1969. "Analytic Categories and Ethnic Genres." *Genre* 2 (3): 275–301.

Bender, Mark. 2019. "Preface." In *The Nuosu "Book of Origins": A Creation Epic from Southwest China*, translated by Mark Bender and Aku Wuwu from a transcription by Jjivot Zopqu, x–xviii. Seattle: University of Washington Press.

Bendi Tso. 2023. "Preface." In *Shépa: The Tibetan Oral Tradition in Choné*, by Bendi Tso, Marnyi Gyatso, Naljor Tsering, and Mark Turin, 1–2. London: Open Book Publishers.

Benson, Sandra. n.d. *Folktale Reader*. Unpublished monograph.

Berglund, Jeff. "'I'm Just as Indian Standing before You with No Feathers Popping out of My Head': Critiquing Indigenous Performativitiy in the YouTube Performances of The 1491s." *AlterNative: An International Journal of Indigenous Peoples* 12 (5): 541–57.

Berry, Chris. 2016. "Pema Tseden and the Tibetan Road Movie: Space and Identity beyond the 'Minority Nationality Film.'" *Journal of Chinese Cinemas* 10 (2): 89–105.

Beyer, Stephen V. 1992. *The Classical Tibetan Language*. Albany: State University of New York Press.

Billé, Frank. 2010. "Sounds and Scripts of Modernity: Language Ideologies and Practices in Contemporary Mongolia." *Inner Asia* 12 (2): 231–52.

———. 2015. *Sinophobia: Anxiety, Violence, and the Making of Mongolian Identity*. Honolulu: University of Hawai'i Press.

Blo brtan rdo rje and Charles Kevin Stuart. 2008. *Life and Marriage in Skya rgya, a Tibetan Village*. New York: YBK Books.

Blo brtan rdo rje, Charles Kevin Stuart, and Gerald Roche. 2009. "Amdo Tibetan Tongue Twisters." *Asian Highlands Perspectives* 1:7–51.

Blommaert, Jan. 2007. "Sociolinguistic Scales." *Intercultural Pragmatics* 4 (1): 1–19.

Børdahl, Vibeke. 2003. "The Storyteller's Manner in Chinese Storytelling." *Asian Folklore Studies* 62 (1): 1–48.

Brag dgon pa dkon mchog bstan pa rab rgyas བྲག་དགོན་པ་དགོན་མཆོག་བསྟན་པ་རབ་རྒྱས|. 1987. *Mdo smad Chos 'byung* མདོ་སྨད་ཆོས་འབྱུང་| (The political and religious history of Amdo). Ziling: Mtsho sngon mi rigs dpe skrun khang.

Briggs, Charles. 1988. *Competence in Performance: The Creativity of Tradition in Mexicano Verbal Art*. Philadelphia: University of Pennsylvania Press.

Briggs, Charles, and Richard Bauman. 1992. "Genre, Intertextuality, and Social Power." *Journal of Linguistic Anthropology* 2 (2): 131–72.

Brodie, Ian. 2014. *The Vulgar Art: A New Approach to Stand-Up Comedy*. Jackson: University of Mississippi Press.

Bronner, Simon. 1978. "A Re-Examination of Dozens among White American Adolescents." *Western Folklore* 37 (2): 118–28.

Brown, Melissa Shani, and David O'Brien. 2020. "Defining the Right Path: Aligning Islam with Chinese Socialist Core Values at Ningbo's Moon Lake Mosque." *Asian Ethnicity* 21 (2): 269–91.

'Brug mo skyid, Charles Kevin Stuart, Alexandru Anton-Luca, and Steve Frediani. 2011. "Stag rig Tibetan Village: Hair Changing and Marriage." *Asian Highlands Perspectives* 6:151–217.

Bruner, M. Lane. 2005. "Carnivalesque Protest and the Humorless State." *Text and Performance Quarterly* 25 (2): 136–55.

Bulag, Uradyn E. 2000. "Alter/native Mongolian Identity: From Nationality to Ethnic Group." In *Chinese Society: Change Conflict and Resistance*, edited by Elizabeth J. Perry and Mark Selden, 261–87. New York: Routledge.

———. 2003. "Mongolian Ethnicity and Linguistic Anxiety in China." *American Anthropologist* 105 (4): 753–63.

Burke, Kenneth. 1973. "Literature as Equipment for Living." In *The Philosophy of Literary Form*, edited by Kenneth Burke, 293–304. Berkeley: University of California Press.

Calkowski, Marcia S. 1991. "A Day at the Tibetan Opera: Actualized Performance and Spectacular Discourse." *American Ethnologist* 18 (4): 643–57.

Caple, Jane. 2019. *Morality and Monastic Revival in Post-Mao Tibet*. Honolulu: University of Hawai'i Press.

Cashman, Ray. 2007. "Genre and Ideology in Northern Ireland." *Midwestern Folklore* 33:3–27.

———. 2008. *Storytelling on the Northern Irish Border: Characters and Community*. Bloomington: Indiana University Press.

———. 2016. "Genre as Ideology-Shaping Form: Storytelling and Parading in Northern Ireland." In *Genre – Text – Interpretation: Multidisciplinary Perspectives on Folklore and Beyond*, edited by Kaarina Koski and Frog with Ulla Savolainen, 387–402. Helsinki: Finnish Folklore Society.

Cai, Shenshen. 2016. "A Culture Hero: *Xiangsheng* (Crosstalk) Performer Guo Degang." *Asian Theatre Journal* 33 (1): 82–103.

Cai, Shenshen, and Emily Dunn. 2020. *Xiangsheng and the Emergence of Guo Degang in Contemporary China*. Singapore: Palgrave MacMillan.

Chen, Ping. 2004. *Modern Chinese: History and Sociolinguistics*. Cambridge: Cambridge University Press.

Chos bstan rgyal. 2014. "Following the Herds: Rhythms of Tibetan Pastoral Life in A mdo." *Asian Highlands Perspectives* 32:1–212.

Clarke, G. E. 1990. "Ideas of Merit (Bsod-nams) Virtue (Dge-ba), Blessing (Byin-rlabs) and Material Prosperity (Rten-'brel) in Highland Nepal." *Journal of the Anthropological Society of Oxford* 21 (2): 165–84.

Clothey, Rebecca, and Elena McKinlay. 2012. "A Space for the Possible: Globalization and English Language Learning of Tibetan Students in China." *Asian Highlands Perspectives* 21:7–32.

Cooke, Susette. 2008a. "Becoming and Unbecoming Tu: Nation, Nationality and Exilic Agency in the People's Republic of China." *Critical Studies* 30 (1): 33–56.

———. 2008b. "Surviving State and Society in Northwest China: The Hui Experience in Qinghai Province under the PRC." *Journal of Muslim Minority Affairs* 28 (3): 401–20.

Cru, Josep. 2018. "Micro-level Language Planning and YouTube Comments: Destigmatizing Indigenous Languages through Rap Music." *Current Issues in Language Planning* 19 (4): 434–52.

Cüppers, Christoph, and Per K. Sørensen. 1998. *A Collection of Tibetan Proverbs and Sayings: Gems of Tibetan Wisdom and Wit*. Stuttgart: Franz Steiner Verlag.

Da Col, Giovanni. 2007. "The View from Somewhen: Events, Bodies, and the Perspective of Fortune around Khawa Karpo, a Tibetan Sacred Mountain in Yunnan Province." *Inner Asia* 9 (2): 215–35.

Dag yig 'di'i rtsom sgring tshan chung དག་ཡིག་འདིའི་རྩོམ་སྒྲིང་ཚན་ཆུང་།. 1979. *Dag yig gsar bgrigs* དག་ཡིག་གསར་བསྒྲིགས། (The new Dagyig dictionary). Ziling: Mtsho sngon mi rigs dpe skrun khang.

Dak Lhagyal. 2019. "'Linguistic Authority' in State-Society Interaction: Cultural Politics of Tibetan Education in China." *Discourse: Studies in the Cultural Politics of Education*. https://doi.org/10.1080/01596306.2019.1648239.

Davies, Christie. 2007. "Humour and Protest: Jokes under Communism." *International Review of Social History* 52 (Suppl. 15): 291–305.

Davis, Sara L. M. 1999. "Singers of Sipsongbanna: Folklore and Authenticity in Contemporary China." Unpublished PhD dissertation, University of Pennsylvania.

———. 2005. *Song and Silence: Ethnic Revival on China's Southwest Borders*. New York: Columbia University Press.

de Heering, Xenia. 2014. "Trouver les mots justes: Échos d'un témoignage écrit sur les années 1950 en Amdo (Tibet)." *Cahiers de littérature orale*, no. 75–76.

DeFrancis, John. 1984. *The Chinese Language: Fact and Fantasy*. Honolulu: University of Hawai'i Press.

Dégh, Linda. 2001. *Legend and Belief: Dialectics of a Folklore Genre*. Bloomington: Indiana University Press.

Denton, Kirk A. 2003. "Literature and Politics: Mao Zedong's Talks at the Yan'an Forum on Art and Literature." In *The Columbia Companion to Modern East Asian Literature*, edited by Joshua S. Mostow, 463–69. New York: Columbia University Press.

Dge 'dun chos 'phel དགེ་འདུན་ཆོས་འཕེལ།. (1926) 2017. *Bla brang la bskur ba'i ka rtsom* བླ་བྲང་ལ་བསྐུར་བའི་ཀ་རྩོམ། (Katsom to Labrang). http://tb.tibet.cn/tb/literature/sg/201801/t20180104_5319298.html.

Diemberger, Hildegard. 2007. "Festivals and Their Leaders: The Management of Tradition in the Mongolian/Tibetan Borderlands." In *The Mongolia-Tibet Interface: Opening New Research Terrains in Inner Asia*, edited by Uradyn E. Bulag and Hildegard Diemberger, 109–34. Leiden: Brill.

Dkon mchog dge legs. 2012. "China's Pastoral Development Policies and Tibetan Plateau Nomad Communities." In Dbang 'dus sgrol ma, Dkon mchog dge legs, Mgon po tshe ring, and Dpal ldan chos dbyings (CK Stuart and G. Roche, eds.), "Environmental Issues Facing Tibetan Pastoral Communities." *Asian Highlands Perspectives* 18:37–72.

Dkon mchog dge legs, Dpal ldan bkra shis, and Kevin Stuart. 1999. "Tibetan Tricksters." *Asian Folklore Studies* 58 (1): 5–30.

Don grub rgyal དོན་གྲུབ་རྒྱལ།. (1980) 1997. "Bod yig slob pa བོད་ཡིག་སློབ་པ།" (Studying Tibetan). In *Dpal Don grub rgyal gyi gsung 'bum* དཔལ་དོན་གྲུབ་རྒྱལ་གྱི་གསུང་འབུམ། (The collected works of Don grub rgyal), 6:43–55. Beijing: Mi rigs dpe skrun khang.

———. 1982. "Sad kyis bcom pa'i me tog སད་ཀྱིས་བཅོམ་པའི་མེ་ཏོག" (A blighted flower, part 1). *Sbrang char* སྦྲང་ཆར། (Light rain), no. 4, 6–28.

———. 1983. "Sad kyis bcom pa'i me tog" (A blighted flower, part 2). *Sbrang char* (Light rain), no. 1, 8–29, 47.

———. (1984) 1997. "Rkang lam phra mo རྐང་ལམ་ཕྲ་མོ" (The narrow footpath). In *Dpal Don grub rgyal gyi gsung 'bum* (The collected works of Don grub rgyal), 6:1–7. Beijing: Mi rigs dpe skrun khang.

———. 1997. "Sprul Sku སྤྲུལ་སྐུ" (The tulku). In *Dpal Don grub rgyal gyi gsung 'bum* (The collected works of Don grub rgyal), 2:119–55. Beijing: Mi rigs dpe skrun khang.

Dong, Jie. 2009. "'Isn't It Enough to Be a Chinese Speaker': Language Ideology and Migrant Identity Construction in a Public Primary School in Beijing." *Language and Communication* 29 (2): 115–26. https://doi.org/10.1016/j.langcom.2009.01.002.

Donyol Dondrup and Charlene Makley. 2018. "'The Body Hair That Grows on the Head': Menla Kyap's 'Views on Hair and Hairstyles' (2009)." *Ateliers d'Anthropologie* 45:1–17.

Dor zhi Gdong drug snyem blo དོར་ཞི་གདོང་དྲུག་སྙེམ་བློ།. 1997. "Rjes dran gyi gtam pad dkar chun po རྗེས་དྲན་གྱི་གཏམ་པད་དཀར་ཆུན་པོ" (A white lotus wreath of recollections). In *Dpal don grub rgyal gyi gsung 'bum* དཔལ་དོན་གྲུབ་རྒྱལ་གྱི་གསུང་འབུམ། 3, edited by Phur kho, Mgon po Dar rgyas, et al. Beijing: Mi rigs dpe skrun khang.

Dpal ldan Bkra shis. 2016. "Amdo Tibetan Language: An Introduction to Normative Amdo Tibetan." *Asian Highlands Perspectives* 43.

Dreyfus, Georges B. 2008. "What Is Debate For? The Rationality of Tibetan Debates and the Role of Humor." *Argumentation* 22 (1): 43–58.

Du, Fachun. 2012. "Ecological Resettlement of Tibetan Herders in Sanjiangyuan: A Case Study of Madoi County in Qinghai." *Nomadic Peoples* 16 (1): 116–33.

Du, Wenwei. 1998. "*Xiaopin*: Chinese Theatrical Skits as Both Creatures and Critics of Commercialism." *China Quarterly* 154 (June): 382–99.

Duara, Prasenjit. 1995. *Rescuing History from the Nation: Questioning Narratives of Modern China*. Chicago: University of Chicago Press.

Dundes, Alan. 1971. "Laughter behind the Iron Curtain: A Sample of Romanian Political Jokes." *Ukrainian Quarterly* 27 (1): 50–59.

Duranti, Alessandro. 1986. "The Audience as Co-Author: An Introduction." *Text* 6 (3): 239–47.

Dwyer, Arienne M. 2007. "Syncretism in Salar Love Songs." In *Cultural Changes in the Turkic World*, edited by Filiz Kiral, Barbara Pusch, Claus Schönig, and Arus Yumrul, 147–60. Würzberg: Ergon.

———. 2013. "Tibetan as a Dominant Sprachbund Language: Its Interactions with Neighboring Languages." In *The Third International Conference on Tibetan Language*, vol. 1, edited by Gray Tuttle, Karma Dare, and Jonathan Wilber, 259–302. New York: Trace Foundation.

Egaña, Andoni. 2007. "The Process of Creating Improvised *Bertsos*." *Oral Tradition* 22 (2): 117–42.

Ekvall, Robert B. 1964a. "Peace and War among the Tibetan Nomads." *American Anthropologist* 66 (5): 1119–48.

———. 1964b. *Religious Observances in Tibet: Patterns and Function*. Chicago: University of Chicago Press.

Falassi, Aldessandro, ed. 1987. *Time out of Time: Essays on the Festival*. Albuquerque: University of New Mexico Press.

Fischer, Andrew Martin. 2008. "'Population Invasions' versus Urban Exclusion in the Tibetan Areas of Western China." *Population and Development Review* 34 (4): 631–62.

———. 2009. "Educating for Exclusion in Western China: Structural and Institutional Dimensions of Conflict in the Tibetan Areas of Qinghai and Tibet." CRISE Working Paper No. 69.

———. 2013. *The Disempowered Development of Tibet in China: A Study in the Economics of Marginalization*. Lanham, MD: Lexington Books.

Foley, John Miles. 1995. *The Singer of Tales in Performance*. Bloomington: Indiana University Press.

Frangville, Vanessa. 2016. "Pema Tseden's *The Search*: the Making of a Minor Cinema." *Journal of Chinese Cinemas* 10 (2): 106–19.

Gaerrang, Kabzung. 2017. "Tibetan Buddhism, Wetland Transformation, and Environmentalism in Tibetan Pastoral Areas of Western China." *Conservation and Society* 15 (1): 14–23.

Gao, Jia, and Peter C. Pugsley. 2008. "Utilizing Satire in Post-Deng Chinese Politics: Zhao Benshan Xiaopin vs. the Falun Gong." *China Information* 22 (3): 451–76.

Gates, Henry Louis. 1983. "The 'Blackness of Blackness': A Critique of the Sign and the Signifying Monkey." *Critical Inquiry* 9 (4): 685–723.

Gayley, Antonia Hollis. 2016. "Controversy over Buddhist Ethical Reform: A Secular Critique of Clerical Authority in the Tibetan Blogosphere." *Himalaya: The Journal of the Association for Nepal and Himalayan Studies* 36 (1): 9.

Gcod pa don grub གཅོད་པ་དོན་གྲུབ། and Chab 'gag rta mgrin ཆབ་འགག་རྟ་མགྲིན།, eds. 2000. "Hor gling g.yul 'gyed stod cha ཧོར་གླིང་གཡུལ་འགྱེད་སྟོད་ཆ།" (The war of Hor and Gling, vol. 1). In *Gling sgrung gces btus* གླིང་སྒྲུང་གཅེས་བཏུས། (Selections of the myth of Gling). Pecin [Beijing]: Mi rigs dpe skrun khang.

Gdugs dkar tshe ring གདུགས་དཀར་ཚེ་རིང་།. 2007. *Bod rig pa'i dpyad 'bras thor bu* བོད་རིག་པའི་དཔྱད་འབྲས་ཐོར་བུ། (Some findings of Tibetology). Pe cin [Beijing]: Mi rigs dpe skrun khang.

Gershon, Ilana. 2010. "Media Ideologies: An Introduction." *Journal of Linguistic Anthropology* 20 (2): 283–93.

Gladney, Dru C. 1987a. "Muslim Tombs and Ethnic Folklore: Charters for Hui Identity." *Journal of Asian Studies* 46 (3): 495–532.

———. 1987b. "Qing Zhen: A Study of Ethnoreligious Identity among Hui Muslim Communities in China." PhD dissertation, University of Washington.

———. 1994. "Representing Nationality in China: Refiguring Majority/Minority Identities." *Journal of Asian Studies* 53 (1): 93–123.

———. 1996. "Relational Alterity: Constructing Dungan (Hui), Uyghur, and Kazakh Identities across China, Central Asia, and Turkey." *History and Anthropology* 9 (2): 445–77.

———. 2004. *Dislocating China: Muslims, Minorities, and Other Subaltern Subjects*. Chicago: University of Chicago Press.

Goffman, Erving. 1981. *Forms of Talk*. Philadelphia: University of Pennsylvania Press.

Goldstein, Melvyn C. 1982. "Lhasa Street Songs: Political and Social Satire in Traditional Tibet." *Tibet Journal* 7 (1): 56–66.

———. 1998. "Introduction." In *Buddhism in Contemporary Tibet: Religious Revival and Cultural Identity*, edited by Melvyn C. Goldstein and Matthew T. Kapstein, 1–14. Berkeley: University of California Press.

———, ed. 2001. *The New Tibetan-English Dictionary of Modern Tibetan*. Berkeley: University of California Press.

Goldstein, Melvyn C., and Cynthia M. Beall. 1989. "The Impact of China's Reform Policy on the Nomads of Western Tibet." *Asian Survey* 29 (6): 619–41.

Goodman, David S. G. 2004a. "The Campaign to 'Open Up the West': National,

Provincial-Level and Local Perspectives." *China Quarterly* 178 (June): 317–34.

———. 2004b. "Qinghai and the Emergence of the West: Nationalities, Communal Interaction and National Integration." *China Quarterly* 178 (June): 379–99.

———. 2008. "Exile as Nationality: The Salar of Northwest China." *Critical Studies* 30 (1): 57–79.

Gorter, Durk, ed. 2006. *Linguistic Landscape: A New Approach to Multilingualism*. Buffalo, NY: Multilingual Matters.

Grewal, Anup. 2016. "Contested Tibetan Landscapes in the Film of Pema Tseden." *Journal of Chinese Cinemas* 10 (2): 135–49.

Griswold, Wendy. 2000. *Bearing Witness: Readers, Writers, and the Novel in Nigeria*. Princeton, NJ: Princeton University Press.

Gunn, Edward. 2005. *Rendering the Regional: Local Language in Contemporary Chinese Media*. Honolulu: University of Hawai'i Press.

Guo, Yingjie. 2004. *Cultural Nationalism in Contemporary China: The Search for National Identity under Reform*. London: RoutledgeCurzon.

Gyatso, Janet. 2011. "Introduction: Moments of Tibetan Modernity: Methods and Assumptions." In *Mapping the Modern in Tibet*, edited by Gray Tuttle, 1–44. Andiast, Switzerland: International Institute for Tibetan and Buddhist Studies.

Hanks, William F. 1987. "Discourse Genres in a Theory of Practice." *American Ethnologist* 14 (4): 668–92.

Hansen, Mette Halskov. 1999. *Lessons in Being Chinese: Minority Education and Ethnic Identity in Southwest China*. Seattle: University of Washington Press.

Harrell, Stevan. 1996. "The Nationalities Question and the Prmi Prblem." In *Negotiating Ethnicities in China and Taiwan*, edited by Melissa J. Brown, 274–96. Berkeley: Institute of East Asian Studies, University of California, Berkeley.

———. 2001. *Ways of Being Ethnic in Southwest China*. Studies on Ethnic Groups in China. Seattle: University of Washington Press.

Harris, Claire. 1999. *In the Image of Tibet: Tibetan Painting after 1959*. London: Reaktion.

Harris-Lopez, Trudier. 2003. "Genre." In *Eight Words for the Study of Expressive Culture*, edited by Burt Feintuch, 99–120. Urbana: University of Illinois Press.

Hartley, Lauran. 1999. "Themes of Tradition and Change in Modern Tibetan Literature." *Lungta* 12 (Summer): 29–44.

———. 2002. "'Inventing Modernity' in A Mdo: Views on the Role of Traditional Culture in a Developing Society." In *Amdo Tibetans in Transition: Social Change in the Post-Mao Era*, edited by Toni Huber, 1–25. Leiden: Brill.

———. 2003. "Contextually Speaking: Tibetan Literary Discourse and Social Change in the People's Republic of China (1980–2000)." PhD dissertation, Indiana University.

———. 2005. "Tibetan Publishing in the Early Post-Mao Period." *Cahiers d'Extreme-Asie* 15:231–52.

———. 2007. "Ascendancy of the Term *Rtsom-rig* in Tibetan Literary Discourse." In *Contemporary Tibetan Literary Studies*, edited by Steven J. Venturino, 7–22. Leiden: Brill.

Hartley, Lauran R., and Patricia Schiaffini-Vedani, eds. 2008. *Modern Tibetan Literature and Social Change*. Durham, NC: Duke University Press.

Hayes, Jack Patrick. 2014. *A Change in Worlds on the Sino-Tibetan Borderlands: Politics, Economies, and Environments in Northern Sichuan*. Lanham, MD: Lexington Books.

He, Chengzhou. 2008. "Women and the Search for Modernity: Rethinking Modern Chinese Drama." *Modern Language Quarterly* 69 (1): 45–60. https://doi.org/10.1215/00267929-2007-024.

Hearne, Joanne. "Indigenous Animation: Educational Programming, Narrative Interventions, and Children's Cultures." In *Global Indigenous Media: Cultures, Poetics, and Politics*, edited by Pamela Wilson and Michelle Stewart, 89–108. Durham, NC: Duke University Press.

Heinrich, Patrick. 2012. *The Making of Monolingual Japan: Language Ideology and Japanese Modernity*. Buffalo, NY: Multilingual Matters.

Henrion-Dourcy, Isabelle. 2017a. "The Art of the Tibetan Actor: *A lce lha mo* in the Gaze of Western Performance Theories." *Revue d'etudes tibétaines*, no. 40 (July), 179–215.

———. 2017b. "Studying the Tibetan Performing Arts: A Bibliographic Introduction (1986–2017)." *Revue d'etudes tibétaines*, no. 40 (July), 5–54.

High Peaks Pure Earth. 2020. "'City Tibetan Is Hip-hop and Also an Attitude'—An Interview with Rapper Uncle Buddhist." May 20, 2020. https://highpeakspureearth.com/city-tibetan-is-hip-hop-and-also-an-attitude-an-interview-with-rapper-uncle-buddhist.

Hill, Jane, and Kenneth C. Hill. 1980. "Mixed Grammar, Purist Grammar, and Language Attitudes in Modern Nahuatl." *Language in Society* 9 (3): 321–48.

Hillman, Ben. 2004. "The Rise of the Community in Rural China: Village Politics, Cultural Identity and Religious Revival in a Hui Hamlet." *China Journal* 51 (January): 53–73.

Hofer, Theresia. 2017. "Is Lhasa Tibetan Sign Language Emerging, Endangered, or Both?" *International Journal of the Sociology of Language*, no. 245, 113–45.

Horlemann, Bianca. 2002. "Modernization Efforts in Mgo log: A Chronicle, 1970–2002." In *Amdo Tibetans in Transition: Society and Culture in the Post-Mao Era*, edited by Toni Huber, 141–70. Leiden: Brill.

Hortsang Jigmé. 2008. "Tibetan Literature in the Diaspora." In *Modern Tibetan Literature and Social Change*, edited by Lauran R. Hartley and Patricia Schiaffini-Vedani, 281–300. Durham, NC: Duke University Press.

Hou, Baolin 侯宝林, ed. 1980. *Hou Baolin xiangsheng xuan* 侯宝林相声选 (Hou Baolin's selected crosstalks). Beijing: Renmin Wenxue Chubanshe.

Hou, Baolin 侯宝林, and Baokun Xue 薛宝琨, eds. 1981. *Xiangsheng yishu lun* 相声艺术论 (On the art of crosstalk). Harbin: Heilong Jiang Renmin Chubanshe.

Hou, Baolin 侯宝林, Baokun Xue 薛宝琨, Jingshou Wang 汪景寿, and Wangpeng Li 李万鹏, eds. 2011. *Xiangsheng suyuan* 相声溯源 (Tracing the sources of crosstalk). Beijing: Zhonghua Shuju.

Hu Jun. 2016. "Wang Min, Zhuoma Yongcuo zhapianzui yishen xingshi juepan shu 王敏卓玛用错诈骗罪一审刑事绝判书" (Judgment in the first fraud trial of Wang Min and Zhuoma Yongcuo). *Zhongguo caipan wenshu wang* 中国裁判文书网 (Chinese judgment documents web), http://wenshu.court.gov.cn/content/content?DocID=feebec25-dfae-4d6c-b93f-b6aa9f8ed159&KeyWord=&from=timeline&isappinstalled=0, accessed DATE (link no longer active).

Hu, Shih. 2013. "The Greatest Event in Life: A Farce in One Act." In *English Writings of Hu Shih: Literature and Society*, edited by Chi-p'ing Chou, 1:33–37. China Academic Library. Berlin: Foreign Language Teaching and Research Publishing.

Huber, Toni. 2002. "Introduction: A Mdo and Its Modern Transition." In *Amdo Tibetans in Transition: Social Change in the Post-Mao Era*, edited by Toni Huber, xi–xxiii. Leiden: Brill.

Hyde, Lewis. 1998. *Trickster Makes This World: Mischief Myth, and Art*. New York: Farrar, Straus, and Giroux.

Inoue, Miyako. 2006. *Vicarious Language: Gender and Linguistic Modernity in Japan*. Berkeley: University of California Press.

Janhunen, Juha. 2004. "On the Hierarchy of Structural Convergence in the

Amdo Sprachbund." In *The Typology of Argument Structure and Grammatical Relations*, edited by Bernard Comrie, Pirkko Suihkonen, and Valery Solovyev, 72–74. Helsinki: John Benjamins.

———. 2005. "The Role of the Turkic Languages in the Amdo Sprachbund." In *Turks and Non-Turks: Studies on the History of Linguistic and Cultural Contacts*, edited by Marzanna Pomorska and Ewa Siemieniec-Gołaś. Studia Turcologica Cracoviensia 10, 113–22.

Ji, Xiaochun 纪小春. 2013. "Qinghai Zangyuwen chuanmei de xianzhuang ji fazhan 青海藏语文传媒的现状及发展" (The present condition and development of Tibetan media in Qinghai). *Qinghai shifan daxue minzu shifan xueyuan xuebao* 青海师范大学民族师范学院学报 (Journal of the Nationalities Teachers College of Qinghai Normal University) 24 (2): 46–50.

Jung, Carl G. 1968. *The Archetypes and the Collective Unconscious*. 2nd ed. Princeton, NJ: Princeton University Press.

Kaikkonen, Marja. 1990. "Laughable Propaganda: Modern Xiangsheng as Didactic Entertainment." PhD dissertation, Stockholm University.

Kapstein, Matthew. 2002. "The Tulku's Miserable Lot: Critical Voices from Eastern Tibet." In *Amdo Tibetans in Transition: Social Change in the Post-Mao Era*, edited by Toni Huber, 99–111. Leiden: Brill.

Khashem Gyal, dir. 2012. *Dpa' bo'i lung pa* དཔའ་བོའི་ལུང་པ། (The valley of heroes).

Kitta, Andrea. 2019. *The Kiss of Death: Contamination, Contagion, and Folklore*. Logan: Utah State University Press.

Kolås, Åshild. 1996. "Tibetan Nationalism: The Politics of Religion." *Journal of Peace Research* 33 (1): 51–66.

Kolås, Åshild, and Monika P. Thowsen. 2005. *On the Margins of Tibet: Cultural Survival on the Sino-Tibetan Frontier*. Seattle: University of Washington Press.

Kondro Tsering. 2012. "A Zorgay Tibetan Childhood/Min tibetanska barndom i Zorgay." Translated by Katrin Goldstein-Kyaga. *Asian Highlands Perspectives* 17 (1): 1–238.

Kongerslev, Marianne. 2020. "Enduring Laughter: Introduction to the Special Issue on Native and Indigenous Humor." *Studies in American Humor* 6 (2): 254–64.

Kroskrity, Paul V. 2000. *Regimes of Language: Ideologies, Polities, and Identities*. School of American Research Advanced Seminar Series. Santa Fe, NM: SAR Press.

Kunsang, Erik Pema, ed. 2003. *The Rangjung Yeshe Tibetan-English Dictionary of Buddhist Culture*, version 3. Boudhanath, Nepal: Rangjung Yeshe Publications.

Kuo, Kaiser. 2017. "Spurning China and Courting Russia: Trump's Dangerous Game." *The China Project*, January 5, 2017. https://thechinaproject.com/2017/01/05/spurning-china-courting-russia-trumps-dangerous-game-2.

Lama Jabb. 2011. "Singing the Nation: Modern Tibetan Music and National Identity." *Revue d'etudes tibétains*, no. 21 (October), 1–29.

———. 2015. *Oral and Literary Continuities in Tibetan: The Inescapable Nation*. Lanham, MD: Rowman and Littlefield.

———. 2020. "The Wandering Voice of Tibet: Life and Songs of Dubhe." *Life Writing* 17 (3): 387–409. https://doi.org/10.1080/14484528.2019.1680247.

Lamotte, Martin. 2014. "Rebels without a Pause: Hip-Hop and Resistance in the City." *International Journal of Urban and Regional Research* 38 (2): 686–94.

Landry, Rodrigue, and Richard Y. Bourhis. 1997. "Linguistic Landscape and Ethnolinguistic Vitality: An Empirical Study." *Journal of Language and Social Psychology* 16 (1): 23–49.

Lee, Haiyan. 2005. "Tears That Crumbled the Great Wall: The Archaeology of Feeling in the May Fourth Folklore Movement." *Journal of Asian Studies* 64 (1): 35–65.

Lee, Leo Ou-Fan. 2001. "Incomplete Modernity: Rethinking the May Fourth Intellectual Project." In *The Appropriation of Cultural Capital: China's May Fourth Project*, edited by Milena Dolezelová-Velingerová and Oldrich Král, 31–65. Cambridge, MA: Harvard University Press.

Leibold, James. 2007. *Reconfiguring Chinese Nationalism: How the Qing Frontier and Its Indigenes Became Chinese*. New York: Palgrave Macmillan.

Levin, Harry. 1987. *Playboys and Killjoys: An Essay on the Theory and Practice of Comedy*. Oxford: Oxford University Press.

Lha sde nyi ma tshe ring ལྷ་སྡེ་ཉི་མ་ཚེ་རིང་།. 2013. *A mdo'i dmangs khrod btags pa phyogs bsgrigs* ཨ་མདོའི་དམངས་ཁྲོད་བཏགས་པ་ཕྱོགས་བསྒྲིགས། (Collected Amdo folk btags pa). Lan gru [Lanzhou]: Kan su'u mi rigs dpe skrun khang.

Lhamo Pemba, comp. 1996. *Tibetan Proverbs*. Dharamsala: Library of Tibetan Works and Archives.

Li, Cheng. 2015. "Xi Jinping's Inner Circle (Part 4: The *Mishu* Cluster I)." *China Leadership Monitor*, no. 46 (March), 1–14.

Li, Chris Wen-Chao. 2004. "Conflicting Notions of Language Purity: The Interplay of Archaising, Ethographic, Reformist, Elitist and Xenophobic Purism in the Perception of Standard Chinese." *Language and Communication* 24 (2): 97–133.

Li, Jianglin. 2016. *Tibet in Agony: Lhasa 1959*. Translated by Susan Wilf. Cambridge, MA: Harvard University Press.

Limusishiden. 2011. "Muulsan Mongghul." *Asian Highlands Perspectives* 10:339–40.

Limusishiden and Jugui. 2010. "Ghalmadi Sgil Da Alog Xosuu: Ghuaisangni Durina Rogshdigu Mongghulni Adal" (Passions and colored sleeves: Mongghul lives in eastern Tibet]." Edited by CK Stuart, Gerald Roche, and Ramona Johnson. *Asian Highlands Perspectives* 7:1–322.

Limusishiden and Gerald Roche. 2017. *Long Narrative Songs from the Mongghul in Northeast Tibet: Texts in Mongghul, Chinese, and English*. London: Open Book Publishers.

Limusishiden and Charles Kevin Stuart. 2010. "Mongghulni Jilaguni Da Adal (Mongghul Memories and Lives)." *Asian Highlands Perspectives* 8:1–119.

Limusishiden, and Kevin Stuart. 1995. "*Larinbuda and Jiminsu*: A Monguor Tragedy." *Asian Theatre Journal* 12 (2): 221–63.

Link, Perry. 1984. "The Genie and the Lamp: Revolutionary Xiangsheng." In *Chinese Literature and Performing Arts in the People's Republic of China, 1949–1979*, 83–111. Berkeley: University of California Press.

———. 2010. "The Crocodile Bird: Xiangsheng in the Early 1950s." In *Dilemmas of Victory: The Early Years of the People's Republic of China*, edited by Jeremy Brown and Paul Pickowicz, 207–31. Cambridge, MA: Harvard University Press.

Litzinger, Ralph. 2000. *Other Chinas: The Yao and the Politics of National Belonging*. Durham, NC: Duke University Press.

Liu, Fei-wen. 2010. "Narrative, Genre, and Contextuality: The Nüshu-Transcribed Liang-Zhu Ballad in Rural South China." *Asian Ethnology* 69 (2): 241–64.

Liu, Hongtao, and Jiening Ruan. 2012. "Foreign Literature Education in China's Secondary Schools from 1919 to 1949." In *Perspectives on Teaching and Learning Chinese Literacy in China*, edited by Cynthia B. Leung and Jiening Ruan, 35–48. New York: Springer.

Liu, Jin. 2008. "Signifying the Local: Media Productions Rendered in Local Languages in Mainland China since 2000." PhD dissertation, Cornell University.

———. 2014. "Alternative Voice and Local Youth Identity in Chinese Local-Language Rap Music." *Positions: East Asia Cultures Critique* 22 (1): 263–92.

Lobsang Yongdan. 2011. "Tibet Charts the World: The Btsan po No mon han's *Detailed Description of the World*, an Early Major Scientific Work." In *Mapping the Modern in Tibet*, edited by Gray Tuttle, 73–134. Andiast, Switzerland: International Institute for Tibetan and Buddhist Studies.

Löhrer, Klaus. 2012–13. "The Quest for Aku Dönpa: The Master-Trickster from Tibet's Lhasa Region." Unpublished draft, IATS conference, https://www.academia.edu/37464978/The_Quest_for_Aku_D%C3%B6npa_The_Master_trickster_from_Tibets_Lhasa_Region_IATS_version.

Lopez Jr., Donald S. 2006. *The Madman's Middle Way: Reflections on Reality of the Tibetan Monk Gendun Chopel*. Chicago: University of Chicago Press.

Ma, Jianzhong, and Kevin Stuart. 1996. "'Stone Camels and Clear Springs': The Salar's Samarkand Origins." *Asian Folklore Studies* 55 (2): 287–98.

Ma, Quanlin, Wanxiang Ma, and Zhicheng Ma. 1993. "Salar Language Materials." Edited by Kevin Stuart. *Sino-Platonic Papers*, no. 43 (December), 1–72.

Ma Yide. 2015. "The Role of Consultative Democracy in a Constitutional System and the Rule of Law in China." *Social Sciences in China* 36 (4): 5–23.

Makley, Charlene. 1998. "The Power of the Drunk: Humor and Resistance in China's Tibet." *Linguistic Form and Social Action* 13 (1): 39–79.

———. 2007. *The Violence of Liberation: Gender and Tibetan Buddhist Revival in Post-Mao China*. Berkeley: University of California Press.

———. 2013a. "The Politics of Presence: Voice, Deity Possession, and Dilemmas of Development among Tibetans in the People's Republic of China." *Comparative Studies in Society and History* 55 (3): 666–700. https://doi.org/10.1017/S0010417513000285.

———. 2013b. "Reb Kong's Klu Rol and the Politics of Presence: Methodological Considerations." In *Monastic and Lay Traditions in North-Eastern Tibet*, edited by Yangdon Dhondup, Ulrich Pagel, and Geoffrey Samuel, 187–202. Leiden: Brill.

———. 2018. *The Battle for Fortune: State-Led Development, Personhood, and Power Among Tibetans in China*. Ithaca, NY: Cornell University Press.

Makley, Charlene, Keith Dede, Hua Kan, and Qingshan Wang. 1999. "The Amdo Dialect of Labrang." *Linguistics of the Tibeto-Burman Area* 22 (1): 97–100.

Mao Zedong 毛泽东. (1953) 1967. *Mao Zedong xuanji* 毛泽东选集 (Selected works of Mao Zedong), vol. 3. Shanghai: Renmin Chubanshe.

McDougall, Bonnie S. 1980. *Mao Zedong's "Talks at the Yan'an Conference on Literature and Art": A Translation of the 1943 Text with Commentary*. Ann Arbor: Center for Chinese Studies, University of Michigan.

Miller, Jeffrey S. 2000. *The Horror Spoofs of Abbot and Costello*. London: McFarland and Company.

Milroy, James. 2001. "Language Ideologies and the Consequences of Standardization." *Journal of Sociolinguistics* 5 (4): 530–55.

Mog chung phur kho མོག་ཆུང་ཕུར་ཁོ. 2010. *Pha mas bdag la 'di skad gsungs: A mdo'i mkhas dbang dang a mdo'i phal skad* ཕ་མས་བདག་ལ་འདི་སྐད་གསུངས། ཨ་མདོའི་མཁས་དབང་དང་ཨ་མདོའི་ཕལ་སྐད། (My parents spoke this language to me: Amdo's intellectuals and Amdo dialect). Beijing: Mi rigs dpe skrun khang.

———. 2013. "Bod kyi kha shags kyi phyi mo—phal skad brtsams chos 'Ja mchod' la rob tsam dpyad pa བོད་ཀྱི་ཁ་ཤགས་ཀྱི་ཕྱི་མོ—ཕལ་སྐད་བརྩམས་ཆོས་ཇ་མཆོད་ལ་རོབ་ཙམ་དཔྱད་པ།" (The first Tibetan comedic dialogue—A brief examination of the vernacular work *The Tea Libation*). In *Kha shags thos pa dga' skyed* ཁ་ཤགས་ཐོས་པ་དགའ་སྐྱེད། (Comedic dialogues produce joyful learning), edited by Mang tshogs sgyu rtsal rtsom sgrig khang, 186–222. Ziling: Mtsho sngon mi rigs dpe skrun khang.

Morcom, Anna. 2008. "Getting Heard in Tibet: Music, Media, and Markets." *Consumption Markets and Culture* 11 (4): 259–85.

———. 2018. "The Political Potency of Tibetan Identity in Pop Music and Dungle." *Himalaya: The Journal of Association for Nepal and Himalayan Studies* 38 (1): 127–44.

Moriarty, Máiréad, and Sari Pietikäinen. 2011. "Micro-Level Language Planning and Grass-Root Initiatives: A Case Study of Irish Language Comedy and Inari Sámi Rap." *Current Issues in Language Planning* 12 (3): 363–79.

Morson, Gary Saul, and Caryl Emerson. *Mikhail Bakhtin: Creation of a Prosaics*. Palo Alto, CA: Stanford University Press, 1990.

Moser, David. 1990. "Reflexivity in the Humor of Xiangsheng." *Chinoperl Papers* 15 (1): 45–68.

———. 2016. *A Billion Voices: China's Search for a Common Language*. Scorsby, Victoria, Australia: Penguin Books.

———. 2018. "Keeping the *Ci* in *Fengci*: A Brief History of the Chinese Verbal Art of *Xiangsheng*." In *Not Just a Laughing Matter*, The Humanities in Asia, vol. 5, edited by King-fai Tam and Sharon R. Wesoky. Singapore: Springer. https://doi.org/10.1007/978-981-10-4960-6_5.

Mu, Aili. 2004. "Two of Zhao Benshan's Comic Skits: Their Critical Implications in Contemporary China." *Concentric: Literary and Cultural Studies* 30 (2): 3–34.

Mullaney, Thomas S. 2004. "Introduction: 55 + 1 = 1 or the Strange Calculus of

Chinese Nationhood." *China Information* 18 (2): 197–205. https://doi.org/10.1177/0920203X04044684.

———. 2010. "Seeing for the State: The Role of Social Scientists in China's Ethnic Classification Project." *Asian Ethnicity* 11 (3): 325–42.

Mullen, Patrick B. 1978. *I Heard the Old Fishermen Say: Folklore of the Texas Gulf Coast.* Austin: University of Texas Press.

Norrick, Neal R. 2000. *Conversational Narrative: Storytelling in Everyday Talk.* Amsterdam: John Benjamins.

Noyes, Dorothy. 2009. "Tradition: Three Traditions." *Journal of Folklore Research* 46 (3): 233–68.

Ó Giolláin, Diarmuid. 2005. *Locating Irish Folklore: Tradition, Modernity, Identity.* Cork, Ireland: Cork University Press.

Oring, Elliot. 1992. *Jokes and Their Relations.* Lexington: University of Kentucky Press.

———. 2004. "Risky Business: Political Jokes under Repressive Regimes." *Western Folklore* 63 (3): 209–36.

Orofino, Giacomella. 2011. "The Long Voyage of a Trickster Story from Ancient Greece to Tibet." *AION: Annali dell'Istituto Universitario Orientale di Napoli* 33:101–16.

Ortiz, Renato. 1996. *Otro territorio: Ensayos sobre el mundo contemporáneo,* translated by Ada Solari. Buenos Aires: Universidad Nacional de Quilmes.

Osumare, Halifu. 2007. *The Africanist Aesthetic in Global Hip-Hop: Power Moves.* New York: Palgrave Macmillan.

Pad ma tshe brtan, dir. 2005. *Lhing 'jags kyi ma Ni rdo 'bum* ཞིང་འཇགས་ཀྱི་མ་ཎི་རྡོ་འབུམ། (The Silent Holy Stones).

Pagliai, Valentina. 2009. "The Art of Dueling with Words: Toward a New Understanding of Verbal Duels across the World." *Oral Tradition* 24 (1): 61–88.

Peacock, Christopher. 2019. "Introduction." In *The Handsome Monk and Other Stories,* by Tsering Döndrup, translated by Christopher Peacock, 1–16. New York: Columbia University Press.

Perks, Liss Glebatis. 2008. "A Sketch Comedy of Errors: *Chapelle's Show,* Stereotypes, and Viewers." PhD dissertation, University of Texas at Austin.

Pema Bhum. 2001 *Dran tho smin drug ske 'khyog* དྲན་ཐོ་སྨིན་དྲུག་སྐེ་འཁྱོག། (Six stars with a crooked neck). Dharamsala: Tibet Times.

———. 2006. *Dran tho Rdo ring ma* དྲན་ཐོ་རྡོ་རིང་མ། (Remembering Rdo rje tshe ring). Dharamsala: Tibet Times.

———. 2008. "'Heartbeat of a New Generation' Revisited." In *Modern Tibetan*

Literature and Social Change, edited by Lauran R. Hartley and Patricia Schiaffini-Vedani, 148–72. Durham, NC: Duke University Press.

———. 2017. "How Dorje Tsering Saved Tibetan." *Words without Borders: The Online Magazine for International Literature*, July 1. https://www.wordswithoutborders.org/article/july-2017-divided-countries-how-dorje-tsering-saved-tibetan-pema-bhum.

Phuntshog Tashi, and Patricia Schiaffini. 2006. "Realism, Humor, and Social Commitment: An Interview." *Manoa* 18 (1): 118–24.

Phur ba ཕུར་བ།. 1993. *A mdo'i kha shags* ཨ་མདོའི་ཁ་ཤགས། (Amdo crosstalks). Ziling: Mtsho sngon mi rigs dpe skrun khang.

Pirie, Fernanda. 2006. "Legal Complexity on the Tibetan Plateau." *Journal of Legal Pluralism*, no. 53–54, 77–100.

———. 2009. "The Horse with Two Saddles: Tamxhwe in Modern Golok." *Asian Highlands Perspectives* 1:213–37.

———. 2012. "Legal Dramas on the Amdo Grasslands: Abolition, Transformation or Survival." In *Revisiting Rituals in a Changing Tibetan World*, edited by Katia Buffetrille, 83–107. Leiden: Brill.

———. 2013. "The Limits of the State: Coercion and Consent in Chinese Tibet." *Journal of Asian Studies* 72 (1): 69–89.

Postiglione, Gerard A. 1992. "China's National Minorities and Educational Change." *Journal of Contemporary Asia* 22 (1): 20–44.

———, ed. 1999. *China's National Minority Education: Culture, Schooling, and Development*. New York: Falmer Press.

———, ed. 2006. *Education and Social Change in China: Inequality in a Market Economy*. London: M. E. Sharpe.

———. 2008. "Making Tibetans in China: The Educational Challenges of Harmonious Multiculturalism." *Educational Review* 60 (1): 1–20.

Ptackova, Jarmila. 2013. "The Great Opening of the West Development Strategy and Its Impact on the Life and Livelihood of Tibetan Pastoralists: Sedentarisation of Tibetan Pastoralists in Zeku County as a Result of Socioeconomic and Environmental Development Projects in Qinghai Province, P. R. China." PhD dissertation, Humboldt University, Berlin.

———. 2019. "Traditionalization as a Response to State-Induced Development in Rural Tibetan Areas of Qinghai, PRC." *Central Asian Survey* 38 (3): 417–31.

Pu Wencheng 蒲文成, ed. 1990. *Gan-Qing Zangchuan fojiao siyuan* 甘青藏传佛教寺院 (Tibetan Buddhist monasteries of Qinghai and Gansu). Xining: Qinghai Renmin Chubanshe.

Rabaka, Reiland. 2013. *The Hip-Hop Movement: From R&B and the Civil Rights Movement to Rap and the Hip-Hop Generation*. Lanham, MD: Lexington Books.

Raheja, M. 2015. "Visual Sovereignty." In *Native Studies Keywords*, edited by Stephanie Nohelani Teves, Andrea Smith, and Michelle Raheja, 25–34. Tucson: University of Arizona Press.

Ramble, Charles. 1995. "Gaining Ground: Representations of Territory in Bon and Tibetan Popular Tradition." *Tibet Journal* 20 (1): 83–124.

Ramsey, S. Robert. 1992. *The Languages of China*. Princeton, NJ: Princeton University Press.

Rdo grags, dir. 2008. *Kha sang gi gtam rgyud* ཁ་སང་གི་གཏམ་རྒྱུད། (Yesterday's story).

Rdo rje tshe brtan. 2013. "A Tewo Tibetan Childhood." *Asian Highlands Perspectives* 23:1–150.

Rea, Christopher. 2015. *The Age of Irreverence: A New History of Laughter in China*. Berkeley: University of California Press.

Rea, Christopher, and Nicolai Volland. 2008. "Comic Visions of Modern China: Introduction." *Modern Chinese Literature and Culture* 20 (2): v–xviii.

Reynolds, Jermay J. 2012. "Language Variation and Change in an Amdo Tibetan Village: Gender, Education, and Resistance." PhD dissertation, Georgetown University.

Rezaei, Afsane. 2016. "'The Superman in a Turban': Political Jokes in the Iranian Social Media." *New Directions in Folklore* 14 (1/2): 89–132.

Rinjing Dorje. 1997. *Tales of Uncle Tompa: The Legendary Rascal of Tibet*. New York: Station Hills Arts/Barrytown.

Robin, Françoise. 2007. "Stories and History: The Emergence of Historical Fiction in Contemporary Tibet." In *Contemporary Tibetan Literary Studies*, edited by Steven J. Venturino, 23–42. Leiden: Brill.

———. 2008. "'Oracles and Demons' in Tibetan Literature Today: Representations of Religion in Tibetan-Medium Fiction." In *Modern Tibetan Literature and Social Change*, edited by Lauran R. Hartley and Patricia Schiaffini-Vedani, 148–70. Durham, NC: Duke University Press.

———. 2014a. "The Increasing Presence in Tibetan Poetry and Films of the Disappearing Herders' Black Tent." Keynote at the 2014 Himalayan Studies Conference, Yale University. https://www.youtube.com/watch?v=nIX3AVJ3Jog.

———. 2014b. "Streets, Slogans and Screens: New Paradigms for the Defense of Tibetan Language." In *On the Fringes of the Harmonious Society: Tibetans and Uyghurs in Socialist China*, edited by Trine Brox and Idilkó Bellér-Hann, 209–34. Copenhagen: Nordic Institute of Asian Studies Press.

Roche, Gerald. 2011. "Nadun: Ritual and the Dynamics of Cultural Diversity in Northwest China's Hehuang Region." PhD dissertation, Griffith University, Australia.

———. 2014. "Flows and Frontiers: Landscape and Cultural Dynamics on the Northeast Tibetan Plateau." *Asia Pacific Journal of Anthropology* 15 (1): 1–25.

———. 2016. "The Tibetanization of Henan's Mongols: Ethnicity and Assimilation on the Sino-Tibetan Frontier." *Asian Ethnicity* 17 (1): 128–49.

———. 2020. "The Alphabetic Order of Things: The Language of Place and the Place of Language in Tibetan Song." In *Presence through Sound: Music and Place in East Asia*, edited by Howard Keith and Catherine Ingram, 72–86. New York: Routledge.

Roche, Gerald, and Lugyal Bum. 2018. "Language Revitalization of Tibetan." In *Routledge Handbook of Language Revitalization*, edited by Leanne Hinton, Leena Huss, and Gerald Roche, 417–26.

Roche, Gerald, and Hiroyuki Suzuki. 2018. "Tibet's Minority Languages: Diversity and Endangerment." *Modern Asian Studies* 52 (4): 1–52.

Roche, Gerald, and Xiangcheng Wen. 2013. "Modernist Iconoclasm, Resilience, and Divine Power among the Mangghuer of the Northeast Tibetan Plateau." *Asian Ethnology* 72 (1): 85–117.

Rossi, Donatella. 1992. "Some Notes on the Tibetan Amdo Love Songs." In *Tibetan Studies: Proceedings of the 5th Seminar of the International Association for Tibetan Studies, Narita 1989*, edited by Ihara Shoren and Yamaguchi Zuiho, 705–9. Narita: Naritasan Shinshoji.

Rwa se dkon mchog rgya mtsho ར་སེ་དཀོན་མཆོག་རྒྱ་མཚོ།. 1996. "A khu bstan pavi byung bar thog mavi bsam gzhigs ཨ་ཁུ་བསྟན་པའི་བྱུང་བར་ཐོག་མའི་བསམ་གཞིགས།" (Thoughts on the origins of A khu bstan pa). *Gangs ljongs rig gnas* གངས་ལྗོངས་ རིག་གནས། (Tibetan culture) 30:92–96.

Sa mtsho skyid and Gerald Roche. 2011. "Purity and Fortune in Phug Sde Tibetan Village Rituals." *Asian Highlands Perspectives* 10:231–84.

Sacks, Harvey. 1992. *Lectures on Conversation*. Oxford: Blackwell.

Sandman, Erika, and Camille Simon. 2016. "Tibetan as a 'Model Language' in the Amdo Sprachbund: Evidence from Salar and Wutun." *Journal of South Asian Languages and Linguistics* 3 (1): 85–122.

Sangs rgyas bkra shis, Qi Huimin, and CK Stuart. 2015. "Being Anything and

Going Anywhere: An A mdo Tibetan Auto-song-ography." *Asian Highlands Perspectives* 39:1–158.

Sangye Gyatso (Gangzhun). 2008. "Modern Tibetan Literature and the Rise of Writer Coteries." In *Modern Tibetan Literature and Social Change*, edited by Lauran R. Hartley and Patricia Schiaffini-Vedani, 263–80. Durham, NC: Duke University Press.

Schein, Louisa. 1999. "Performing Modernity." *Cultural Anthropology* 14 (3): 361–95.

Schweig, Meredith. 2014. "Hoklo Hip-Hop: Resignifying Rap as Local Narrative Tradition in Taiwan." *CHINOPERL: Journal of Chinese Oral and Performing Literature* 33 (1): 37–59.

Scott, James C. 1985. *Weapons of the Weak: Everyday Forms of Peasant Resistance*. New Haven, CT: Yale University Press.

———. 1990. *Domination and the Arts of Resistance: Hidden Transcripts*. New Haven, CT: Yale University Press.

Seeberg, Vilma. 2008. "Girls First! Promoting Early Education in Tibetan Areas of China, a Case Study." *Educational Review* 60 (1): 51–68.

Seitel, Peter. 1999. *The Powers of Genre: Interpreting Haya Oral Literature*. Oxford: Oxford University Press.

Seizer, Susan. 1997. "Jokes, Gender, and Discursive Distance on the Tamil Popular Stage." *American Ethnologist* 24 (1): 62–90.

Shakya, Tsering W. 1993. "Whither the Tsampa Eaters?" *Himal* 6 (5): 8–11.

———. 1994. "Politicization and the Tibetan Language." In *Resistance and Reform in Tibet*, edited by Robert Barnett and Shirin Akiner, 157–65. Bloomington: Indiana University Press.

———. 2000. "The Waterfall and Fragrant Flowers: The Development of Tibetan Literature Since 1950." *Manoa* 12 (2): 28–40.

———. 2008. "The Development of Modern Tibetan Literature in the People's Republic of China in the 1980s." In *Modern Tibetan Literature and Social Change*, edited by Lauran R. Hartley and Patricia Schiaffini-Vedani, 61–85. Durham, NC: Duke University Press.

Shohamy, Elana, and Durk Gorter, eds. 2009. *Linguistic Landscape: Expanding the Scenery*. New York: Routledge.

Shokdung. 2016. *The Division of Heaven and Earth: On Tibet's Peaceful Revolution*, translated by Matthew Akester. London: Oxford University Press.

Shugart, Helene A. 2001. "Parody as Subversive Performance: Denaturalizing

Gender and Reconstituting Desire in *Ellen*." *Text and Performance Quarterly* 21 (2): 95–113.

Shuman, Amy. 1986. *Storytelling Rights: The Uses of Oral and Written Texts by Urban Adolescents*. Cambridge: Cambridge University Press.

Si Hongxia and Li Xiaohua. 2013. "Use of Language in Radio and Television Broadcasting." In *The Language Situation in China, Volume 1, 2006–2007*, edited by Li Yuming, 85–96. Berlin: De Gruyter.

Sichuan Sheng Minjian Wenyi Yanjiu Hui 四川省民间文艺研究会, ed. 1980. *A kou dengba de gushi* 啊叩登巴的故事 (Stories of Uncle Tonpa). Chengdu: Sichuan Minzu Chubanshe.

Silverstein, Michael. 1979. "Language Structure and Language Ideology." In *The Elements: A Parasession on Linguistic Units and Levels, April 20–21, 1979: Including Papers from the Conference on Non-Slavic Languages of the USSR, April 18, 1979*, edited by Paul R. Clyne, William F. Hanks, and Carol L. Hofbauer, 193–247. Chicago: Chicago Linguistic Society.

———. 1996. "Monoglot Standard in America: Standardization and Metaphors of Linguistic Hegemony." In *The Matrix of Language: Contemporary Linguistic Anthropology*, edited by Donald Lawrence Brenneis and Ronald K. S. MacAulay, 284–306. Boulder, CO: Westview Press.

Slater, Keith W. 2003. *A Grammar of Mangghuer: A Mongolic Language of China's Qinghai-Gansu Sprachbund*. Curzon Asian Linguistics Series 2. London: Routledge Curzon.

Sman bla skyabs སྨན་བླ་སྐྱབས།. 1985. *Sgyu rtsal pa* སྒྱུ་རྩལ་པ། (The artist). *Mtsho sngon mang tshogs sgyu rtsal* མཚོ་སྔོན་མང་ཚོགས་སྒྱུ་རྩལ། (Qinghai folk arts) 1 (1985): 70–75.

———. 1989. *Sgyu rtsal pa* སྒྱུ་རྩལ་པ། (The artist). Beijing: Zhongyang minzu chuban she yinxiang bu.

———. 1990. *Kha shags snying bsdus* ཁ་ཤགས་སྙིང་བསྡུས། (Selected comedic dialogues). Xining: Qinghai Kunlun Yinxiang Chubanshe.

———. 1993a. *Lhasar 'gro* ལྷ་སར་འགྲོ། (Going to Lhasa). Xining: Qinghai Kunlun Yinxiang Chubanshe.

———. 1993b. *'Tshol* འཚོལ། (Searching). Xining: Xihai Minzu Yinxiang Chubanshe.

———. 1995. *Brag ri'i sras mo* བྲག་རིའི་སྲས་མོ། (Princess of the stone mountain). Lanzhou: Kansu mi rigs dpe skrun khang.

———. 1996a. *Cang shes rta bshad* ཅང་ཤེས་རྟ་བཤད། (Horse speech). Xining: Xihai Minzu Yinxiang Chubanshe.

———. 1996b. *Ribong blo ldan* རི་བོང་བློ་ལྡན། (The clever rabbit). Xining: Xihai Minzu Yinxiang Chubanshe.

———. 1996c. "Sems chung sde ba'i mna' ma སེམས་ཆུང་སྡེ་བའི་མནའ་མ།" (Careful Village's bride). In *Ru sde khra mo* རུ་སྡེ་ཁྲ་མོ། (The colorful nomad camp). Ziling: Nub mtsho mi rigs sgra brnyan par skrun khang. Audiocassette.

———. 1996d. "Sems chung sde ba'i rkun ma སེམས་ཆུང་སྡེ་བའི་རྐུན་མ།" (Careful Village's thief). In *Ru sde khra mo* རུ་སྡེ་ཁྲ་མོ། (The colorful nomad camp). Ziling: Nub mtsho mi rigs sgra brnyan par skrun khang. Audiocassette.

———. 1996e. "Sems chung sde ba'i rtsod སེམས་ཆུང་སྡེ་བའི་རྩོད།" (Careful Village's grassland dispute). In *Ru sde khra mo* རུ་སྡེ་ཁྲ་མོ། (The colorful nomad camp). Ziling: Nub mtsho mi rigs sgra brnyan par skrun khang. Audiocassette.

———. 1996f. "Sems chung sde ba'i ston mo སེམས་ཆུང་སྡེ་བའི་སྟོན་མོ།" (Careful Village's wedding). In *Ru sde khra mo* རུ་སྡེ་ཁྲ་མོ། (The colorful nomad camp). Ziling: Nub mtsho mi rigs sgra brnyan par skrun khang. Audiocassette.

———. 2000. *Dpon po mnkhyen* དཔོན་པོ་མཁྱེན། (Please, wise leader). Ziling: Nub mtsho mi rigs sgra brnyan par skrun khang.

———. 2006a. "Gesar rta rdzi གེ་སར་རྟ་རྫི།" (Gesar's horse herder). In *Gser mdog gi pha sa* གསེར་མདོག་གི་ཕ་ས། (My golden homeland). Ziling: Nub mtsho mi Rigs sgra brnyan par skrun khang.

———. 2006b. *Gser mdog gi pha sa* གསེར་མདོག་གི་ཕ་ས། (My golden homeland). Ziling: Nub mtsho mi Rigs sgra brnyan par skrun khang.

———. 2006c. "Sems bde mgron khang སེམས་བདེ་མགྲོན་ཁང་།" (At Ease Hotel). In *Gser mdog gi pha sa* གསེར་མདོག་གི་ཕ་ས། (My golden homeland). Ziling: Nub mtsho mi Rigs sgra brnyan par skrun khang.

———. 2006d. "Sgo tshong སྒོ་ཚོང་།" (Door-to-door sales). In *Gser mdog gi pha sa* གསེར་མདོག་གི་ཕ་ས། (My golden homeland). Ziling: Nub mtsho mi Rigs sgra brnyan par skrun khang.

———. 2006e. "Skad gtong ba སྐད་གཏོང་བ།" (Sending a message). In *Gser mdog gi pha sa* གསེར་མདོག་གི་ཕ་ས། (My golden homeland). Ziling: Nub mtsho mi Rigs sgra brnyan par skrun khang.

———. 2006f. "Zur gnyis ཟུར་གཉིས།" (Twenty Cents). In *Gser mdog gi pha sa* གསེར་མདོག་གི་ཕ་ས། (My golden homeland). Ziling: Nub mtsho mi Rigs sgra brnyan par skrun khang.

———. 2010. *Rol mo pa dang gyer 'don pa* རོལ་མོ་པ་དང་གྱེར་འདོན་པ།" (The musician and reciter). Ziling: Minzu Yinxiang Chubanshe.

———. 2012. *Gser gyi skar tshoms—Sman bla skyabs kyi glu gzhas brtsams chos dgong tshogs* གསེར་གྱི་སྐར་ཚོམས། སྨན་བླ་སྐྱབས་ཀྱི་གླུ་གཞས་བརྩམས་ཆོས་དགོང་ཚོགས། (The golden constellation: An evening of Menla Jyab's musical works). Ziling: Minzu Yinxiang Chubanshe.

———. 2014. *Bod kyi na chung byis pa'i glu gzhas gzi yi phreng ba* བོད་ཀྱི་ན་ཆུང་བྱིས་པའི་གླུ་གཞས་གཟི་ཡི་ཕྲེང་བ། (Onyx prayer beads of Tibetan children's songs). Ziling: Minzu Yinxiang Chubanshe.

Sonam Tsering. 2016. "Introduction." In *The Division of Heaven and Earth: On Tibet's Peaceful Revolution*, by Shokdung, translated by Matthew Akester, vii–xvi. London: Hurst and Company.

Sorensen, Majken Jul. 2008. "Humor as a Serious Strategy of Nonviolent Resistance to Oppression." *Peace and Change* 33 (2): 167–90.

Sørenson, Per K. 1990. *Divinity Secularized: An Inquiry into the Nature and Form of Songs Ascribed to the Sixth Dalai Lama*. Wiener Studien zur Tibetologie und Buddhismuskunde, Heft 25. Vienna: Arbeitskreis für Tibetsiche und Buddhistische Studien, Universität Wien.

Sørenson, Per K., and Franz Xaver Erhard. 2013a. "An Inquiry into the Nature of Tibetan Proverbs." *Proverbium* 30:281–309.

———. 2013b. "Tibetan Proverbial Literature: Semantics and Metaphoricity in Context." In *Nepalica-Tibetica Festgabe for Christoph Cüppers*, edited by Franz-Karl Ehrhard and Petra Maurer, 2:237–52. Andiast, Switzerland: International Institute for Tibetan and Buddhist Studies.

Sprel nag pa rig 'dzin grags ldan སྤྲེལ་ནག་པ་རིག་འཛིན་གྲགས་ལྡན།. 2009. *Dpal Don grub rgyal la zhib 'jug byas pa'i dpyad rtsom phyogs bsgrigs* དཔལ་དོན་གྲུབ་རྒྱལ་ལ་ཞིབ་འཇུག་བྱས་པའི་དཔྱད་རྩོམ་ཕྱོགས་བསྒྲིགས། (Collected essays of research on Don grub rgyal). Lan gru'u [Lanzhou]: Kan su'u mi rigs dpe skrun khang.

Squint, Kirstin L. 2012. "Gerald Vizenor's Trickster Hermeneutics." *Studies in American Humor* 3 (25): 107–23.

Stam, Robert, with Richard Porton and Leo Goldsmith. 2015. *Keywords in Subversive Film/Media Aesthetics*. Malden, MA: Wiley Blackwell.

Stein, Rolf Alfred. 2010. *Rolf Stein's Tibetica Antiqua with Additional Materials*. Edited and translated by Arthur P. McKeown. Leiden: Brill.

Stirr, Anna. 2008. "*Blue Lake:* Tibetan Popular Music, Place, and Fantasies of the Nation." In *Tibetan Modernities: Notes from the Field on Cultural and Social Change*, edited by Robert Barnett and Ronald Schwartz, pp. 305–32. Leiden: Brill.

Stuart, Kevin, and Limusishiden. 1994. "China's Monguor Minority: Ethnography and Folktales." *Sino-Platonic Papers* 59 (December): 1–193.

Su, Buer. 2019. "Locating Selves in 21st Century Tibet: Tibetan Youth Identity and Hip Hop in the People's Republic of China." *Georgetown Journal of Asia Affairs* 5:54–72.

Sujata, Victoria. 2005. *Tibetan Songs of Realization: Echoes from a Seventeenth-Century Scholar and Siddha in Amdo*. Brill's Tibetan Studies Library 7. Leiden: Brill.

Sulek, Emilia. 2012. "'Everybody Likes Houses. Even Birds Are Coming!'—Housing Tibetan Pastoralists in Golok: Policies and Everyday Realities." In *Pastoral Practices in High Asia: Advances in Asian Human-Environmental Research*, edited by Herrmann Kreutzmann, 235–55. New York: Springer Science+Business Media B.V.

Sulek, Emilia, and Jarmila Ptackova. 2017. "Introduction, Mapping Amdo: People and Places in an Ongoing Transition." *Archiv Orientalni* 10:9–22.

Sulek, Emilia Roza. 2019. *Trading Caterpillar Fungus in Tibet: When Economic Boom Hits Rural Area*. Amsterdam: Amsterdam University Press.

Sullivan, Jonathan, and Yupei Zhao. 2021. "Rappers as Knights-Errant: Classic Allusions in the Mainstreaming of Chinese Rap." *Popular Music and Society* 44 (3): 274–91.

Sun, Fuhai 孙福海. 2007. *Dou ni mei shangliang—Xiangshengjie qiwen qushi* 逗你没商量：相声界奇闻趣事 (I didn't mean to tease you: Strange and interesting things from the world of Xiangsheng). Tianjin: Baihua Wenyi Chubanshe.

Suoci 索次. 2004. "Lun Zangyu xiangsheng de lishi yu xianzhuang" 论藏语相声的历史与现状 (On the history and present state of Tibetan-language crosstalk). *Xizang Yishu yanjiu* 西藏艺术研究 (Research on art in Tibet) 3:13–24.

Tam, Gina Anne. 2016. "'Orbiting the Core': Politics and the Meaning of Dialect in Chinese Linguistics, 1927–1957." *Twentieth-Century China*. 41 (3): 1–24.

Tan, Gillian G. 2016. "'Life' and 'Freeing Life' (*tshe thar*) among Pastoralists of Kham: Intersecting Religion and Environment." *Études mongoles et sibériennes, centrasiatiques et tibétaines* 47. http://journals.openedition.org/emscat/2793.

Tedlock, Dennis, trans. (1978) 1999. *Finding the Center: The Art of the Zuni Storyteller*. Lincoln: University of Nebraska Press.

Thomas, George. 1991. *Linguistic Purism*. London: Longman.

Thurston, Timothy. 2012. "An Introduction to Tibetan Sa Bstod Speeches in A Mdo." *Asian Ethnology* 71 (1): 49–73.

———. 2013. "'Careful Village's Grassland Dispute': An A Mdo Dialect Tibetan Crosstalk Performance by Sman Bla Skyabs." *CHINOPERL: Journal of Chinese Oral and Performing Literature* 32 (2): 156–83.

———. 2017. "On Artistic and Cultural Generation in Northeastern Tibet." *Asian Ethnicity* 19 (2): 143–62.

———. 2018a. "A Careful Village: Comedic Dialogues and Linguistic Modernity in China's Tibet. *Journal of Asian Studies* 77 (2): 453–74.

———. 2018b. "A Korean, an Australian, a Nomad, and a Martial Artist Meet on the Tibetan Plateau: Encounters with Foreigners in a Tibetan Comedy from Amdo." *Journal of Folklore Research* 55 (3): 1–24.

———. 2018c. "The Purist Campaign as Metadiscursive Regime in China's Tibet." *Inner Asia* 20 (2): 198–218.

———. 2019. "An Examination of the Poetics of Tibetan Secular Oratory." *Oral Tradition*. 33 (1): 23–50.

Thurston, Timothy, and Caixiangduojie, trans. 2016. "The Ne'u na Village Wedding Speech." *Asian Highlands Perspectives* 40:301–53.

Thurston, Timothy, and Tsering Samdrup. 2012. "An A Mdo Tibetan Pastoralist Family's Lo Sar in Stong Skor Village." *Asian Highlands Perspectives* 21:33–69.

Tian, Xi. 2014. "Uncertain Satire in Modern Chinese Fiction and Drama: 1930–1949." PhD dissertation, University of California Riverside.

Toelken, Barre, and George Wasson. 1999. "Coyote and the Strawberries: Cultural Drama and Intercultural Collaboration." *Oral Tradition* 13 (1): 176–99.

Tong, Q. S. 2010. "Global Modernity and Linguistic Universality: The Invention of Modern Chinese Language." *Eighteenth-Century Studies* 43 (3): 325–39.

Tournadre, Nicolas. 2003. "The Dynamics of Tibetan-Chinese Bilingualism." *China Perspectives*, no. 45 (January–February). http://chinaperspectives.revues.org/231.

Tournadre, Nicolas, and François Robin. 2006. *Le grand livre des proverbes tibétains* (The great book of Tibetan proverbs). Montreal: Presses du Châtelet.

Tsau, Shuying. 1980. "Xiangsheng and Its Star Performer Hou Baolin." *Chinoperl Papers* 9 (1): 32–78.

Tsering Bum. 2013. "A Northeastern Tibetan Childhood." *Asian Highlands Perspectives* 27:1–117.

Tsering Döndrup, translated by Christopher Peacock. 2019. *The Handsome Monk and Other Stories*. New York: Columbia University Press.

Tsering Samdrup and Hiroyuki Suzuki. 2019. "Humilifics in Mabzhi Pastoralist Speech of Amdo Tibetan." *Linguistics of the Tibeto-Burman Area* 42 (2): 222–59.

Tshe brtan rgyal ཚེ་བརྟན་རྒྱལ།. 2010. *A mdo'i goms srol nyung bsdus* ཨ་མདོའི་གོམས་སྲོལ་ ཉུང་བསྡུས| (A few collected Amdo customs). Lan gru'u [Lanzhou]: Kan su'u mi rigs dpe skrun khang.

Tshe dbang bsod nams ཚེ་དབང་བསོད་ནམས|. 2006. "Precious Juniper *rtsa che ba'i shug sdong* རྩ་ཆེ་བའི་ཤུག་སྡོང་།." In *Tibetan-English Folktales*, edited by Tshe dbang rdo rje, Allie Thomas, Kevin Stuart, dPal ldan bKra shis, and 'Gyur med rgya mtsho, 64–65. Unpublished textbook.

Tshe dbang rdo rje, Alexandru Anton-Luca, and Charles Kevin Stuart. 2009. *Tibetan Weddings in Ne'u na Village*. New York: YBK Publishers.

Tshe dbang rdo rje, Allie Thomas, Kevin Stuart, dPal ldan bKra shis, and 'Gyur med rgya mtsho, eds. n.d. *Tibetan-English Folktales*. Unpublished monograph.

Tuohy, Sue. 1999. "The Social Life of Genre: The Dynamics of Folksong in China." *Asian Music* 30 (2): 39–86.

Tuttle, Gray. 2005. *Tibetan Buddhists in the Making of Modern China*. New York: Columbia University Press.

———. 2010. "The Failure of Ideologies in China's Relations with Tibetans." In *Multination States in Asia: Accommodation or Resistance*, edited by Jacques Bertrand and André Laliberté, 219–43. Cambridge: Cambridge University Press.

Upton, Janet. 1996. "Home on the Grasslands? Tradition, Modernity, and the Negotiation of Identity by Tibetan Intellectuals in the PRC." In *Negotiating Ethnicities in China and Taiwan*, edited by Melissa J Brown, 98–124. Berkeley: University of California Press.

———. 1999. "The Development of Modern School-Based Tibetan Language Education in the PRC." In *China's National Minority Education: Culture, Schooling, and Development*, edited by Gerard A. Postiglione, 281–340. New York: Falmer Press.

———. 2000. "Notes towards a Native Tibetan Ethnology: An Introduction to and Annotated Translation of dMu dge bSam gtan's Essays on Dwags po (Baima Zangzu)." *Tibet Journal* 25 (1): 3–26.

Venturino, Steven J. 2008. "Signifying on China: African-American Literary Theory and Tibetan Discourse." In *Sinographies: Writing China*, edited by Eric Hayot, Haun Saussy, and Steven G. Yao, 271–99. Minneapolis: University of Minnesota Press.

Verdery, Katherine. 1991. *National Ideology under Socialism: Identity and Cultural Politics in Ceausecu's Romania*. Berkeley: University of California Press.

Virtanen, Riika. 2008. "Development and Urban Space in Contemporary Literature." In *Modern Tibetan Literature and Social Change*, edited by Lauran R. Hartley and Patricia Schiaffini-Vedani, 236–62. Durham, NC: Duke University Press

———. 2011. "Tibetan Written Images: A Study of Imagery in the Writings of Dhondup Gyal." PhD dissertation, University of Helsinki.

Volosinov, Valentin N. 1973. *Marxism and the Philosophy of Language*. New York: Seminar Press.

Wallenböck, Ute. 2016. "Marginalisation at China's Multi-Ethnic Frontier: The Mongolian Autonomous County in Qinghai Province." *Journal of Current Chinese Affairs* 45 (2): 149–82.

Wang Jue 王决, Wang Jingshou 汪景寿, and Teng Tianxiang 藤田香. 2011. *Zhongguo xiangsheng shi* 中国相声史 (A history of Chinese xiangsheng). Tianjin: Baihua Wenyi Chubanshe.

Wang Shiyong. 2013. "Towards a Localized Development Approach in Tibetan Areas of China." *Asian Highlands Perspectives* 28:137–63.

Wang Shuangcheng 王双成. 2012. *Zangyu anduo fangyan yuyin yanjiu* 藏语安多方言语音研究 (Research on the phonology of the Tibetan language's Amdo dialect). Shanghai: Zhongxi Shuju.

Wang, Xianzheng, Yongzhong Zhu, and Kevin Stuart. 1995. "'The Brightness of the World': Minhe Monguor Women Sing." *Mongolian Studies* 18:65–83.

Wang, Yuxiang, and JoAnn Phillion. 2009. "Minority Language Policy and Practice in China: The Need for Multicultural Education." *International Journal of Multicultural Education* 11 (1): 1–14.

Warner, Cameron David. 2013. "Hope and Sorrow: Uncivil Religion, Tibetan Music Videos, and YouTube." *Ethnos: Journal of Anthropology* 78 (4): 543–68.

———. 2019. "Tibetan Heritage in Urban China." *Volume* 55 (1): 30–33.

Weber, Eugen. 1976. *Peasants Into Frenchmen: The Modernization of Rural France, 1870–1914*. Stanford, CA: Stanford University Press.

Weiner, Benno Ryan. 2012. "The Chinese Revolution on the Tibetan Frontier: State Building, National Integration, and Socialist Transformation, Zeku (Tsékhok) County, 1953–1958." PhD dissertation, Columbia University.

———. 2020. *The Chinese Revolution on the Tibetan Frontier*. Ithaca, NY: Cornell University Press.

White, Linda. 2003. "Basque *Bertsolaritza*." *Oral Tradition* 18 (1): 142–43.

Willock, Nicole D. 2011. "A Tibetan Buddhist Polymath in Modern China." PhD dissertation, University of Indiana.

Winkler, Daniel. 2013. "Review: Transforming Nomadic Resource Management and Livelihood Strategies." *Asian Highlands Perspectives* 28:387–92.

Woolard, Kathryn A., and Bambi B. Schieffelin. 1994. "Language Ideology." *Annual Review of Anthropology* 23:55–82.

Wu Qi. 2013. "Tradition and Modernity: Cultural Continuum and Transition among Tibetans in A Mdo." PhD dissertation, University of Helsinki.

Yang, Eveline. 2016. "Tracing the *Chol kha gsum*: Reexamining a Sa skya-Yuan Period Administrative Geography." *Revue d'etudes tibétaines*, no. 37 (December): 551–68.

Yangdon Dhondup. 2000. "Song of the Snow Lion: New Writing from Tibet." *Manoa* 12 (2): 144–49.

———. 2008a. "Dancing to the Beat of Modernity: The Rise and Development of Tibetan Pop Music." In *Tibetan Modernities: Notes from the Field on Cultural and Social Change*, edited by Robert Barnett and Ronald Schwartz, 285–304. Leiden: Brill.

———. 2008b. "Roar of the Snow Lion: Tibetan Poetry in Chinese." In *Modern Tibetan Literature and Social Change*, edited by Lauran R. Hartley and Patricia Schiaffini-Vedani, 32–60. Durham, NC: Duke University Press. Yangdon Dhondup, Ulrich Pagel, and Geoffrey Samuel, eds. 2013. *Monastic and Lay Traditions in North-Eastern Tibet*. Leiden: Brill.

Yao, Wang. 1994. "Hu Yaobang's Visit to Tibet, May 22–31, 1980." In *Resistance and Reform in Tibet*, edited by Robert Barnett and Shirin Akiner, 285–89. Bloomington: Indiana University Press.

Yau, Wai-ping. 2016. "Reading Pema Tseden's Films as Palimpsest." *Journal of Chinese Cinemas* 10 (2): 120–34.

Yeh, Emily T. 2003. "Tibetan Range Wars: Spatial Politics and Authority on the Grasslands of Amdo." *Development and Change* 34 (3): 499–523.

———. 2013a. "Blazing Pelts and Burning Passions: Nationalism, Cultural Politics and Spectacular Decommodification in Tibet." *Journal of Asian Studies* 72 (2): 319–34.

———. 2013b. *Taming Tibet: Landscape Transformation and the Gift of Chinese Development*. Ithaca, NY: Cornell University Press.

You, Ziying. 2012. "Tradition and Ideology: Creating and Performing New *Gushi* in China, 1962–1966." *Asian Ethnology* 71 (2): 259–80.

Young, Katharine. 1978. "Indirection in Storytelling." *Western Folklore* 37 (1): 46–55.

Yü, Dan Smyer. 2006. "Emotions under Local Nationalism: The Primordial

Turn of Tibetan Intellectuals in China." *Pacific Rim Report* 42. San Francisco: USF Center for the Pacific Rim.

———. 2013. "Subaltern Placiality in Modern Tibet: Critical Discourses in the Works of Shogdong." *China Information* 27 (2): 155–72.

Yu, Zongqi. 1991. "One Hundred Jests of Afanti." MA thesis, Missouri State University.

Yulha Lhawa. 2019. "Language Revitalization, Video, and Mobile Social Media: A Case Study from the Khroskyabs Language amongst Tibetans in China." *Language Documentation and Conservation* 13:564–579.

Zenz, Adrian. 2010. "Beyond Assimilation: The Tibetanisation of Tibetan Education in Qinghai." *Inner Asia* 12 (2): 295–315.

———. 2014. *"Tibetanness" under Threat: Neo-Integrationism, Minority Education and Career Strategies in Qinghai, P. R. China*. Inner Asia Book Series 9. Leiden: Brill.

Zhang, Daqing, and Paul U Unschuld. 2008. "China's Barefoot Doctors: Past, Present, and Future." *Lancet* 327 (9653): 1865–67.

Zhang Yisun 张怡荪, ed. 1985. *Bod rgya tshig mdzod chen mo* བོད་རྒྱ་ཚིག་མཛོད་ཆེན་མོ། (The great Tibetan-Chinese dictionary). Pe cin [Beijing]: Mi rigs dpe skrun khang.

Zhogs dung ཞོགས་དུང་། 2008. "Bag chags dong sprug བག་ཆགས་དོང་སྤྲུག" (Overturning propensities). In *Dpyod shes rgyang 'bod* དཔྱོད་ཤེས་རྒྱང་འབོད། (The call of examination and knowledge), 2nd ed., 25–41. Lanzhou: Gansu Minzu Chubanshe.

Zhou Decang 周德仓. 2007. "Mao Zedong yu Xizang dangdai xinwen shiye de chuangjian 毛泽东与西藏当代新闻事业的创建" (Mao Zedong and the construction of a contemporary Tibetan news industry). *Mao Zedong sixiang yanjiu* 毛泽东思想研究 (Mao Zedong thought studies) 24 (3): 28–31.

Zhou, Minglang. 2004. "Minority Language Policy in China: Equality in Theory and Inequality in Practice." In *Language Policy in the People's Republic of China: Theory and Practice since 1949*, edited by Minglang Zhou and Hongkai Sun, 71–96. New York: Kluwer Academic Publishers.

Zhu Yongzhong, Huimin Qi, and Kevin Stuart. 1997. "Mirror-Bright Hearts and Poor Lives: Minhe Mangghuer Kugurjia Songs." *CHIME* 10–11:62–78.

Zhu Yongzhong, and Kevin Stuart. 1996. "Ritual Village Songs from East Qinghai: Minhe Monguor Nadun Texts." *CHIME* 9: 89–105.

Index

1958, 13-14
2008 demonstrations, 122

Ache Lhamo opera, 22
"Adri Topa" (story), 24-25, 30, 32
Afanti, 34
"Alalamo" (song), 136-41; excerpts, 137-38; intertextuality, 140; music video, 137; *zurza* and, 139-40
Amdo: cultural production, 57; dialects, 9-10, 102; education in, 105; hospitals in, 79, 87; illiteracy in, 64, 76, 124, 165n4; language purism in, 124; population, 9; *sprachbund*, 13; traditionalization, 104-5
animals: comparisons to, avoided in dokwa, 27; living alongside, 110; misfortune of, 29; trickster and, 34
Anti-Rightist Campaign, 53
Arik Lenpa, 34
"Artist, The" (script), 81. *See also* jyutselpa
audiences: expectations of, 54, 95-96, 57-58, 62, 64; reaching wider, 76, 77, 104, 121, 144, 145–46, 147. *See also specific media, apps, and platforms*

Bauman, Richard, 23, 37
bertsolari (Basque poetic dueling), 22
boasting, 7, 32, 33
Bod, 12, 129. See also *wol*
Bongdzi, 84
btags pa, 21. See also *dokwa*
"Buying Monkeys" (performance), 53

"Careful Village" (fictional community): conversational storytelling, 84, 96; critiques of religion, 82; education in, 83; linguistic critiques in, 89-92; marriage in, 78, 82-83, 86, 88, 91 166n10; metonym, 93-96; and modernity, 82, 87-89, 92-93; popularity of, 77, 96; quoted speech in, 84-85
"Careful Village's Bride," 74
"Careful Village's Grassland Dispute," 67-74, 82-83
"Careful Village's Thief," 75-76
"Careful Village's Wedding," 75-76
caterpillar fungus, 18-23, 106, 123, 125. *See also* yartsa gunbu
CCTV, 119
Chen Duxiu, 83
chol kha sum (three Tibetan cultural regions), 10-11, 141-42

Choné, 123
Chunwan (TV show), 119
City Tibetans (album), 129, 131, 136; critique in, 133, 142; excerpts from, 133, 135; video in, 131-32
clothing: and culture, 107-8, 133-34; modern/Chinese, 3, 18, 69; and poverty, 29; proverb about, 43, 63; styles of, 68-69; of Uncle Buddhist, 127
Colorful Nomad Camp, The (album), 68, 93
communicative economy, 94, 139
contrasto (Tuscan verbal dueling), 22
Coyote (trickster), 34
Cultural Revolution, 14-15, 19, 51

Dai people, 22
deities: comparisons to, avoided in dokwa, 27; encounters with, 110; invoked in wedding speeches, 91; rituals for, 140
Dekyi Tsering, 120-21
Deng Xiaoping, 50, 64
development: economic, 11, 48; ethnic, 52; national, 122, 165n20; of society, 65; technological, 88, 126
dokwa (extemporaneous poetry): definitions of, 21-22; importance of a response, 32; keys to performance, 23; narratives about, 24-26, 28-30; poetics of, 30; pronunciations and spellings, 21; and verbal dueling traditions, 22-23
Dondrup Jya: influence of, 51; and *larjya*, 59, 60, 66; linguistic critiques, 64-65; major works, 51, 82; and proverbs, 63; references to, 129, 139; vernacular writing of, 63, 165n19
dozens, the, 22-23, 33
dranyen (instrument), 126
Drijya Yangkho (character), 18-21, 42
Drowa zangmo (Tibetan opera), 54
Drukmo (King Gesar's wife), 100, 110
Dubhe (singer), 62
dueling, verbal/oral, 22-23, 33, 38, 52; via songs, 21, 28; specific instances, 42
dunglen (music genre), 62, 126

ecological conservation, 102, 105, 108-11
ecological migration, 105
economies of fortune, 89, 100-101, 110-11
education: boarding schools, 42, 78, 79, 112-13, 134; and "Great Open the West Campaign," 105; and harvest season, 18; during Maoist period, 14-15, 39; during post-Mao period, 15, 48, 56-57, 64; Menla Jyab and, 74, 75, 81, 83, 86-89, 91; pastoralist attitudes toward, 78-79, 87; policies, 123, 125, 152; Tibetan-language, 15, 64, 124
"ethnic identification" project, 12, 64, 161n2
ethnic pride, 58, 61-62, 65, 66; Menla Jyab's, 96; and zurza, 151-52. See also *larjya*

farming dialects, 9
fengci, 6, 63; Mao and, 39; as translation for *zurza* and *satire*, 39-40, 63

folksong, 26, 28; meter in Tibetan, 28. *See also* lushag
folktales, 2, 33-34, 53-54; collectors of, 40; decreasing place of, 147; reimagining, 148
footings, discursive, 85
Four Modernizations (goals), 50, 64, 165n20

Gansu, 9, 12-14
garchung (sketches): definition, 103-4; new social critiques in, 115-16, 118; and television, 106
Gates, Henry Louis, 8, 33-34
Gendun Chopel, 37-38
Gesar, King, epic of, 90, 101, 110, 123, 137, 140, 146
"Gesar's Horse Herder," 107; and ecological critiques, 108-9; and language purism, 115-16; metonymy in, 109-10; nationalism in, 116; popularity of, 107; social critique in, 111, 113
Golok, 23-24, 26, 56, 79
Gomang, 1
Goméla, 23
"Gonpo Dorje's Tea Prayer," 55
grassland warfare, 70 80
"Great Leap Forward" (campaign), 14
"Great Open the West Campaign," 105-6
Gungthang Tenpa Dronme, 55
gushi (stories), 164n12
gzi, 25

Haló, 23
He Chi, 53

hidden transcripts, 130, 141
hip-hop, 6, 16; in China, 126-27; and dialect, 126; and language planning, 142; in Tibetan exile, 121
Hou Baolin, 54, 164,n14
Hu Yaobang, 56
Hui people, 13
humilifics, 86

indirection: definition of, 32-33; in hip-hop, 127-28, 141-43; and zurza, 8
Inner China, 48, 54, 164n13
intangible cultural heritage, 113, 116, 138-42; UNESCO program, 106, 123
intellectuals; in Amdo, 11, 15-16; debates among, 52, 83-84, 104-6; and cultural production, 52, 57-58; and *larjya*, 58-61; linguistic purism in, 111-13, 121, 124; and nationalism, 116; and *zurza*, 9

Jamyang Lodree, 16-17, 118, 125
Jason J, 136-43
Jigme Rigpai Lodro, 60
jokes, 9, 38, 49, 52. See also *kure*; *tséwa*
jyala (modern clothing), 3, 18
Jyanang, 164n13
Jyoktrin (social media app), 146
jyutselpa: as a concept, 16; title of *khashag*, 81

katsom, 37
"Katsom to Labrang," 37-38
khatak, 68

204   INDEX

kenre, 22
khabde, 31-32, 42
Kham region, 9-11, 127, 129, 138, 141
khamtshar, 33
khashag: contested origins of, 55; definition of *shag*, 52; difference from *garchung*, 103; etymology, 51-52; links to *xiangsheng*, 52-55, 65; verbal art in, 63, 65; *zurza* in, 62-63, 65-66, 76
khatak (silk scarves), 68
khel, 21
Khenpo Tsultrim Lodree, 124
Kuaishou (online platform), 146
Kumbum Monastery, 14
kure, 7

labjyagpa, 7, 33
Labrang Monastery, 14, 56; monastic community as target of poetic critique, 37-38
Laji Shan, 23
Langdarma, King, 94
language ideology; China's monoglot, 92; language purism and, 112, 115, 131
language mixing, 111-12
larjya, 56, 61, 65, 95; definitions, 58, 61; *mirik gi larjya*, 58-59; and *zurza*/satire, 95-97
laye, 21, 28, 49
Lhalung Hualdor, 94-95
Lhasa dialect, 9-12, 22, 39, 54, 56, 122
Liang Qichao, 84
Lin Biao, 48, 64
Lobzang (computing company), 123
Lobzang Dorje, 54

Losar Gongtsog, 106, 119
love songs, 21, 28, 49
lu, 110
Ludrub Jyamtso, 129. *See also* Uncle Buddhist
Lujya Rati, 148
lungta, 24, 166n12
lushag, 21-22, 33, 52

Ma Sanli, 53
Makley, Charlene, 9, 12, 14, 16, 56, 82, 88, 112
Malho Mongolian Autonomous County, 23, 170
marriage, 83, 88. *See also* "Careful Village's Bride"
Mangra County, 1, 81
May Fourth Movement, 84
Menla Jyab, 9, 21, 67-80; critiques of religious clerics, 82-83; early years, 80-81; physical deformity, 80-81; pseudoynms, 81
metonymic referentiality, 110, 139
minzu shibie, 12
modernity, 7, 24, 88-89, 93, 96-97, 115, 141
Monguor people, 13
My Golden Homeland (album), 113

Namlha Bum, 21-22, 144-45
narrated/narrative event, 86-87
nationalism; music and, 126; Tibetan cultural, 116-18, 143; and tradition, 105;
national pride, 58-61, 62. See also *larjya*
ndrokhkel (nomad dialects), 9

"new people," 84
"new prose style," 84
"New Ten Virtues, the" (movement), 125
"New Thinkers" (movement), 83-84; critiques of, 84; parallels with May Fourth Movement, 105
New Youth (magazine), 83-84

oath swearing, 86, 89
oral dueling. *See* dueling, verbal/oral
oratory, 127-8, 162n4; parodies of, 75-76, 91-92; poetic features of, 26-27, 92

Pakmo Drashe, 67, 83-84, 87, 94, 105
Panchen Lama, the, 60, *165n6*
parody, 10, 22, 33, 36, 92
Pema Bhum, 14, 83
Pema Tsetan, 125
phalké (vernacular language), 55
Phuntsog Tashi, 56
Pig's Head Soothsayer, The (TV show), 105
pride. See *larjya*
proverbs (*tamhwé*), 21, 65
Putonghua standard Chinese, 14, 92, 112, 142

Qinghai, 9, 12, 23; dialect, 142; illiteracy in, 78-79, 165n4; media in, 53, 119; monasteries in, 13-14; social conditions in, 78-79

radio, 51, 53; comedy broadcasts, 55-6, 76-77, 104, 106
rap music. *See* hip-hop; *shuochang*; *zheematam*

Rebgong, 7, 23, 122
Reform and Opening Up period, 15, 55-56
religion: and Cultural Revolution, 14; Menla Jyab on, 83, 88, 93; restricted in popular media, 140; Sinicization of, 123; and Tibetan identity, 10, 148; "Uncle Horse Herder" and, 101
reported speech, 85, 88
riddles, 21
ronghkel (farming dialects), 9
Rudé Tramo (album), 68, 93
Ruyong Riglo (character), 18-21, 41-42

Salar people, 13, 161n5
Samlo sarwa. *See* "New Thinkers"
satire, 6-7, 38-41, 53, 63, 95-97, 114, 151; as Chinese *fengci*, 39; government support, 41; theory, 8; Yan'an talks, 39
Scott, James C., 130
Secretary Wangchen (character), 45-48, 50, 66
[Sengcham] Drukmo, 100, 110
Serta Larung Gar, 124
Shakya, Tsering, 57, 130
Shar Kalden Jyamtso, 8, 38, 82
shengtai baohu, 102, 108. *See also* ecological conservation
Shépa speech tradition, 123
Shidé Nyima, 105, 119 [Q AU: "y" added on 105 & glossary, deleted on 119]
Shokdung (author-intellectual), 83-84
shuochang (speaking singing), 121, 167n1 (ch5). *See also* hip-hop

Sichuan, 9, 12, 16, 22, 124
signifying, 8, 33-34, 40
Sinophobic purism, 112
social ills, 82-83, 87
Sokdzong, 23. *See also* Malho
Soktruk Sherab, 105
speeches: *tamshel*, 21; wedding, 27, 91
"Studying Tibetan" (script): excerpts from, 43-50; lack of scholarly attention to, 51, 163n9; proverbs in, 65; *zurza* in, 64, 66
Suoci (writer), 54–55

tamhwé (proverbs), 21, 65
tamshel (speeches), 21
tangka paintings, 69
television: and *garchung*, 104-5, 106-7, 119; ownership in Amdo, 76; Tibetan terms for, 111; and *xiangsheng*, 55-56
tellability, 106, 107
Tibetan sign language, 130
Tibetophone: intellectuals, 51; media, 77
traditional formulae, 129-30
Tri Ralpachen, 69, 165n2
tricksters: narratives, 35-36; theoretical approaches to, 34, 166n7; Tibetan intellectuals as, 17, 82, 84, 147-49. *See also* Uncle Tonpa
Trika County, 1
tsampa (food), 127, 130
"Tsampa" (song), 141; excerpts from, 128, 131; music video, 127-28; social critique in, 129-30, 142
Tsekhog County, 141, 162n6

Tsering Döndrup, 82
tsétar, 34
tséwa (play), 7
Tsolho Nationalities Normal School, 15, 81
Tsultrim Lodree, Khenpo, 124

Uncle Buddhist, 127-30, 134-36, 141-42, 149
Uncle Tonpa, 2, 8, 34-40, 82; film about, 148; satirists as modern version of, 149-50
UNESCO, 106, 123, 168n4
United Work Front, 13
Ü-Tsang, 10-11, 56, 129, 138, 141

Valley of Heroes (film), 124
verbal dueling. *See* dueling, verbal/oral
vernacular language, 55, 165n19
"Vowels and Consonants" (song), 120-21

WeChat/Weixin (app), 17, 120, 125
wind-horses, 24
wod or *wol* (term), 12. *See also* Bod

xiangsheng tradition: in the countryside, 52-53; expressive arts of, 63; and *khashag*, 55; localization of, 65; origins of, 55
xiaopin (skits), 167n1 (ch4). *See also garchung*
Xin qingnian (magazine), 83-84
xin min ("new people"), 84
xin wenti ("new prose style"), 84
Xining, 134. *See also* Ziling

Yan'an Forum, 39
"Yangsel" (song), 120-21
yartsa gunbu: sketch comedy about, 18-20, 23, 30, 32, 41, 43; trade in, 106, 123-25. *See also* caterpillar fungus
Yesterday's Story (TV show), 105
Yi people, 22
Yongzin (search engine), 123, 168n2
Younghusband expedition, 101-2

Zalejya (character in "Careful Village" series), 74, 86, 96
zhadgar (comedic plays), 103. See also *garchung*
zheematam: Chinese *shuochang* and, 121; links to world hip-hop, 126. *See also* hip-hop
zheng nengliang (positive energy), 126
Zhonghua minzu (Chinese nation-race), 12
Ziling, 1, 11, 15, 23, 59, 67, 80-81, 119, 136-38. *See also* Xining
Zonthar Gyal, 125
zurza, 6-8; and access to media, 40, 62, 97, 116, 142; audience expectations of, 95-96; changes to, 142; definitions, 6-8; as expressive resource, 64-65, 107, 142; and *fengci*, 40, 63; government support for, 41; and indirection, 8, 33-34, 127, 140; and signifying, 33, 40; social critique in, 77, 93; and tricksters, 34, 37-38; *zurza ye*/doing zurza, 6, 8, 20, 34, 65, 95-6, 136, 142-43

Studies on Ethnic Groups in China
Stevan Harrell, Editor

Cultural Encounters on China's Ethnic Frontiers, edited by Stevan Harrell
Guest People: Hakka Identity in China and Abroad, edited by Nicole Constable
Familiar Strangers: A History of Muslims in Northwest China,
    by Jonathan N. Lipman
Lessons in Being Chinese: Minority Education and Ethnic Identity in Southwest China, by Mette Halskov Hansen
Manchus and Han: Ethnic Relations and Political Power in Late Qing and Early Republican China, 1861–1928, by Edward J. M. Rhoads
Ways of Being Ethnic in Southwest China, by Stevan Harrell
Governing China's Multiethnic Frontiers, edited by Morris Rossabi
On the Margins of Tibet: Cultural Survival on the Sino-Tibetan Frontier,
    by Åshild Kolås and Monika P. Thowsen
The Art of Ethnography: A Chinese "Miao Album," translation by David M. Deal and Laura Hostetler
Doing Business in Rural China: Liangshan's New Ethnic Entrepreneurs,
    by Thomas Heberer
Communist Multiculturalism: Ethnic Revival in Southwest China,
    by Susan K. McCarthy
Religious Revival in the Tibetan Borderlands: The Premi of Southwest China,
    by Koen Wellens
Lijiang Stories: Shamans, Taxi Drivers, and Runaway Brides in Reform-Era China, by Emily Chao
In the Land of the Eastern Queendom: The Politics of Gender and Ethnicity on the Sino-Tibetan Border, by Tenzin Jinba
Empire and Identity in Guizhou: Local Resistance to Qing Expansion,
    by Jodi L. Weinstein
China's New Socialist Countryside: Modernity Arrives in the Nu River Valley,
    by Russell Harwood

Mapping Shangrila: Contested Landscapes in the Sino-Tibetan Borderlands,
   edited by Emily T. Yeh and Chris Coggins
A Landscape of Travel: The Work of Tourism in Rural Ethnic China,
   by Jenny Chio
The Han: China's Diverse Majority, by Agnieszka Joniak-Lüthi
Xinjiang and the Modern Chinese State, by Justin M. Jacobs
In the Circle of White Stones: Moving through Seasons with Nomads of Eastern Tibet, by Gillian Tan
Medicine and Memory in Tibet: Amchi *Physicians in an Age of Reform*,
   by Theresia Hofer
The Nuosu Book of Origins*: A Creation Epic from Southwest China*, translated
   by Mark Bender and Aku Wuwu from a transcription by Jjivot Zopqu
Exile from the Grasslands: Tibetan Herders and Chinese Development Projects,
   by Jarmila Ptáčková
Pure and True: The Everyday Politics of Ethnicity for China's Hui Muslims,
   by David R. Stroup
Satirical Tibet: The Politics of Humor in Contemporary Amdo,
   by Timothy Thurston